Chaya Feuerman, LCSW
Rabbi Simcha Feuerman, LCSW

DIRECTION:

Finding Your Way in Relationships,
Parenting & Personal Growth

DIRECTION:

L'Chaim
Publications
TO LIFE!

CHAYA FEUERMAN, LCSW
RABBI SIMCHA FEUERMAN, LCSW

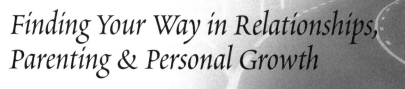

Finding Your Way in Relationships,
Parenting & Personal Growth

Distributed by:
L'Chaim Publications
521 Fifth Avenue, Suite 1740
New York, NY 10175
Email: lchaim@att.biz

Cover design:
D.C. Design

Book design, printing and binding:

© copyright
Simcha and Chaya Feuerman
(718) 793-1376
simcha_chaya@excite.com

ISBN# 0-9766946-2-X

With gratitude to the A-lmighty,
we thank our rebbeim and teachers,
as well as our parents and family
who have provided us with the
inspiration and guidance
from which the ideas in this book
have developed.

The Copy-Editing and Cover Design of this book
were made possible by a generous grant from

"CONSULTING PLUS … עצה הוגנת ועוד"

www.cyberconsultingplus.com

Contributions toward the publication of this book
were made in memory of our dear departed grandmoter
MRS. CHANA RUTH ALTHEIM ע״ה
לזכר נשמת סבתנו היקרה חנה רות בת ר׳ מאיר בעריש ז״ל

and in memory of our dear departed parents
Mr. Abe. and Mrs. Frieda Feuerman ע״ה
ולזכר נשמות הורינו היקרים
ר׳ אברהם ב״ר חיים ז״ל
ואשתו היקרה מרת פריידע בת ר׳ אברהם לייב ז״ל

and in memory of our dear departed parents
Rabbi Abraham I. and Mrs. Shifra Twersky ע״ה
ולזכר נשמות הורינו היקרים
מוהר״ר אברהם יצחק בן מוהר״ר משה מרדכי ז״ל
ואשתו היקרה מרת שפרה בת מוהר״ר אלטער ישראל שמעון ז״ל

BY RABBI CHAIM AND MRS. CHANA FEUERMAN

RABBI SHLOMO WAHRMAN
ROSH HAYESHIVAH

ב"ה

3 Tishrei 5764

Rabbi Simcha Feuerman, CSW
136-70 72nd Avenue
Kew Gardens Hills, NY 11367

Dear Reb Simcha, Shlit"a:

I received the material you sent me and I read it from cover to cover.* I enjoyed it immensely and feel that your approaches in these areas are second to none. You elaborate extensively on all aspects of each problem and leave no stone unturned.

Unfortunately, due to my hectic schedule, I simply cannot comply with your request that I review the manuscript in its entirety. However, at first glance, your material is well coordinated, and if the rest of it is written as the portions I have reviewed, your book will be of great value to the readers.

May Hashem grant you and yours a Gmar Chasima Tova.

Rabbi Shlomo Wahrman

*This includes the following sections from your manuscript on parenting, Torah, and psychology:

Pushkas and Pedagogy

A "Shanda on a Honda": When the Rabbi's Children Misbehave

A Hypothetical Debate Between a Baal Mussar and a Psychotherapist

Kibbud Av V'em: Psychological and Halachic Implications for Modern Times

בס״ד

Congregation Poale Zedeck

Rabbi
Yisroel
Miller
Spiritual Leader

The Feuermans give us dozens of "recipes for living", presented with clarity, humor and warmth. It's a book for any Jewish parent — and grandparents too!

[signature]

בע״ה יא"ח

Note: These comments were written upon Rabbi Miller's review of the sections of the book that pertain to parenting.

6318 Phillips Ave.
Pittsburgh, PA
15217-1808
tel. (412)421-9786
fax (412) 421-3383

TABLE OF CONTENTS

Introduction

People today feel conflicted, concerned and confused. Even as we cling to the anchoring morals and structure of our tradition, strong currents tug at all of us — parents and children, individuals and families. How can we maintain and impart religious morals and observance while accommodating children's emotional needs? And then there's the pressure to measure up to the standards of the people around us, Jewish or secular.

This book is written to serve as a guide to help sincere and devoted religious people resolve psychological and social conflicts within the parameters of their religious values. We address the areas of intersection between religion, values, and feelings, and share our discoveries that come from our personal and professional experience as Orthodox Jews and psychotherapists. We will discuss typical relationship issues, parenting problems, and personal conflicts that we have seen repeatedly in our therapy sessions and in correspondence with many of our readers.

INDIVIDUALS HAVE ASKED US:

- ‣ How can Jewish traditions and values guide us in promoting emotional health in our loved ones and ourselves?

- ‣ How do personal and relationship ethics relate to Torah ethics?

- ‣ How has the Holocaust affected us psychologically and religiously?

▸ How do parents set limits for their children to control the harmful influences of secular society, without overdoing it?

▸ How can parents apply the wisdom of our tradition to modern parenting dilemmas?

▸ Which secular psychological theories about child rearing are beneficial and helpful to parents and which are destructive?

▸ What steps can parents take to insure their children will remain faithful to our religion?

▸ What steps can parents take to produce successful, happy and morally grounded children in a society where there is much immorality?

We thank our many readers who took the time to write to us with questions, some of which served as a basis for the chapters found in this book. We hope our readers find this book helpful and instructive. The ideas in this book are not a substitute for professional or *halachic* guidance; they merely serve as a starting point for meaningful inquiry and exploration.

We gratefully acknowledge the skillful work of our copy editor, Elky Langer.

SECTION ONE
You and Your Significant Other

For a religion system to survive, it needs to invest heavily in promoting positive relationships. Religious values can only be transmitted effectively through functional families and communities. The wisdom of the Torah and the accumulated wisdom of centuries of ethical introspection by our sages offer a rich resource for enhancing relationships. But sometimes it is difficult to adapt age-old wisdom to modern circumstances. How do we integrate our religious values into relationship issues that confront us today?

In this section, we will begin with a number of questions we have received about the dating and courtship process, and then segue into issues related to marriage.

1

The Ten Commandments of Dating

Later in this section, we will discuss at length Rabbi Avigdor Miller's "Ten Commandments of Marriage", which focuses on loyalty to a spouse, making every effort to avoid cycles of hurt and resentment. Dating, however, is a different story.

Why be loyal to someone whom you may not marry? The dating process allows you to filter unsuitable prospects and reject them before marriage even becomes an option. Why should you learn to forgive and overlook flaws if you can wait for Miss or Mr. Perfect?

But here the line blurs. Your filtering process may be wise and prudent — or perhaps it is picky and selfish. Here are some useful guidelines to help you navigate through this difficult chapter in your life.

COMMANDMENT #1: *Stay in the Here and Now*

When dating, concentrate on the experience of being with the prospective partner. Forget about past relationships; don't dream about future possibilities. Just listen to your date, share your thoughts, and enjoy the moment. After the date you can spend as much time as you like analyzing it.

COMMANDMENT #2: *Assess Your Ability to Solve Problems Together*

The single most important quality of a successful relationship is the ability to solve problems together. Even the best of marriages and the most compatible people experience serious and difficult challenges over the years. Ask yourself, "Is this the person I want with me during the bad times as well as the good?"

COMMANDMENT #3: *Don't Give Up*

No matter how long it takes for you to find your predestined match, don't become jaded or cynical. Easier said than done, but it's the plain and simple truth. There is absolutely nothing helpful or constructive about giving up.

COMMANDMENT #4: *Look for*
A Positive Fit with Family Styles and Similar Values

While someone from a different background shouldn't be ruled out entirely, the chances for success are higher when there are basic similarities. Aside from investigating the individual, also inquire about the family to determine if you'd be comfortable with them as well. In an ideal situation, your spouse's family will become like your own.

COMMANDMENT #5: *Don't Confuse*
Values with Religious Customs and Practice

Though it helps to share religious practice, the main thing is that you share common values. If she is more *yeshivish* and you are a learner earner, but you're both serious about fulfilling your purpose in life, the details can be resolved. Of course, don't wait until the kids are of age to work on it! Some matters of religious practice are non-negotiable. Find a rabbi respected by both of you whose rulings you will both accept.

COMMANDMENT #6: *Have A Low Tolerance for Abuse*

If your prospective mate broke a confidence, was deceitful in any major way or was abusive, this is a bad sign that there will be future problems. To be sure, you should always give a person the benefit of the doubt and state what he or she did wrong, but if it is part of a recurring pattern, cut that fish loose before it's too late!

COMMANDMENT #7: *Ask Yourself if You Can Trust This Person*

Trust is a key ingredient in a relationship. If over time you are not getting the feeling that you trust this person, follow your instincts and leave while you can.

COMMANDMENT #8: *Don't Be Afraid to Succeed*

Though it is difficult to admit, some people are afraid to succeed. Having a successful relationship may inadvertently hurt other family members. A youngest or only child of a widowed parent might find it difficult to marry and abandon his parent. A younger sibling might feel bad about getting married before an older sibling. If you let these fears run your life, no one will be happy. But if you bravely do what is healthy and appropriate for you, this may actually liberate others in your family to live their lives to the fullest.

COMMANDMENT #9: *Trust Your Friends*

Getting an objective opinion can be crucial when you are making serious life decisions. Don't be afraid to share your anxiety and ask for their thoughts.

COMMANDMENT # 10: *Don't Be Swayed by Romance and Passion*

Romance is a great thing if you have it, but it does not necessarily predict or assure success in a relationship. You can have strong feelings for someone who ultimately is not the best choice for a marriage partner. Some people are attracted to those who hurt them, and others start off relationships being attracted to the same qualities that they ultimately end up despising. Shared values, mutual respect, and an ability to enjoy each other's company override attraction, which can quickly wear off, leaving the relationship nowhere if there is nothing of substance beneath the surface.

2

To Tell the Truth

Dear Feuermans,
I recently went out with a guy who had an illness and
he only told me after several dates. I think this was
unfair and dishonest. Can you offer your opinion about
this matter?

OUR RESPONSE

Though your feelings are understandable, your date chose the most realistic option. Could he really tell every single person about his illness before he dates them — or even on a first date? Feelings aside, this is a *halachic* question and ultimately needs to be referred to an authority on Jewish law.

Rav Moshe Feinstein in his responsa (*Igros Moshe, Orach Chaim* IV:118) counseled a woman with a serious flaw about how and when she should tell a prospective marriage partner. "Of course you must tell him …but not on the first date …only after you know he wants to marry you …then he will recognize your other virtues." There is an obligation to disclose serious flaws to a marriage prospect, but this sensitive topic can wait until the relationship edges close to engagement.

Rav Moshe recommended delaying disclosure so the other party "will recognize your other virtues." This is good advice for dating in general. During initial dates, you do not have to be so forthright about your shortcomings, lest it overshadow your good qualities.

Although Rav Moshe's ruling was in reference to a woman with a serious flaw, the same applies to a man. In terms of emotional pain, both sides invest in the relationship. In terms of financial losses incurred via the wasted dates, usually the man pays the expenses for the date. If Rav Moshe had no objection to the woman withholding this negative information for several dates, surely there should be no objection in the reverse situation.

Rav Moshe in no way permitted actual falsehood. A person may withhold information on initial dates, but he may not provide misleading information.

Everyone has negative qualities to some degree. In seeking a marriage partner, you have to get to know the person as a whole, to consider the negative qualities in the context of the overall personality. How can you judge a marriage prospect if all his flaws were disclosed to you before you even met him?

Another point to consider is whether Rav Moshe would apply his ruling beyond the specific case of the responsa. The woman in the responsa had a religiously subjective flaw. A serious medical condition is objective, and sometimes more substantial. Under what circumstances would a healthy person agree to marry someone with a terminal illness, or an individual medically incapable of having children?

Second-hand sources relate that Rav Moshe's attitude was the same regarding all flaws, objective or subjective — to be revealed only when engagement appears to be imminent and forthcoming.

Even healthy persons with relatively minor problems (real or imagined!) can find dating to be anxiety provoking and difficult. You can imagine how stressful this can be for someone with a handicap to negotiate this process. If an issue arises, it is best to seek counsel from a competent rabbinic authority.

3

The Shy Date

Dear Feuermans,
What is a fellow to do when a girl simply does not speak
on a date? Recently I went out with a girl who was
almost totally silent. It was very uncomfortable for me
because I had no idea what she was thinking, or even if
she was interested in spending time with me. I am
certain this situation repeats itself with many people.

OUR RESPONSE

Before we discuss the girl, let's talk about you. Some people believe in the pre-arranged dating system and some don't. We aren't going to advocate one position or another, but if you do engage in arranged dates it is important to use the system in the most advantageous manner. And that means doing as much research as you can about the proposed date and her family. The female portion of the equation should do the same.

You should have a good idea about the type of person you are looking for. Aside from level of observance and religious outlooks, consider emotional maturity. What personality traits are important to you? Decide what age bracket of women you are willing to meet — before you go out. Find out about their current or planned educational and life goals.

Being shy or unusually quiet is not necessarily an impediment to being a good parent or life partner, although it might have its drawbacks. For some, shyness is the embodiment of modesty, but it might be too extreme for others.

In any case, you need a picture in your mind of the ideal match before you even go out. This allows for the maximum benefit from the *shidduch* system and saves all concerned parties much time and heartbreak.

Now, let's discuss the girl. Everyone has a bad day — even confident people go through an occasional bout of stage fright. But the extreme shyness you describe certainly casts doubt about this person's emotional maturity and development. Even if she is new to dating and will eventually warm up, there probably will be other circumstances in life where this problem will inconveniently resurface.

This situation could have been prevented with adequate research about the prospective date. Is this behavior anomalous or typical? Is this social disability limited to meeting new people, or is she withdrawn even among people she knows well?

The girl's parents also need to play a role. Before they send their daughter on a date, particularly a shy girl, they should try to prep her. Either the parents are unaware of their daughter's problem or unwilling to take it seriously. There's a certain amount of passivity and neglect in this situation. All in all, these do not sound like the best candidates for in-laws and grandparents.

DATING WITH A GOAL

But, as you asked, "What is a fellow to do once he is on such a date?" There are general strategies that encourage fruitful dates.

People have different ideas of what they should feel before they are ready to marry someone. Some people want to feel "fireworks" and a sense of falling in love. Others, more practical, look for a basic sense of compatibility. But whatever it is you are looking for, the single most important factor in the long-term success of your relationship is the ability to work together to solve problems.

Even the most ideal marriage has problems every day. Money, kids, work — the list is endless. On a date, you need to ask yourself, "Is this person someone I can work with to solve problems?" No matter what the topic or entertaining locale, keep this question in the back of your mind.

Not that you should deliberately test your date — that would be unfair and patronizing. Plenty of situations arise naturally. What happens when you get lost on the road — how do you solve that? When you come late to the date, completely by accident, are you made to feel comfortable or do you feel judged?

Even finding a topic of conversation can be the first problem in your relationship. Despite the stiff and formal atmosphere, these first few moments can teach you a great deal about yourself and your partner. How will you both manage to solve this problem? Is your partner withdrawn? Is your partner concerned about how you are feeling? Is your partner overly nervous? Is your partner suspicious and cynical, or clever and creative?

None of these single items has to be the deciding factor in your relationship. But how you solve this first problem indicates your compatibility to solve other problems together.

Keep this in the back of your mind — but don't focus on this exclusively. If you are preoccupied with testing your date instead of relating to her, she may pass your test, but you will probably fail hers! Who wants to marry a guy who is remote and judgmental?

So in your efforts to start a conversation, try to invite your date to work collaboratively with you. "Where should we go tonight?" should not be viewed as the chauffeur's polite question, but as a problem you should work on jointly.

The main function of a date is to work together on solving a problem. If you see things from this perspective, whatever you do and whatever you talk about is preparation for a future successful relationship.

4

Rerun Date

Dear Feuermans,
Recently, someone suggested that I go out with a
woman whom I dated two years ago. We went out
three times and after that, she was not interested in
seeing me again. I was not heartbroken in any way,
but I was ready to continue dating her. Now, after
she rejected me, I am not so sure. Is it that she is
desperate, so she is going through her files to recall
her runner up choices? My thinking is to say no,
but others have advised me to see her again. What
do you think?

OUR RESPONSE

Your question calls for a response on two levels. First, your letter reveals a particular outlook that may be interfering with your success in dating. Second, there are a number of general psychological and relationship factors to consider when assessing whether to re-date someone you dated previously.

You seem overly concerned about why this woman wants to date you again, and why she discontinued your relationship in the first place. You assume she rejected you because she saw you as second rate, and now she's reconsidering only because she is desperate. Neither of these assumptions may be true. She probably broke off dating you because she thought you lacked a desired quality. But certain qualities can be subjective, and can differ even for the same person as time passes.

A younger, more idealistic woman may put *"yeshivishness"* and commitment to Torah study as a higher priority relative to wage earning ability. After a few years of life experience, perhaps even from observing her relatives' and friends' marriages, she may have reordered her priorities.

Of course, this is just an illustration. The exact opposite reordering of priorities may also occur, too. People change over the years. Maybe she is interested in you again not out of desperation, but out of a renewed focus.

Although we really do not know you, we might conjecture that this slightly paranoid and pessimistic attitude can potentially interfere with all relationships, not just this particular rerun date. If you view the dating process as a chance to be accepted or rejected, it becomes a tension producing experience — making you less attractive and less emotionally involved. Though it is easier said than done, it would be helpful for you to see the dating process in a more objective manner, and not let it serve as a personal measure of whether you are likable or attractive.

On the other hand, some of your hesitation may also be valid. As the saying goes, "Sometimes when you are paranoid, they really are out to get you." Let us consider some general relationship factors to consider when contemplating a "rerun date."

COMMUNICATION IS KEY

Whether you have dated someone five times, or are married for twenty years, both situations are relationships, and their success or failure depends heavily on being able to communicate feelings and needs and working to address them. You are entitled to share your concerns about re-dating someone who turned you down a few years ago.

Be forthright and direct, but phrase your question in a pleasant and respectful manner. You can ask, "Before we go out again, I would like to understand what has changed now that I am being considered again as a date." Try to use the less accusatory "what," instead of the more challenging "why."

More important than the actual answer is how you are answered. Is your question welcomed, or treated with suspicion? Does the other party become defensive, or sympathetic and interested in responding to your concerns? This will help give you a better idea of how this potential marriage partner will respond to other communication difficulties should your relationship broaden.

Compare this to the type of questions asked on job interviews, such as, "Why are you leaving your current job?" No interviewer is really naïve enough to expect an honest answer. "Well, actually I am leaving my current position because I am incompetent and about to be fired," or, "I am greedy, disloyal, and just want to get paid more money." Imagine how that would sound!

The interviewer just wants to see how the interviewee answers the question — if he planned a plausible explanation ahead of time, if he reacts well under pressure. In your situation, the answer provided may not be the absolute truth, but it can still reveal important information about the person's sincerity and mindset.

5

Picking Up the Pieces

*Every relationship is bashert (predestined). It makes no
difference whether it lasts for a moment or for a lifetime;
there always is something we can learn from being
involved with another person.*

— Rav Nachman

Ending a relationship, whether by divorce, broken engagement,
or stopping to date someone, brings disturbing feelings that are difficult to contend with. Someone who chooses to end a serious
relationship either made a great decision or a huge mistake. It's
hard to imagine anything in between. And for the one being, as
they say, "dumped" — this requires some serious introspection too.

REJECTION

Rejection is one of the most painful experiences you can have.
To mutually end a relationship is one thing. But when a person rejects you when you still want to continue the relationship — that's
a bitter pill to swallow.

After experiencing rejection, you may feel that something must
be terribly wrong with you. You must be ugly or dumb or boring or
unsuccessful. Even the most emotionally healthy person might experience temporary self-doubt in the face of a devastating rejection.

This can be a constructive response. Perhaps there were good
reasons for the rejection. If you really want to grow, you must take
a good look at yourself and see if any of the criticisms have validity. Sometimes it is necessary to read between the lines, because the

other person may have been less than candid in order to preserve your feelings.

But recognizing flaws and realizing mistakes are not reason to reject yourself. Someone chose to reject you, but you do not have to choose to do the same! A mother does not reject a child who makes mistakes. She guides him to become better. You must be your own good parent. If you make a mistake, you have to accept the reality, but also support and encourage yourself to make improvements.

Sometimes you hold out hope for reconciliation. This is not altogether unreasonable, but in many situations, it can be destructive and hurtful. The Torah addresses a parallel issue. A man is allowed to remarry his divorced wife as long as she did not marry anyone in between. But once the wife married another man, her original husband may never remarry her even after she divorces her second husband.

Perhaps one aspect of this Torah directive signals to us that once a decision is made, it is unhealthy to keep looking back. Note that the Torah defines this point for a marriage relationship, but not for a pre-marriage relationship. It is worthwhile to seek objective advice from a friend to prevent long term obsessing over something that cannot be changed.

BREAKING IT OFF

When you break off a relationship with someone, be firm and clear that you are not interested in continuing the relationship. Mixed messages imply that perhaps you're really not as sure about ending this relationship as you think you are. It's important to be as polite and inoffensive as possible — not just out of decency, but because provoking hostility ironically prolongs relationships instead of shortening them.

You must let go of your hate. Even if you have succeeded in physically separating from the person, as long as you are filled with hate, your former loved one is always with you, making you as miserable as you were when you were together.

AFTER IT'S OVER

Even when it's mutual, it is still worthwhile to reflect on the past relationship. If you don't make an effort to understand what went wrong, you're likely to experience similar problems in future relationships. It's only logical.

You find particular personality traits attractive. These personality traits have positive aspects and negative aspects. The problems your ex-friend or ex-spouse had are not only about him — the way you reacted and the way you perceived these traits played a major role. History will repeat itself unless you are insightful and honest with yourself.

You may be attracted to the way a person is open-minded and seemingly unconcerned with the way others think. His personality complements your own shyness and self-consciousness. Family therapists call this complementarity; opposites attract, balancing out each other's flaws.

As life evolves, this same trait, which once was endearing to you now is offensive and embarrassing. You used to admiringly think, "Wow, what confidence, what guts." Now you wonder, "How could he act that way? Doesn't he care about the way others think?" To avoid an endless cycle of attraction and repulsion, you must try to understand how to make peace with what attracts you but also disgusts you.

Before beginning a second relationship, there must be honest analysis and inner probing of the first.

- What is the real reason the relationship failed? Relationships fail because of many complex reasons, but it is helpful to isolate one key issue. When you begin your next relationship, you need a clear picture of what to avoid.

- Why did I not see that problem early in the relationship? What can I do differently to either notice or fix the problem in future relationships? People have difficulty seeing themselves and others objectively. Contrary to how we'd like to imagine it, often whatever was wrong in a relationship was a problem from the very beginning. Problems can be overcome, but it is best to view the problems clearly from the very outset, so they can be dealt with.

- If the person of my interest became unattractive to me, what caused it? Is it that he really changed or is it that my needs changed? In all probability, your needs changed. Someone you once found attractive usually doesn't change — how you feel about that person changes.

- If my needs changed, what am I doing in the future to make sure that my next relationship will meet my needs?

The Confused Yeshiva Bochur

Dear Feuermans,

I'm a 22-year-old boy, and I'm not sure if I should be dating. The problem is that I switch my hashkafos (religious outlook) from time to time. Most of the time, especially when yeshiva is out, I'm not so frum. For example, I watch videos and listen to the radio. From time to time, I get back into learning — I used to be a very serious learner — and I become more frum. I could change from day to day to all different levels of observance.

I don't know if I will ever be sure. Should I stop dating and wait indefinitely? I assume that when I leave yeshiva I will be the way I am most of the time. Another reason why I don't want to stop is because my parents might get divorced and I want to get engaged before that happens.

Please advise me if you can. I am quite confused about this matter.

OUR RESPONSE

It seems you are confused about two things. You are confused about how you want to live your life, but you also are confused about whether you should date someone if you aren't sure what your final *hashkafos* will be. We will try to address both issues.

Your confusion about how you want to live may be related to your parents' pending divorce. As a psychological defense, sometimes a person will create a smoke screen, a superficial problem that hides a more difficult and painful issue. Perhaps your confusion about religion is a cover for a more deeply troubling question — like the institution of marriage in general.

You probably have justifiable doubts about your own relationship skills, understandably so since your parents were probably not the best role models. Even if we assume your parents valiantly and selflessly tried to keep their marriage together for the benefit of their children, you are not secure in your knowledge of how to create a truly loving and vibrant relationship. Perhaps you should take some time to think about this more, and explore this with someone who can give you guidance.

Now, whether you should date or not. Ultimately, you said you will leave the yeshiva and engage in non-*yeshivish* practices. From a traditional yeshiva perspective, which considers secular values and entertainment detrimental to the soul, your lifestyle is anathema.

But this is not an impediment to getting married. Pragmatically speaking, there are those who identify themselves as *yeshivish* — wear black hats and daven in *yeshivish minyanim* — who nonetheless watch videos and listen to pop music. These people are externally comfortable with the practices, styles and ideology of the yeshiva world, but are not stringent in their rejection of secular culture. And there are young women who fall into this category as well.

Though your practices might not be particularly in line with what your family and/or rosh yeshiva want, there should be a sufficient supply of prospective marriage partners. Matchmakers have worked out a euphemistic code for this kind of thing — a girl who is worldly or a husband who knows more than just Gemara. You get the picture.

If you are otherwise ready for marriage, there is no reason to hold yourself back just because you might want to become more frum later on. Just be honest with yourself about what you really want. Don't marry someone on the basis of what kind of level of observance you wish you are, or significant others wish you would be. Look for a mate who is similar to you in your family background, your personal beliefs and practices. Over time, you will have the opportunity to grow together. But if you delay marriage in order to wait until you have worked everything out, time passes by quickly and opportunities can be lost.

The Ten
Commandments of Marriage

Some therapists are uncomfortable when rabbis encroach on their territory, claiming they provide unlicensed psychotherapy to their congregants. But in reality, rabbis have been marital counselors for centuries. Rabbi Avigdor Miller ZT"L's famous taped lecture series, "The Ten Commandments of Marriage," supplies us with a sound *mussar* perspective as well as psychotherapeutic advice.

"Even the idle conversation of Torah sages requires study" (*Avoda Zara* 19b). Honed by study of Torah logic and ethics, a Torah scholar automatically exudes Torah and we must treat even his idle remarks with great respect. How much more so ethical advice and admonition from the mouth of a Torah scholar!

Though we approach Rabbi Miller's teachings with great trepidation, we feel it is important to analyze and understand them. Regarding Torah commandments for which we do not know their meaning, Rambam states, "Though all the laws of the Torah are decrees [and not subject to debate] … it is fitting to contemplate them and, to whatever extent possible, try to find reasons for them" (*Mishneh Torah*, *Hilchos Temurah* 4:13).

Why is it important to find reasons for Torah laws, if we must adhere to them whether they are logical or not? Making the effort to understand the laws helps us think in consonance with the morals and ethics of the Torah.

In our analysis of Rabbi Miller's Ten Commandments of Marriage, we attempt to identify psychological or traditional sources, in order to enhance and deepen the effect of his words.

And if we are unable to find an adequate explanation, this by no means signals a diminishment of our respect for his teachings. Like Rambam in his introduction to his commentary on *Avos (Shemonah Perakim)*, we depend even on secular sources that help us understand the subject matter at hand.

COMMANDMENT #1: DO NOT TELL EVERYTHING

> *A man once approached Rabbi Miller with a dilemma. "My wife thinks I am a big tzaddik but I'm really not. What should I do? Shouldn't I tell her my faults?"*
>
> *To this Rabbi Miller responded, "Absolutely not. If only you could keep fooling her for the next one hundred and twenty years!"*

There is a similar situation presented in the Talmud. (*Chulin* 94b) The sages debate whether this is *geneivas daas*, theft of knowledge, being misleading or dishonest. The question can be resolved with an insight into the psychodynamics of this couple, which Rabbi Miller seemed to have gleaned in his great wisdom.

Sometimes a person is afraid of the success he is experiencing and might unconsciously look for the security of failure. Many times, after someone becomes significantly successful, there is a subsequent and suspicious failure. Someone gets a new job and a significant raise, but then crashes his car. A mother finally achieves control and stabilizes the behavior of one child, and shortly after that, another child begins to misbehave.

There is a strange and powerful force that draws people toward self-destruction and self-induced failure.

> Dared to perform a stunt, a young man rode his bike down a steep, scary hill. Midway down the hill, he panicked and let go of the handlebars, resulting in a serious injury. "It was so scary I just couldn't take it anymore," he later explained. "Somehow I felt better causing the accident to happen than experiencing the anxiety of waiting for it to happen."

People have an instinctive drive to seek control, to have mastery over their lives. On a primitive psychological level, a person feels more control if he can engineer his demise, instead of struggling, only to fail when he least expects it.

This may be the same principle behind beginner's luck. Why is it that a person new to a sport or endeavor is often relatively successful? The novice has nothing to lose. There's no pressure to perform; he is relaxed and able to concentrate on the task at hand. But should the beginner bowler bowl a few strikes, he suddenly becomes nervous and starts to fail.

Problems in relationships often stem from this same unconscious resistance to success. If a person is mediocre in his spouse's eyes, there's no pressure to perform. Whatever he does is okay, as long as he is doing a fair job. He is accepted, flaws and all.

But if his spouse feels he is really a great person, there is pressure to live up to that image. The husband who approached Rabbi Miller felt uncomfortable being held on a pedestal — because then he has to live up to his reputation.

And Rabbi Miller placed value in the wife's assessment, too. She was probably right, at least insofar as his potential. That's why Rabbi Miller told him not to disillusion her.

COMMANDMENT #2: DO NOT DISRUPT THE ROUTINE OF MARRIAGE

No matter how angry a person feels, he or she should never go on strike and withhold essential duties and services. Both the husband and wife should work and assist in household chores, as is the usual routine. Fights and arguments are not positive, but a relationship can survive disputes as long as the basic routine is maintained.

There was a landmark study that scientifically analyzed the ingredients of a successful marriage. Among couples tracked over a period of several years, the overall number of arguments had little bearing on whether the relationship survived. The critical feature in lasting marriages was a five-to-one ratio of positive interactions to negative interactions.

Yankel and Sorah fight like cats and dogs, but ultimately, they are happy with each other because they have five times as many good experiences together. Shmuel and Rivkie maintain a calm enmity and rarely fight, but they rarely share pleasure either — their relationship is in serious danger.

If the husband and wife constantly work together on raising the children and managing the home, even if there is much resentment and anger, there is a likelihood of a high ratio of positive experiences to overcome the negative.

Rabbi Miller's advice also makes sense on a pragmatic level. If a husband or wife withholds a basic service, or refuses to share an area that is part of normal married life, in effect he is teaching the spouse to live without it. Once the spouse learns to live without, the possibility of divorce draws nearer. So if a spouse wants to hold the relationship together, it is always wise to continue the routines and roles of the marriage.

COMMANDMENT #3: BE REALISTIC

Newlyweds' feelings of romance and excitement inevitably wear off over time. People are not head over heels in love with their spouse forever. At times, a person might feel quite disgusted and angry. This is a normal part of relationships. Ride these feelings out, make the best of it, because there will be more joy and pleasure to come.

Success in a relationship is different than success as an individual. As therapists, we sometimes encounter a person who begins treatment in individual therapy, and then wants to bring in his spouse or fiancé for couple's therapy. Treatment changes radically at that point.

When treating an individual, his needs are the center of attention. If a person complains about his spouse or parent, we explore his feelings about the matter, how it relates to his earlier relationships in life, what his choices are, and what unconscious resistance prevents him from accomplishing his stated goal.

When treating a couple, neither one is the client. The marriage is the client. Often, what is good for the relationship as a whole is not always good for the individual, and vice versa. Anyone entering a relationship needs to know that to make a relationship work requires sacrifice.

An individual need not forgo all personal goals and needs in order to have success in a relationship, but he might have to sacrifice some of them. A man might wish his wife was prettier, or a woman might wish her husband was more clever or financially successful.

When the emotional climate in a relationship sours, charming and endearing quirks suddenly transform into enormous blemishes. Small shortcomings balloon into major faults. The trick is not to focus on these. If there are truly no redeeming qualities, a person may feel divorce is an option. But nearly every spouse has some good qualities, and if one focuses on them, there is a good chance for long-term happiness.

COMMANDMENT #4: NEVER SAY THE WORD DIVORCE

Rabbi Miller intended this advice quite literally. Divorce must be out of the realm of possibility. Even mentioning divorce in jest can plant a seed that could eventually grow into a reality. Within the "Ten Commandments of Marriage," divorce is heresy.

Even in the Torah, desperate situations require desperate measures. The Talmudic dictum testifies, "When there is a time to act on behalf of Hashem, the Torah can be broken" (*Berachos* 54a). Divorce is like the atomic bomb of relationship tools, only to be used as a doomsday weapon of last resort.

If a spouse is wounding the relationship mortally, being abusive, unfaithful, or completely uncooperative in solving problems, divorce or threat of divorce, may be the only solution. The problem, whatever it may be, must be stated clearly, allowing at least one final chance to change.

But a dissatisfied spouse who chronically threatens divorce destabilizes the family emotionally. When he finally means divorce, there's no chance of effecting a change. If it never was meant seriously until now, why should it suddenly be taken seriously?

So when it comes to divorce, better not to say it. But if it must be said, it must be meant! And it should be accompanied by clear conditions — what must change in order to keep the relationship together. To minimize the likelihood of a hostile and unproductive response, such a declaration shouldn't be made in anger or with intent to hurt. It should be related in a serious, neutral tone, at a time when there are no potential distractions.

A couple can spend their lives fighting each other and still be better off not divorcing. Some couples are only able to express their intimacy through hostility. Although they fight bitterly and belittle each other, there is a certain comfort and closeness they have with each other.

From a psychodynamic perspective, this deep fear of intimacy is sometimes based on a past loss. Some are afraid to express and admit too much love, for if they lose the loved one, they will feel devastated and abandoned. As an unconscious defense, people will be cranky, intolerant and hostile.

Almost everyone has a married friend, relative or family member like this. Their continuous fighting is its own rhythm and dance. But if they were separated from each other, they would feel lonely and despondent.

The therapeutic goal for such a couple would be to help them learn to express feelings of intimacy in a more direct manner. But as much as each party wishes to divorce, it's just a sham, a defense against the fear of being close to another human being. People like this who get divorced and then remarry often wind up in similar relationships. It's not their choice of spouse; it's their emotional limitations.

COMMANDMENT #5: HAVE A PERSONAL RABBI

Rabbi Miller tells us that he is frequently approached by women who are unhappy with a particular behavior of their husbands. When he advises the woman to seek advice from her husband's rabbi, she reports, "Well, we don't really *daven* in just one *shul*, and anyway, my husband does not speak much to the rabbi. His rosh yeshiva is in Israel, but he hasn't spoken to him in several years."

It is important for every young couple to establish a rabbi from whom they can seek counsel — before problems crop up. "Make for yourself a rabbi and acquire a friend" (*Avos* 1:6).

Rabbi Miller endorses living among a community. As part of a group, members are subjected to certain standards of decency. It helps to hold impulses in check.

The American way of life is so different — socially — than the way Jews lived just a couple generations back. Jews were part of a close-knit community, surrounded by immediate family and close relatives and friends. Often, married children, parents, and siblings lived under the same roof. The stability and security this provided cannot be underestimated.

Within this warm, supportive environment, many of the challenges of observant life were mitigated. The ethical imperative to marry young and produce as many children as possible is accomplished much more easily as a member of an extended family.

A young mother recuperating from childbirth didn't just move into her mother's house for a couple weeks — she actually lived next door! They did not need lactation specialists or Lamaze classes — the wisdom of the *bubbes* and village elders were right at hand.

Today, young women admirably, and at times even stoically, fulfill the same ethical imperatives for reproduction — with barely a trace of the social support their counterparts had in earlier times. And some of these women also manage to bravely hold down jobs to support their families. We gratefully acknowledge the many advantages our ancestors did not have — bountiful wealth, freedom from persecution. But still, family and community support is critical for a healthy marriage.

Part of the initial evaluation process in marital therapy includes an assessment of familial and community supports available to the couple. Often in cases of marital dysfunction, there is some type of unnatural emotional or geographical distance from potential familial caregivers. To augment treatment, couples need to marshal their resources and support, leaving them free to work on their relationship.

If necessary, a troubled couple should bravely ask their parents or siblings for help — a babysitter once a week, for example, so they can spend a distraction-free evening together. Even children and parents or siblings who are not on the best of terms can learn to put disagreements to the side for the overriding concern of a troubled marriage.

COMMANDMENT #6 & #7:
BE LOYAL AND DISPLAY YOUR REGARD TO YOUR MATE

A wife must always stick up for her husband in front of others; a husband must always stick up for his wife — especially in front of relatives. Many couples experience difficulties dividing their loyalties between their parents and spouse, leading to issues with in-laws.

When two people marry, their respective originating families are like two separate and distinct nations, each with its own particular culture and customs. With marriage, these two nations must join together and form an alliance. In this process, there is an instinctive struggle for the continuity of the values and morals of each nation.

For parents marrying off a child, it is emotionally stressful to let go of the son or daughter they raised and hand him or her over to a foreigner. Most families are flexible enough to make the emotional transition — partially let go of one of their own citizens, and allow a new citizen to immigrate into the system.

There is a natural give and take as the two nations blend together. Common ground is found, and if accommodations are necessary, certain rules, values, and customs are modified and adjusted. Many in-law problems contain aspects of the basic unvoiced question: "Whose values will endure? Which family will have itself replicated in the future generation?"

Where to live, what school the children will attend, how they should behave, career paths — all these conflicts are really about who gets to control and shape the future generation. Parents invest an incalculable amount of energy in the nurturing and education of their children, and it is only natural that they develop an almost territorial stance regarding their grandchildren, too.

From this perspective, many seemingly petty arguments are understandable. If a couple argues about such matters, they probably have unwittingly become pawns in this tribal war over the future generation.

Although we must be diplomatic with our family of origin, we should never tolerate any slander about our spouse. Our loyalty must lie with our spouse and we must make the rest of our family aware of that.

And the children. Some people wittingly or unwittingly belittle their spouses in front of their children, involving them in complicated family politics — with damaging results. Parents must avoid disagreeing about discipline in front of their children. Differences should be settled first in private, and a unified front should be presented to the child so he cannot play one parent against the other.

COMMANDMENT #8 & #9:

ALWAYS MAINTAIN YOUR APPEARANCE AND DON'T BE SLOVENLY

This commandment applies to both men and women. Much to the surprise of his pious students, the wife of one great sage always greeted her husband adorned with jewelry. He explained her behavior to his disciples, "It is so that I not be tempted to look at other women" (*Taanis* 23b).

After marriage, men sometimes gain significant weight; women put less energy into maintaining their attractiveness. Why? Aside from aging, the burdens of earning a living and parenthood make it difficult for a man or woman to devote as much attention to personal grooming, diet and exercise like the old single days.

More cynically, she (or he) already snared a marriage partner so there is no need keep up appearances. The peacock displays its plumage during the mating season to attract a partner, but has little use for the feathers when the season is over. No doubt there is an element of truth to all of the above points, but psychodynamically it goes somewhat deeper.

In relationships, people often find themselves in highly frustrating situations where they have little chance to express their frustration, much less address it. A wife loves her husband most of the time — so she is too embarrassed to point out the occasional insensitivity. Or she may have tried to tell her husband about it a few times, but he became hostile or defensive due to his insecurity. Perhaps she feels selfish or spoiled because she has particular needs.

Many men are outwitted by the seemingly endless attention their wives spend on caring for the children. "What happened to the good old days, when I used to be the center of attention instead of this two-year old prince?" It would be most tyrannical and controlling to express these selfish thoughts. But the feelings are there. Where do they go?

Many people put these feelings into food. The religious community offers few alternative "kosher" outlets. Food is a source of immediate soothing and gratification that helps pacify the emptiness and frustration felt by many. Just watch some fathers in restaurants — the kids are screaming, the bills are running up. What can dad do? Order an extra helping! Women do the same thing.

Some neglect their appearance out of unconscious hostility. Deep down they think, "Why bother struggling to look beautiful for him, when he hardly does anything romantic?" Though it is a bit offensive, in a certain aspect there is some truth to the French saying: "There is no such thing as an ugly woman, only a lazy woman." Of course, this commandment is directed at both men and women.

COMMANDMENT #10: LOVE YOUR NEIGHBOR AS YOURSELF

This Torah directive is particularly applicable — and very important — between husband and wife. Two people who live together have a great opportunity to constantly fulfill — or constantly violate — this commandment. There is an interesting psychological mechanism that comes into play here.

Being good to a spouse is not merely loving your neighbor — it is loving yourself, in the most literal sense! Sometimes a person's ability or inability to be kind to his spouse is a direct reflection of his ability or inability to be kind to himself. What does this mean psychologically?

A wife complains her husband never does anything romantic on their anniversary and doesn't verbalize his affection for her. But when the husband finally buys her roses, a fight erupts. He made a significant gesture, albeit with minor mistakes, and his wife simply squashes his progress.

Some people have a natural resistance to enjoying themselves, perhaps from fear of intimacy, or perhaps reflective of a deeper fear of endearment and subsequent loss. If the wife has to appreciate her husband now, there will be a greater feeling of loss should anything happen to him.

This woman's resistance to her husband's overtures is as much about her own inability to be good to herself as they are about his faults. She does not treat her husband in accordance with "love your neighbor as yourself" because of her own resistance to receiving pleasure.

To put the commandment in practice, this woman must show love to her husband, and also prepare herself to receive the love that her husband will inevitably reciprocate. This heartfelt give and take brings emotional growth and development in its wake.

◇ 8

How To Argue
with Your Spouse

Believe it or not, there really is a simple formula for han-
dling marital disputes respectfully. Follow these rules and
you will have more productive and less hurtful arguments.

ACTIVE LISTENING

When discussing a difficult issue, you and your spouse must
both agree to employ active listening: You make a statement. Your
spouse must repeat the statement until you are satisfied that your
point is correctly understood. Then your spouse can proceed with
a response.

Do not confuse understanding with agreeing. Many marital
spats run afoul on this nuance. Unless one or both of you are psy-
chotic, you may strongly disagree with your spouse, but still
comprehend and relate to your spouse's view. Frankly, you can
only disagree in good conscience if you really understand the
other's viewpoint thoroughly.

This wonderful technique is effective on many levels. First, it reduces misunderstandings that often are the cause of arguments,
because it forces both parties to pay close attention to the other
side of the argument. Second, even if there still is major disagreement, husband and wife feel respected and understood, defusing
rising tensions and anger.

This technique is supported by the Talmud:

> Why was the *halacha* ruled in accordance with the opinion of
> Bais Hillel? Because they were gentle and forgiving in nature,

and they studied their opinion as well as Bais Shammai's opinion. Furthermore, they would state Bais Shammai's opinion first. (*Eruvin* 13b).

If the issue raised is a matter of *halacha* and intellect, how can the character traits of the sages factor into the decision? The *halacha* should be decided based on intellectual acumen and prowess. And it was Bais Shammai that excelled in this area! (*Yevamos* 14a)

One who respects both opinions is most likely to arrive at the more accurate answer. Bais Hillel studied and considered both their own view and Bais Shammai's, so the *halacha* was decided in favor of Bais Hillel. This has obvious implications for how we should conduct ourselves in all disagreements.

I VERSUS YOU, FEELINGS VERSUS JUDGMENTS

The "simple formula" we described above is not so simple. You cannot use abusive language such as name-calling. "So your point is that I am an idiot and a fool..." This type of statement is not conducive to a productive argument. Both parties must avoid "You statements," and stick with "I statements." You should express your feelings instead of passing judgment.

Yosef and Bracha — this couple might remind you of people you know, but any resemblance is purely coincidental. Bracha hates going to her in-laws for the holidays because her mother-in-law is highly critical.

> **Bracha**: Yosef, why do you want us to go to your parents for Yom Tov? Your mother is so mean!

> **Yosef**: Well, why do you have to be so sensitive? And anyway, sometimes you act so crazy, of course my mother gets upset!

Do you notice all the "You statements" and the judgmental language? Well, of course we are well on the way to a horrible fight. Compare it to this next version.

> **Bracha**: Yosef, I do not want to go to your parents for Yom Tov. When your mother speaks to me she makes me feel criticized.

Yosef: Well, I hear you saying that you do not want to go my parents for Yom Tov, but I miss them and I feel guilty if we don't go.

True, no one likes to hear that their spouse and mother don't get along, so this is still somewhat threatening to Yosef. Nevertheless, the language itself is less threatening and tends to reduce tension. Do you notice the abundance of feelings? No one is being called any names or negative adjectives. Each person is sharing feelings about themselves. Yosef even validated his wife's viewpoint before he went on to say his own.

Because of this simple formula, the conversation is on the road to some sort of compromise. At the very least, no one's feelings are being unnecessarily hurt. With a little thought and a lot of listening, disagreements don't have to be arguments anymore.

When a Couple
Just Can't Stop Fighting

There are methods for healthy arguments, but why do couples fight in the first place? Well, obviously because they disagree! All husbands and wives, parents and children will disagree at times. But for some people, disagreements are resolved quickly and fairly, while others have fights that are degrading, painful and destructive.

Husband and wife know what they should and shouldn't say, but they just can't control their tempers or choice of words. After a particularly nasty and damaging fight, the couple may promise each other to speak more calmly in the future. But eventually the couple will succumb to this compulsion to argue and fight mercilessly, like moths drawn to a flame.

Abusive relationships are in a completely different category from terrible and damaging fights. The distinction lies in the power differential. In abusive relationships, one party has the upper hand and the other party is the victim. A squabbling husband and wife are equals, capable of inflicting equal damage on each other.

Many couples that have these types of horrible fights also feel a great deal of love toward each other. When they are not squabbling they even feel close. Nasty arguments do not mean the marriage is doomed. But most people will not put up with misery forever. Sometimes, there are too many hurt feelings to allow for continued relationship. Like a flame, love can be extinguished if not tended carefully.

But if these couples do divorce and then continue on to remarry, these relationship problems resurface. The problem is not necessarily the marriage. There can be deeper personality, communication and relationship issues. Without any change, history repeats itself in a new marriage.

THE ANATOMY OF A MARITAL SPAT

As therapists, we have identified three elements in a typical marital or family argument. (1) *Argumentum ad hominem*, insults and demeaning words are used instead of discussing issues to resolve; (2) a pattern of escalating insults, instead of honest reflection and validation of the other's comments; and (3) an underlying emotional theme.

No matter how hostile or insulting the remark, you must first honestly evaluate if there is any measure of truth to the accusation. If there is some truth, take responsibility for it and apologize, no matter how angry and frustrated you are about the way in which it was said.

And after honest reflection, if the statement is found to be false, validate your spouse's remark regardless.

> A wife accuses her husband of being wasteful and careless because he left the lights on all over the house. He is sure that he shut them off, and the cleaning lady left them on. His initial response is to flat out deny the accusation. Instead he can say, "I understand that it really bothers you when we waste electricity."
>
> *He shows her that he is supportive and empathetic. And he just de-escalated a confrontation.*

Many times couples think they are fighting about one thing, but really it is a deeper issue. This is not at all obvious and takes practice to recognize. Certain couples fight about the same things over and over again without resolving anything. They are not fighting about what is really bothering them. Sometimes the fight is induced to serve as a distraction from painful or disturbing emotions, which the couple is not ready to face.

> **Yosef**: You always are spoiling the kids and are too weak-willed to discipline them!

Bracha: You don't spend enough time with them, and anyway you aren't stuck at home all day, so don't judge me!

Yosef: Boy, I wish I could be stuck at home! Do you realize how hard my job is? All you do is nag and complain. You are just lazy and immature!

Bracha: You have some nerve! You waltz home after eight every night and grumble without saying a kind word to anyone. I wish for once you would come home early and help out!

Yosef: I wish for once you would stop whining and actually do some work around here.

[Fight degrades into incoherent hollering and screaming.]

Yosef and Bracha certainly should have acknowledged the other's feelings and spoken with more tact and respect. But let's focus on another aspect of the fight. The fight escalated because of a few underlying emotional themes that neither one was able to tune into.

When Yosef accused Bracha of not disciplining the children, is it really because he is concerned about their upbringing? If he is so concerned about his children's development, Yosef should certainly reflect on the effect of belittling their mother! He is probably jealous that Bracha indulges the children more than he does. There is a clue supporting this in the remark he makes later on about how hard his job is.

Bracha complains that Yosef "waltzes home after eight every night" and does not spend enough time with the children. This is projection. Bracha projects her own inner feelings — that she herself doesn't get to spend enough time with Yosef — and places it on the children.

This is just one possible set of underlying issues. Bracha and Yosef essentially have the same complaint. They feel neglected and isolated; they feel that they are working too hard. If either one, or both, could tune into the underlying issues, the fight could be more easily resolved.

Bracha and Yosef need to let go of their anger and resentment and work together on meeting this common emotional need. A couple can learn to tune into these emotional currents and respond to them, resulting in less fighting. And the disagreements they do have can be resolved more quickly and fairly.

10

Revenge in Marriage

When you are hurt, humiliated, or wronged, you have an urge to seek revenge. Although logically, revenge does not usually bring about an improvement or correction to the situation, somehow it feels good to let the other party have a taste of their own medicine.

Most consider revenge an immoral and ugly act. But morals aside, revenge is the cause for many difficulties within marriages and other family relationships. Often a resentful family member's behavior is motivated by the need to get even. And often the parties involved are more interested in evening the score than working toward a fresh and positive solution.

THE DRIVE

Evolutionary psychologists seek to explain human behavior and emotions in terms of how a particular response enhances the chances of survival. The behaviors and response that work are passed down — genetically — to the next generation. Although evolutionary psychologists think of this in terms of Darwinian natural selection, a religious person can see these survival traits as evidence of the wisdom of the Creator. (Such an approach has support in the words of Rambam, *Mishneh Torah*, *Yesodei HaTorah* 4:12)

The need to seek revenge, according to evolutionary psychologists, occurs in order to neutralize and prevent any future dangers to the organism. An animal that seeks to completely destroy its enemies and attackers — even after the current threat is removed —

has a greater chance of surviving than an animal that merely responds defensively to an impending attack. Hence the existence of revenge. Revenge is at least partially instinctive, but not necessarily adaptive to modern civilization.

The psychoanalytic approach interprets revenge as an ego defense against other painful emotional states, such as depression or a feeling of impotence. After you suffer humiliation, you seek to deflect this pain by directing it outward against the perceived aggressor. The very act of revenge artificially bolsters an illusion of strength, competence and power. Although this is an effective short-term defense against painful feelings, it is not the best approach for personal growth and character development.

Most people would claim to be familiar with the Torah view on revenge — namely that it is forbidden. As it states, "Do not take revenge nor bear a grudge" (*Vayikra* 19:18). Actually, the Torah philosophy regarding revenge is much more complex. Surprisingly, there are instances when it may be permitted to respond in kind to an attacker.

The Talmud (*Yoma* 22b) defines the parameters of revenge and grudge bearing.

> What is taking revenge, and what is bearing a grudge? Taking revenge is when you ask your neighbor to lend you his saw and he says, "No." The next day, your neighbor asks to borrow your ax and you say, "I will not lend it to you just as you did not lend to me." That is taking revenge. What is bearing a grudge? That is when you ask your neighbor to lend you his ax and he says, "No." The next day, your neighbor requests to borrow your garment and you say, "Here, take it. I am not like you who did not lend me." That is bearing a grudge.

Not only is it forbidden to retaliate in response to mistreatment, it also appears that it is even forbidden to inform the person about your resentments.

As further encouragement to let go of past resentments, the Talmud (*Yoma* 87b) states, "One who overlooks his honor when offended will be forgiven for all his sins." It is considered cruel to withhold forgiveness from someone who is sincerely apologetic. (Rambam, *Mishneh Torah*, *Hilchos Teshuva* 2:10)

The verse in *Vayikra* that precedes the prohibition of revenge indicates another course of action entirely. "Do not hate your friend in your heart, rebuke him and do not bear a sin on his behalf." The Torah commands you to tell the person directly what he has done wrong so you won't come to hate him.

Similarly, the Rambam (*Mishneh Torah, Hilchos Deos* 6:6) states:

> When one person wrongs another, the latter should not remain silent and despise him. This is the way of the wicked, as *Shmuel* II (13:22) states, "And Avshalom did not speak to Amnon neither good nor bad, for Avshalom hated Amnon." Rather, one is commanded to make the matter known and ask him, "Why did you do this to me? Why did you wrong me regarding that matter?"

How do we reconcile these two imperatives? You are obligated to inform your neighbor how he wronged you. Yet, when he requests to borrow something from you, you are forbidden to remark on his ungenerous behavior of the past.

There are two critical differences between bearing a grudge and telling someone how you were mistreated. The first is time related. If you respond immediately by telling the person what he did wrong, this is not bearing a grudge. But if you keep silent for a while, hatred builds up in your heart. And then, only when he asks you for a favor, you inform him of your resentment. This is bearing a grudge.

Second, there is an opinion that an act of retaliation is classified as revenge only when it is monetary-related (*tzarah dimemona*). (*Yoma* 22b) If your neighbor refuses to lend you his saw, you may not respond in kind — that would be revenge. But if he causes emotional pain, it is permitted to respond and inform him how you resent his actions. Still, you must take care not to violate the prohibitions against slander or verbally hurtful remarks.

This Torah approach is beneficial psychologically as well. The Torah encourages people to express their resentments appropriately, not to let them simmer. This prevents buildup of anger and its destructive release. Expressing feelings and reflecting on past actions increases the possibility of growth and change.

According to this approach, the Torah draws a line between emotional issues and social cooperation. Revenge is forbidden when it is in response to the withholding of a physical service or object. This maintains stability in relationships, not allowing someone to retaliate "tit for tat" against another who has not loaned an object or withheld a similar good or service.

PRACTICAL ADVICE

This approach provides an excellent guideline for couples who are experiencing serious disagreements and fights. The long-term goal is to reduce fighting and increase marital satisfaction. But in the short term, it is essential that neither party retaliate by withholding necessary services.

Whatever issues and disagreements are going on between a couple, if a husband always goes grocery shopping and helps out with the housekeeping, he should continue to do so. If a wife always cooks dinner, let her cook dinner no matter how angry she is.

Basic operations and infrastructure of the relationship should function as normal, so that when and if the other resentments are solved or smoothed over, there won't be new problems, grudges, and resentments.

11

Giving Gifts with Words

G-d sent three angels to visit Avraham after his circumcision. One angel had the specific task of informing Avraham and Sarah of the impending birth of a child. Why did G-d deem it necessary to send an angel bearing this news? Surely Sarah would soon determine she was with child. Then she and Avraham would recognize G-d's miraculous kindness.

There is an important lesson in *derech eretz* (proper behavior). "When one gives a gift to his friend, he is obligated to inform him" (*Shabbos* 10b). There are psychological benefits to this rabbinic dictum, but many retain an unconscious resistance to it.

SPEECHLESS

A husband sends his wife a dozen roses every year on their anniversary. Surprisingly, she hardly seems happy about it. But it is not so surprising. He never says, "Here are a dozen roses because I love you. These roses celebrate the wonderful day we started our life together."

If this husband were asked why his loving gesture is not accompanied with words, he would respond, "Well, of course I love her! Obviously, I am happy we are married. Why else would I send her roses?"

Words that accompany a gift are as important as the gift itself. The Meiri says that it fosters friendship and love. When you tell someone you are giving him a gift, it enhances the act. By extension, any small or great act of kindness is enhanced with a loving verbal message.

An extra household chore due to an unfortunate circumstance — like a spouse's illness — can be turned into a loving gift by saying, "I am happy to do this because I love you." The same with children. Young children require a lot of extra attention — they are not self-sufficient. Verbalize it. As supper is served say, "Here is a delicious dinner for you because I love you. I'm happy I can take care of you."

THE UNSPOKEN MESSAGE

Why is it so difficult for many people to follow this advice? In some cases, there may be unconscious or conscious resentment that prevents someone from expressing love or caring.

The husband who sends the anniversary flowers — he may appreciate his wife for many things, but there may be certain things he resents. And these prevent him from being extra solicitous. Instead of letting the relationship stagnate, he should productively discuss his resentments. Likely his wife also has disappointments of her own and he should be ready to hear her side.

It may not be easy to discuss problems, but it can ultimately be very rewarding. He may be afraid of stirring up a hornet's nest. In this case, maybe he should consider letting go of his resentment altogether and turning over a new leaf. If he can manage this, it may also bring beneficial results. When he changes his behavior for the better and becomes more attentive, she may automatically do the same.

Saying, "I am doing this because I love you," raises the bar and creates an expectation that further acts of kindness will follow. There's no resentment, only love. But people don't want to commit themselves to this level of performance.

Emotional limitations like these often result from childhood experiences. They can be remedied over time, first by becoming aware of this fear, and then by consciously taking small steps toward greater levels of verbal and personal expressions of commitment.

Love and Hate are Closer Than You Think

Love and hate are at opposite ends of the spectrum. Behavior toward a loved one versus an enemy is miles apart. But if love and hate are so unrelated, how can people hate someone they used to love so much? Some of the bitterest feuds occur between family members. Crime statistics show a great prevalence of violence toward friends and relatives.

PHENOMENON SINCE BIBLICAL TIMES

The Torah calls attention to this paradox as well, in reference to Amnon's enmity for Tamar. "For his hatred for her was even greater than the love he used to have for her" (*Shmuel* II 13:15). What psychological mechanisms account for this human dynamic?

Hatred usually requires a certain amount of closeness. You can't hate someone you have nothing to do with. The most horrible villains in the Torah are also close to G-d. The Talmud relates that G-d grabbed Yeravam ben Nevat by his clothes and offered, "Repent, and you and I and the son of Yishai [King David] will stroll together in the Garden of Eden." (*Sanhedrin* 102a)

Yeravam declined because G-d only offered to give him second place, behind King David. Yeravam's personal qualities and potential must have been such that in his own way, he was as close to G-d as he was distant — if he only repented. He certainly had high standards and aspirations, if he refused to be second only to Dovid HaMelech.

Amalek, the reviled nation descended from Esav, son of Yitzchak, also had aspects of greatness. The Torah anthropomorphically describes G-d swearing by His throne to eradicate the memory of Amalek. (*Shemos* 17:16) In a way, this paradoxically ensures that Amalek will be remembered forever! The villainous nation of Amalek must have had significant qualities — which they unfortunately used for their villainous aims — to merit this personal attention.

APPLYING IT TODAY

The deepest truths of the Torah are beyond our comprehension, but we see a significant connection between the haters and the hated. The closer you are with a friend, the more physical and emotional pain he can inflict. We hate people because they hurt us, perceived or real. And if we hate them, this defends us from suffering further pain. In an allegorical sense, wicked biblical personalities also had great potential to serve and be close to G-d, and therefore their sins caused a greater spiritual cataclysm.

Hatred often happens automatically and instinctively; it is therefore highly destructive to families and relationships. When a behavior is understood, we exercise greater conscious control over it, and we can make rational and thoughtful changes. But many times we are unaware of hatred felt toward a spouse or a child.

Objectively, we exhibit behavior that is clearly hatred. Because hatred is such an ugly emotion, however, we have difficulty admitting it to ourselves. "How can I hate someone who I am supposed to love?" In reality, we usually only hate the people whom we can or did love!

But our first reaction need not be recoiling in shame when we find ourselves hating a loved one. We need to analyze and understand it. Why is the hatred so strong? Are there any ways to change the situation?

A friend can provide a more objective outlook. In more difficult to resolve cases, therapeutic counseling should be sought. But realize that the depth of hate that exists right now in the relationship may be an indicator of the great potential for love.

The Husband
Who Wouldn't Study Torah

Dear Feuermans,

I am married to a loving husband and caring father, but I have one problem. I always imagined that my husband would spend time every day studying Torah and would eventually become knowledgeable and well-versed in Talmud and halacha. This is what I always admired about my father.

I don't expect my husband to be a great rabbi or brilliant halachic authority. I just wish he could say an intellectually challenging Torah thought at the Shabbos table and know enough to guide us on the everyday halachic questions that arise.

When we were dating, my husband was learning and I never had any reason to be concerned that he would not continue to make time in his life to study Torah. The way it works now, I am the one who recalls the halacha from how my father conducted himself, and I tend to challenge the children to look at the deeper issues in the Torah thoughts they repeat at the Shabbos table. I encourage my husband to study but he is too tired at the end of the day, and on Shabbos he wants to relax and read the newspaper. Is there any way to get my husband to change?

When someone's yarmulka falls off his head, it is very difficult for another person other than the wearer to place it back on correctly. Sometimes, the more you pressure a person to do something, the less he feels like doing it. It must be very painful for you that your husband falls short of your expectations. But the fact that he senses it only exacerbates the situation.

Psychologically speaking, laziness is rare. More likely, laziness is a conscious or unconscious decision to step down from a challenge, avoiding potential failure. It is easier to tell ourselves, "I choose not to do this because I am lazy," than to face a feeling of incompetence if we try to do something and fail.

Assuming that in your community the norm is for men to display prowess in Talmud and *halacha*, your husband is opting out, likely due to feelings of inadequacy and prior failures in Torah study. Your personal expertise and your inadvertent comparison of your husband to your father only make him feel more inadequate.

Although unquestionably the yeshiva system has promoted Torah growth and scholarship throughout the Jewish community, with certain individuals it has the opposite effect. Torah can potentially include a broad range of philosophy, literature, mathematics, ethics and commerce. It can appeal to almost any individual's interests or tastes. But this gets lost in the emphasis on traditional Talmudic scholarship that the yeshiva stresses.

The Talmud itself recommends, "One should always study in an area that his heart desires" (*Avoda Zara* 19a). Your husband probably views Torah study as a burden instead of a pleasure because of his experience in the yeshiva system. If he would study whatever arouses his curiosity, he will develop a natural taste for the inherent pleasure of learning Torah. Language should not be a barrier either, as today there are hundreds of Jewish classics available with superb English language translations.

If this has provided you with some insight into the nature of your husband's problem, you still must be cautious. Avoid patronizing your husband, but do encourage him when he does express interest. Be attentive and show your respect for his scholarship. Men have a need for their wives to respect and support their abilities, regardless of their actual standing in the community.

The Talmud makes a wry observation about a wife's loyalty to her husband regardless of his profession. The Talmud tells us of a woman who was first married to a scholar, and then to a tax collector. "When she was married to the Torah scholar she assisted him by tying his *tefillin* to his arm. When that same woman was married to a tax collector she assisted him by tying a tax signet to his arm" (Avoda Zara 39a).

The Should Syndrome

Many people fall into the "should" trap. A wife is angry with her husband because he "should" spend more time with her. A husband is annoyed because his wife "should" be nicer to his brother and sister-in-law. In healthy relationships, husband and wife communicate and work through incompatibilities, but certain issues resist change.

Getting hung up on "should's" interferes with constructive and practical ways of moving past the problem. The spouse is completely focused on the notion that she is correct. "If only he would just realize that he is wrong, then he would do it the right way."

Even if, objectively speaking, the person is correct, the world of relationships is subjective. Every opinion has validity, and in relationships, we have to learn how to respect others' opinions. People who obsess over what they believe others "should do" are lapsing into primitive emotions of anger and fear instead of employing more mature emotions such as empathy and compassion.

If an issue comes up, you should communicate feelings of anger and hurt to prevent resentments from building to a toxic level. But if after repeated attempts there is no resolution, it may be more healthful to just let go. Letting go is not to compromise or to control your temper; it does not mean swallowing your anger while you continue to seethe with resentment. Letting go means to completely overlook any wrongdoing committed against you. It means forgetting about what "should" be.

Letting go can be quite rewarding. Someone who learns to let go of even legitimate resentments creates an environment of acceptance and love.

Help,
My Wife is a Chessed-aholic!

Dear Feuermans,

You know how some men are workaholics, so addicted to their work that they ignore their personal lives? Well, I am in the opposite position. I earn a decent salary, do not have to work crazy hours and actually enjoy spending time with my family. But my wife is too busy to spend time with me.

It's not my wife's job that keeps her away; it's all the different community activities she is selflessly devoted to. Every weekend, either it's a tea, or a matchmaker's meeting, or a speech. And during the week, the phone rings off the hook with people who need various forms of assistance or advice.

Don't get me wrong, I am very proud of my wife's dedication and chessed. But where do my needs fit in? Doesn't charity begin in the home?

OUR RESPONSE

You compare your wife's involvement in *chessed* to a workaholic. What are the psychodynamics behind the behavior of a workaholic? Looking at the root of the word, it is obviously borrowed from the term alcoholic. Just as some people can become addicted to a drug, others can become addicted to work.

Many mental health professionals agree that addictive behavior is reinforced in part by the avoidance of pain or discomfort. Addicts use drugs or alcohol to numb themselves from internal emotional pain.

What does this have to do with a workaholic? Some people are uncomfortable or anxious around their family. If a person has resentment toward his spouse, he may not wish to feel or recognize this resentment. After all, most people do not like to fight. He might feel that the situation is hopeless — his dissatisfactions will never be resolved. He'll try to find a way to avoid it all.

Unconsciously, the workaholic evades his home life. He comes home late when everyone is too tired to fight. He might have the best excuses for why he is so busy, but deep down, he only allowed himself to become so busy in order to avoid the painful feelings he gets being around his family.

The *chessed*-aholic you describe is no different. There may be no better excuse than being involved in a *mitzvah*, but if the behavior is excessive then it is fair to presume that deep down, this serves a need to avoid.

Now What?

You may be tempted to confront your spouse and say, "See, this proves something is wrong with you! Why can't you spend more time with me?" Bad idea. The workaholic — or *chessed*-aholic — will only justify his behavior. "You don't understand how hard I work, everyone leaves the burden to me."

No one appreciates being psychoanalyzed by his or her spouse. So why are we explaining the psychodynamics? This is to help you understand and become sensitized to changes you may need to make in your relationship.

Instead of accusing your spouse of not spending time with you, set aside time for a serious discussion about your spouse's personal needs and goals. Are there aspects of your relationship that are dissatisfying? What can be done to change them?

If sincere efforts to communicate and work on this problem are not effective, try a different approach. Instead of accusing her or being argumentative, make yourself into a *chessed* project in order to get her attention. She likes to do *chessed*! Something — maybe guilt — is compelling her to help everyone else in town.

Try saying something like, "I feel very lonely when you are gone," or, "I miss your company." She may not respond right away. But if you say it with emotion — and it doesn't work well if you fake it — then maybe she'll start to feel guilty for not spending time with you.

SECTION TWO
Raising Children to be Mentschen

Religious parents feel a responsibility to raise their children not only to become successful people, but also good Jews. Every parent wants his child to grow up to be a mentsch, a fully mature person with sterling character traits capable of living a productive and meaningful life. Presumably this is the goal of Torah chinuch as well. But how do we incorporate the choices provided by modern society into the richness of our tradition?

16

How to Raise Healthy Children

Psychology books and articles speak mostly about problems and illnesses. They do not concentrate on which factors promote well-adjusted families and children. In this article, we attempt to identify features that healthy families display, and ways in which they engender mental health in their children. Whether the families are rich or poor, stressed out or relaxed, strict or lenient, there are three key features they all share — emotional flexibility, boundaries, and communication.

EMOTIONAL FLEXIBILITY

Parents should respond to situations in an emotionally real manner, and not slavishly adhere to rigid rules. *Koheles* mentions (3:1-8) that there is an appropriate time for every type of behavior and every emotion. Though in general disciplining should be consistent, there is always an exception to the rule.

Letting go of anger and forgiving, even when the other person is "totally wrong," is another important example of emotional flexibility. Spouses who respect each other, who do not hold long-standing grudges, are good models for their children.

For children to feel comfortable with themselves, they need parents who possess this emotional freedom. A person who trusts in himself can change his mind, admit a mistake, and think creatively. Such a person will be able to adapt to all types of stresses and show resilience in the face of the vicissitudes of life.

BOUNDARIES

Boundaries mean there are clear rules in the home for how to behave, with minimum expectations. Parents should be treated with respect, and responsibilities such as chores should be appropriately assigned. Even a three-year-old child can be responsible for putting his clothes in the hamper or throwing away a younger sibling's diaper. Children develop self-confidence when they play a role in the maintenance of the family.

Personal space is another boundary. Adults should certainly have privacy, but children are also entitled to some degree of respect at an age appropriate level. If a door is closed, other members of the household should knock before entering. Of course, if boundaries are too strict, this would infringe on emotional flexibility.

COMMUNICATION

A healthy family must have a system where family members can communicate with each other. Even families that are very busy should set aside time — a designated day and hour to eat supper without any interruptions. Parents should reserve special time to spend with each child. Some families hold meetings where each of the family members gets a chance to talk and share opinions. We know people are very busy these days, so this presents a real challenge.

Some parents fear that giving their children a chance to express their opinions about family rules would lead to disrespect and is not in consonance with Torah values. But Dr. Haim Ginot made an important distinction: "Children are given a voice, but not a vote." Parents can express interest in their children's thoughts and opinions, but they reserve the right to make the ultimate decision.

Rambam discusses the respectful treatment of a servant:

> However, even though the letter of the law is such [that it permits one to work his servants intensively], it is the way of the scrupulous in the commandments …to be a merciful person and to abstain from excessive screaming or anger. Rather, the master should speak to the servant in a gentle tone and listen to his complaints …The children of Avraham, the Jewish people upon whom G-d bestowed the goodness of the Torah, are merciful to all. (*Mishneh Torah, Hilchos Avadim* 9:8)

If this is how one is advised to treat his servants, one should obviously treat his children with at least as much respect.

17

Children and the Media

We live in an age where we are bombarded by media. Even without watching TV, listening to the radio, or reading a newspaper, we are exposed to outside influences from advertisements on billboards and buses. Aside from religious objections to the content of today's media, parents should be concerned about the effects and influence these often lurid and graphic displays have upon a child's developing mind.

TECHNOLOGY CHANGES OUR SOCIAL VALUES

As technology advances it becomes harder to erect protective barriers between our families and the outside world. You can refuse to own a TV, or place limits on the degree of access children have to it. Some religious communities even ban computers because of the Internet.

But what will you do when the telephone itself merges into a universal communications device that is a computer and television all in one? Without it, your limited access to communications will severely hamper your business. This technology is already here, so be prepared!

Changing communications technology will bring new moral and social implications, along with increased access to others' personal lives. Twenty years ago, no one expected a physician to be available for emergencies twenty-four hours a day. Today, with beepers and cell phones, a doctor who is out of touch and unreachable might be held liable. In the same way, changing technology will reach into our homes and force us to come to terms with it.

If you don't own an answering machine, people are annoyed that they cannot reach you or leave a message. In the same way, we can reasonably speculate that if everyone uses a videophone, you would be anti-social to use an audio-only phone. No employer would want to hire someone who refused to show his face on a phone interview.

The next generation is comfortable with personal lives being documented in public. There are those whose social lives revolve around on-line contacts and role-playing games. Evolving technology brings societal changes — some positive, such as the availability of thousands of *shiurim* on-line as electronic audio files; and some negative. There will be no way to shut it out. As society changes, you will have no choice but to find your — and your family's — place within the new social reality.

THE ELECTRONIC BABYSITTER

Many parents use television, videos or video games for babysitting purposes. Parents can buy as much as two to three hours of relief time by depositing their children in front of these devices. Parents, you do deserve a break, but these non-activities have a negative impact on child development. There are healthier options available for parental relief.

Studies show that American children are overweight and out of shape. Many attribute this to the numerous sedentary hours children spend in front of the television. Reading a book is also sedentary, but it is by no means passive. Kids have to process new words and idea, they have to turn the pages. Video games, though they require concentration and mental agility, are repetitive and lacking in the educational value that books possess.

If your child was not watching television or playing a video game, perhaps you might spend some time talking together.

EDUCATIONAL BROADCASTING

Everyone agrees that movies with violent or immodest content are unsuitable for children. But public television and children's videos? They're harmless, maybe even beneficial!

Not necessarily. Even relatively benign children's movies carry with them many cultural assumptions, and indoctrinate children with the values and morals of writers and producers whose lifestyles and beliefs differ drastically from your own.

Comparing some Disney movies, parents are portrayed as unthinking and unaware at best, foolish buffoons at worst. The child or teen hero always knows best. Even the wonderful and squeaky-clean *Mary Poppins*, with the enchanting music and choreography, portrays the father to be a foolish tyrant. At the end of the movie, he must let it all hang loose and risk his job in order to be redeemed as a parent. The only adult who behaves admirably and acts emotionally stable is Mary Poppins — and she is, quite literally, a witch!

In *The Lion King*, Father behaves honorably, but he gets murdered early on — the nice, ethical adult finishes last. The rest of the adults are either evil like Uncle Scar, or passive and ineffectual. The only resolution is a violent showdown between Simba and Scar.

Not all these movies are absolute moral poison. Even *The Lion King* has many important moral lessons in it. But a parent cannot plunk a child down in front of a video and assume that no supervision is required.

Stories in *Tanach* and *Midrash* require parental supervision and discussion, too. But Torah stories are learned under the guidance of a teacher. The lessons and morals are explored within the context of our traditions. Children in a trance-like state, without an adult's guiding presence to help them exercise critical thinking, are more susceptible to absorb the values and morals presented in videos and movies.

The PG rating stands for parental guidance. Have you ever seen a parent who actually gives a child parental guidance after a movie? If you find it acceptable for your children to watch PG videos, be sure to take the time to watch it with them and then ask them afterward what they learned from it. Try it out, and you may be surprised at what your child understands and misunderstands from what he has viewed.

Recent children's cartoons depict a distorted image of women and girls. Who knows what disastrous effect this picture of physical perfection has on the perception of young children?

Educational programs, such as *Magic School Bus* or *Electric Company*, make science and literature exciting with hyperactive characters, explosion-a-minute programming, and comic relief injected at every opportunity. The sobering and awe-inspiring wonders of creation or the emotions evoked in a story are just too powerful for the shows' writers and producers — they need to inject distraction. Children are trained to expect a punch line every minute, while the Jewish approach to wisdom and knowledge requires an appropriate degree of respect and restraint. (See *Mishneh Torah, Hilchos Yesodei HaTorah* 4:1,12,13.)

There may be a good deal of worthwhile content in these shows. And children do need to be entertained when they learn. But these shows can go too far and become subtly damaging.

VIDEO GAMES

Video games are not viewed as advertisements in a conventional sense, but they are advertisements nonetheless. Whether the video game is a promotion for the cards or the movie or the other way around is an enigma. All three are advertisements for each other and amazingly, you pay for all of them!

The newest generation of video games brings a level of graphics and realism that is astounding. While video games may be less harmful than television, the social and emotional implications from extended use are not unknown. There is one recent study reported in *The New York Times* (January 23, 2001, page F7) that shows a strong link between aggression and violent video games and television shows.

As children mature, assuming they have a core sense of values developed from a stable family life, they are able to separate fantasy from fiction. Games played in moderation at an age-appropriate level are probably harmless. But as a form of entertainment, they are of limited social and educational value. It is much better for children to engage in recreation that is more socially and physically interactive than video games.

THE INTERNET

The Internet is a revolutionary tool for communication, information retrieval and commerce. It is probably responsible for the longest lasting economic expansion in history.

But despite the Internet's obvious utility and value, more than fifty percent of Internet commerce is composed of pornographic and adult content. That can be a serious problem if you want to allow your child to surf the net.

Computerized censors are not able to filter out all content because of the complexity and constantly changing nature of the world wide web. The onus rests in the hands of the parents to monitor if and when children are allowed to use the Internet. You will need to take an active role in monitoring your children's use of the Internet and educating them about its potential dangers.

Mommy, I'm Bored!

Without these forms of entertainment your children will be fighting, whining and complaining, right? Not necessarily. Being bored is also an opportunity for personal growth and development. Children who squabble because of boredom need to learn how to soothe and calm themselves. If children are constantly tranquilized with mindless activities, they miss this opportunity for growth.

Most needs tend to be defined by the environment. If there is a television in the room and a child wants to watch it, he is bored and has nothing to do. But if there is no TV, books, crayons, papers, and toy cars suddenly become more appealing. Being bored is only the initial response and withdrawal symptom.

As with any developmental task, parents should be supportive and sympathetic but not overly involved. As a parent, you should communicate your expectations in a firm but empathetic manner, stating your conviction that children can learn how to occupy themselves. Tell your eight-year-old, "You feel like you have nothing to play with this afternoon. That can be hard for you. But if you keep thinking, I'm sure you can come up with something."

As long as you supply your child with a reasonable and age appropriate selection of toys, games, and activities, there's no reason to feel guilty — no matter how much whining you hear. If you make it clear that his boredom is not your problem, rather his own developmental challenge, over time you will hear fewer and fewer complaints.

Our Final Take

Of course, the best protection against outside influences is just that — keep it outside. Yet it is becoming increasingly difficult to shut these influences out of our homes. Parents must therefore be aware of the dangers and set appropriate limits.

Thankfully, the largest influence on a child's character is his family's own values. As Jews, we belong to a larger community that has always been able to preserve traditions. We have a moral compass to bequeath our children. We must model appropriate behavior and engage our children in guided discussions and exposure to media. Advertisements, news, and other media should be discussed with children. We have to develop their critical thinking skills to inoculate them against the media's powerful influence.

From a psychological perspective, when a child is either over-gratified or under-gratified, there usually is a delay in development. Parents who want their children to mature in their ability to handle these influences need to find the right balance of access and limits. Though there are no perfect answers for this, common sense and thoughtful discussion should be your guide.

Motivational Charts

A chart or reward system is a commonly used method to motivate children to change their behavior. Many parents fail to utilize this tool either because they find it ineffective, or because they feel it trains children to expect bribes. But such motivational charts can be extremely helpful — when applied appropriately.

A BRIBE?

Some might argue that children should obey parents out of fear, respect, and gratitude. If you constantly reward your child with treats, he will not develop fear for his parents. But the proper application of a reward system does not contradict this development. A proper reward system bolsters and reinforces the authority of a parent. If a parent has not established a presence of authority and respect, no chart or reward will be effective.

A chart should be implemented as an incentive to help a reasonably obedient child apply his energy to changing one aspect of his behavior at a time. If the child is not reasonably obedient and respectful, the chart will not work. But if the child wants to be good anyway, why bother with the chart?

> Moshe is defiant and uncooperative. He does not get dressed on time, talks back to his parents, and leaves his room a mess. Moshe's parents are very upset about his behavior and cannot get him to change it.
>
> Yaakov is not particularly disrespectful, but he is constantly late getting dressed for school and he leaves his room a mess. Many

mornings his mother or father scold him, sometimes resulting in cooperation on Yaakov's part, sometimes in heated arguments and disrespectful back-talk.

Moshe will not respond well to a reward system because the foundation of cooperation and parental respect is not present. His parents first need to understand what is causing this undermining of parental authority.

But Yaakov has a basic will to please his parents. Bad habits, lack of personal and parental attention, and other factors contribute to his pattern of misbehavior. Yaakov will respond well to a carefully crafted and applied reward system.

Yaakov is like the chronic nail biter. He really wants to stop biting his nails, but he just can't for various reasons. Yaakov does not want to misbehave, but he has bad habits. He needs reinforcement and incentive to change them.

Rambam gives us a tangential glimpse of an appropriate behavior modification program. In his introduction to *Perek Chelek*, Rambam maintains that the descriptions of physical pleasure in the afterlife are merely metaphors. The pleasures that the soul experience are far better and non-comparable to any worldly pleasure. But the Torah uses the metaphor of physical pleasure to help people appreciate and be motivated toward the ethereal reward that awaits them.

Rambam compares this approach to the manner in which young children were educated in his time:

> It is assumed regarding a young child who begins to study Torah with a teacher, even though the study of Torah itself is a great and ultimate benefit, because of his young age and pithy knowledge he will not recognize its value or what it will bring him. Therefore, it is necessary for the teacher who is more developed than he to encourage him to study by means of something that is valuable to the young student, due to his tender age. He will say to him, "Study and I will give you nuts or figs," or, "I will give you a piece of sugar." Then he will put his effort into his studies, not for the Torah itself because he does not yet recognize its value, but in order to obtain that treat. And to the child that reward is surely greater than the study of

Torah …As he gets older and his intellect matures, the treats he was offered earlier become devalued in his eyes, and then we must offer other rewards. We offer something else that is now important in his eyes. His teacher says, "Study, and I will buy you nice shoes or a particular item of clothing." Then the child will put his efforts once again into his studies not for the Torah itself, but for the item of clothing that is in his eyes more important than the ultimate purpose of his studies. And when his intellect matures further and this too becomes devalued, we offer a greater reward. His teacher says, "Study this portion and I will give you a coin or two coins." Once again he will study in order to obtain this money. The receipt of this money is more important to him than the Torah itself, and he studies merely to obtain the money promised him. Once he reaches an even higher level of development and even this becomes of minimal value to him, we say to him, "Study in order to become a rabbi or a judge, and people will honor you and stand up in your presence. You will become famous and people will talk about you even after your death, such as so and so." Then the student will study in order that he accomplishes this goal. All this is actually repugnant, however it is necessary due to the intellectual weaknesses of man …Our rabbis already warned that one should not serve G-d in order to obtain a reward (*Avos* 1:3) …However, they permitted this approach as we do with a child when he begins Torah study …This approach serves the purpose of helping people prepare themselves to ultimately make the transition to the truth, which is to serve G-d out of love. As our rabbis have said, "One should study Torah even for an ulterior motive and gain, because from this, eventually one will come to study Torah for its own sake."

IDENTIFYING BEHAVIORS THAT NEED CHANGE

The first step is to target behaviors that need correcting. It is important to break down such behaviors into concrete and specific elements. The motivational chart will be more effective if used to address a specific behavior instead of a global problem.

If your child does not get ready on time for school in the morning, this is a global problem composed of a number of smaller elements — going to sleep on time, waking up on time, washing *nagel vasser* (ritually required morning hand washing), brushing teeth, getting dressed, organizing knapsack, eating and cleaning up breakfast, and being mindful of the passing time.

In order to implement an effective behavior modification plan, you should select the critical element of the morning routine. For some children, the problem may be waking up on time; for others it may be deciding on what to eat and eating within a reasonable span of time.

The chart should be built to track the key component alone, or one or two of the key components, instead of addressing the global behavior. A child needs to focus his energy directly on changing the problematic behavior, instead of diffusing his energy into the whole project.

If a child does not do his homework assignments, this may be composed of several behaviors — copying down and retrieving the assignment correctly, paying attention in class, writing neatly, monitoring time so he stays on task, and knowing how to skip questions that he does not know instead of getting hung up on one problem. In order to help focus the child's energies, the specific behavior should be targeted instead of the general problem.

Targeting a specific behavior takes careful analysis and discussion, but it is well worth it. At first it may appear that the child is doing everything wrong. A closer and more detailed inspection will usually show areas of competency and areas of deficiency. As a parent, when you see areas of competency, it is important to compliment and praise that behavior as well.

ESTABLISHING A BASELINE

Once the specific behavior is targeted, a baseline of the child's behavior must be established. Parents may feel that their child never listens, but after a closer and more careful investigation, they usually will find that this is not entirely accurate. Monitor and track the behavior for a week to see what the child does on his own, and then set appropriate goals.

The initial reward or prize should be within the child's ability to achieve with a modest amount of effort and within a relatively short time span. This helps build confidence and induces behavioral momentum. Even a modest improvement helps set the pace for continued improvement.

The parental concept of behavioral momentum was discovered by monitoring parent-child interactions. If a parent asks a child who has been categorized as disobedient to do something relatively benign first, and then immediately follows it with a more difficult request, the child is more likely to comply.

For example, a parent might say, "Please turn on the light." The child turns on the light, and the parent continues, "Thank you. Please put your shoes away." This is parallel to the rabbinic dictum of "*Mitzvah gorreres mitzvah*, one *mitzvah* leads to another" (*Avos* 4:2).

When the targeted behavior has improved, a new chart can be set up to include a different area to improve. It is best to work on one behavior at a time. To help prevent backsliding, there also should be some reward system for maintaining performance in newly acquired skills.

> *Tehila cannot wake up on time for school. Her behavior needs to be quantified and measured in some manner. How many times do her parents have to wake her up every morning? Tehila's parents track this problem behavior for a week.*
>
> *With one week of observation, Tehila gets up once when the alarm went off. Twice, she needs the alarm and a parental reminder. The remaining school days, Tehila has to be dragged out of bed.*
>
> *When Tehila's parents set up the reward system, the goal is not to wake up on time every single day. The goal is only slightly higher than the current baseline. Twice a week she must wake from the alarm clock, and the rest of the week after one parental reminder.*

SELECTING A REWARD

The chart should have a goal that can be achieved by a child with a moderate effort and a relatively short time span. You should not offer a lavish reward. Discuss the reward and chart with your child and allow him or her to select a small but significant initial prize.

After this initial period, a more significant prize over a longer duration can be set, depending on the child's emotional maturity and ability to delay gratification. Intermediate goals can be more motivational. After successfully completing each weekly chart's goals, you can offer your child a small prize, and after four small prizes, your child can receive a bigger prize.

Aside from the actual reward, part of the motivational aspect of a chart is the sense of completion.

> *There was a man who went to sleep every night after hearing his upstairs neighbor pull off his boots. "Clump, clump." One night the neighbor pulled off one boot, but the other boot he placed on a chair. The man downstairs heard, "Clump..." Then silence. And he could not fall asleep. His day was just not complete without the second clump.*

The chart should have a visual dimension that shows a graph building up to a picture of the prize. For some children, the natural urge to complete the chart is sufficient motivation to improve their behavior.

DO'S AND DON'TS

- ▸ Clearly discuss prizes in advance and have an alternate set up in case the first choice prize is not available. As parents, you must honor the deal, or risk a loss of credibility with future rewards.

- ▸ Do not goad or challenge the child. Be aware of the subtle difference between being supportive and encouraging, as opposed to being competitive and antagonistic.

- ▸ Do not give up or be provoked if a child says, "I don't need that dumb prize anyway!" As a parent, if you did your "homework", and carefully selected a baseline and appropriate behavioral goal, chances are this child is just putting on a show of defensive bravado. When he is more calm, give your child gentle encouragement.

- ▸ Do not deduct points for misbehavior. Whatever is achieved must remain despite other misdeeds.

19

Making the Most of Family Vacations

Some of the fondest childhood memories are of family vacations. Vacation can be a wonderful way for family members to strengthen their bonds and develop confidence and maturity. In relaxed vacation mode, parents are less distracted. Children take advantage of new opportunities to explore and learn about the world.

But family vacations can potentially become a misery and emotional torture for parents. Whining and ungrateful children demand the most expensive attractions and activities, without any regard or respect for their parents' or siblings' feelings. Long hours in a car or waiting on line may be punctuated by bickering, name-calling, and even physical fights among siblings.

Sometimes, the more money parents spend on an activity, the more ingratitude and selfishness children reciprocate. After all, most vacation resorts and attractions are designed to please and stimulate its participants. It's easy for children to slip into a self-centered, bratty mode. What can parents do to alter this selfish dynamic and foster a vacation environment that is positive and character building?

CHILDREN TAKING PART

In day-to-day life, younger children perceive adults as all knowing, while teenagers act all knowing. Children do not play a role in navigating or planning a day's activity — the adults plan the schedule of the day. Even if a child has a good idea, adults on a tight schedule don't have patience to hear out their child's thoughts or suggestions.

But on a family vacation, school-age children have an opportunity to make real contributions, such as reading a road map or studying a tour book to learn about the various local attractions. You should encourage your children to get involved in a significant way.

Placing real responsibility on their shoulders makes children less self-centered. Assign older siblings as buddies to the younger kids. The younger kids are entertained and responsibly cared for. Even relatively young children can make sandwiches and pack their own clothes.

Before the trip, have children prepare a written or oral assignment such as, "How I will use my vacation to improve a *midah* (character trait)." If the trip involves a good deal of time in a car or waiting on lines, you can instruct your children to think of activities they can do when they are bored.

BUDGETING

On trips, money often becomes an issue. Children can get greedy and want every toy and treat in sight. You can ward this off ahead of time by giving each child a trip allowance, to be spent any way he or she would like. This way, the kids won't pester you every time they want a chocolate bar, trinket or souvenir. And children learn how to budget and plan expenses.

Even children as young as four and five years old could have an allowance. You may prefer to hold onto the money and dole it out in smaller portions on a daily basis, rather than one large lump sum for the whole vacation.

Your children may balk at these suggestions, but discuss it with them seriously — they will get the message. Your hard-earned time and money are going into this vacation and you have every right to expect your children to earn it in some way. The more children contribute to their own vacation, the more they will respect their parents' efforts.

20

Sibling Rivalry

Sibling rivalry is a parenting problem dating back to Kayin and Hevel; Yosef and his brothers. We don't normally project modern day problems onto biblical figures, but in this particular case, even the Talmud lends its legitimacy: "A person should never single out a child among his other children, for it was just two coins' worth of silk [Yosef's coat] which caused the brothers to become jealous and sell Yosef into slavery" (*Shabbos* 10b).

Sibling rivalry occurs when one child feels that another sibling is loved more than he. In some cases, parents are substantively unfair or show favoritism toward one child over others. But more often, children have unrealistic and even paranoid views about their parents' affection. It would be difficult for parents to always respond in a manner that will satisfy a child's hunger for attention.

ACKNOWLEDGING THE PROBLEM

As a parent, you cannot simply disregard a child's complaint, no matter how hard it may be to appease him. Listen carefully to your son's or daughter's complaint, and own up to it — if there is some truth to it. You may have to work to change the situation.

There is one potential pitfall to this approach. You could get caught up in a never-ending game, always precisely tabulating and calculating dosages of love and affection. It's impossible to change the whole family around because one child perceives your behavior as unfair.

To forestall this scenario, validate your child's feelings. "It must really make you jealous when I praise Dovid. You feel he gets more attention than you do. That must be very sad for you." Usually this suffices to calm your child. You recognized the child's feelings and took him seriously.

Sometimes children are persistent in demanding corrective action. If you feel the demand is unfair or out of proportion, remain sympathetic but firm. You might say, "I try to be as fair as I can, and I certainly want all my children to get the love and attention they need, but perhaps for you it does not feel that way." Don't fake it or be patronizing. To be effective, muster genuine empathy.

WHY IT EXISTS

Sibling rivalry is based chiefly on one false assumption — that parental love is a finite commodity that parents are responsible for distributing. Like a cake sliced on a dessert platter, once it's gone, it's gone.

In reality, of course, parental love is an infinitely renewable resource. Children themselves play a primary role in generating this love and attention. Instead of it being the sole responsibility of the parents to ration this scarce commodity, children can be invited to see it as the responsibility of the entire family unit to create and preserve an emotional climate that facilitates this love and attention.

We should be comforted by the fact that sibling rivalry has been a problem since ancient times. We realize that to some extent it is an intractable feature of family life. But there are still some important steps you can take to minimize sibling rivalry. You can even utilize its dynamics for your children to develop emotionally.

▸ Encourage your children to work out rivalry issues among themselves. For example, if your children argue and vie for your attention when you spend time with them, you might say the following: "I have an hour to spend playing with you. You can either split the time equally, or have me spend it with all of you together. Why don't you discuss it and let me know what you decide." You shift the impossible burden of "making it fair" from you to them.

▸ Do not get overly involved in their rivalry. You want all your children to feel loved, but you cannot measure and monitor every toy or praise to see that it is equally distributed. If your children are arguing, only intervene if a family rule is being broken — like hitting, name-calling, or shouting at the dinner table. Even then, do not get sucked into being the judge and jury; you should assume the role of a referee to enforce the rules for a fair fight.

▸ Do not buy doubles of toys or other presents just because the children refuse to share.

▸ Be honest in your praise, even if it means one child is praised and another is not. Children usually can tell what is real and what is false. False praise will only decrease a child's self-esteem, not increase it.

▸ Definitely do not make comparisons from one sibling to another. Praise each true accomplishment for what it is worth.

▸ Adults in the family should model respectful behavior. Do you and your spouse share well? Do you talk with respect toward each other? Do you talk with respect about others — neighbors, parents, and community figures? Children learn from how you act, and not from how you tell them to act.

▸ Encourage siblings to complain to each other instead of to their parents. Yonah complains, "It's my turn to sit next to you. Shira *always* gets to sit next to you." Instead of getting involved in the argument, tell Yonah to ask Shira directly if she can move over and let him sit next to you. You may need to monitor the conversation, and if you find that Shira is being unfair, talk to Shira about it — out of Yonah's company — and encourage her to be more generous.

▸ Create boundaries where family members can have privacy without older or younger siblings bothering them, a "no teasing" zone. For example, a comfortable chair in the living room can be established for quiet reading. If someone is sitting there it means, "Do not disturb."

FAMILY DISCUSSIONS

Although parents tire of hearing complaints about favoritism, children, especially older children, must be given a chance to express their gripes. First, the gripes might be legitimate. Perhaps you are unfairly favoring one child over another. Second, even if they do not appear to be objectively true, children, like all people, need basic respect and a chance to express their feelings.

After hearing the complaint, you should encourage the child who is complaining to discuss this with the family as a whole. Time should be set aside where the matter can be discussed rationally and maturely with parents and siblings together. You do not need to cede your authority to a democracy. You remain as a firm leader in the discussion; you make the final assessment about what to do.

A lot of important information can be gleaned from hearing siblings talk to each other about their rivalry and jealousy. Sometimes parents are surprised to find that the child who is accused of receiving favoritism agrees! This makes it much easier for parents to implement a change, since there will be less cries of protest from the other party.

In other instances, two siblings may accuse the other of receiving favoritism. They may both be right in different ways. From the discussion, each emerges with a more balanced perspective.

> *Noam and Hadassah were brother and sister. Noam got a lot of attention. He received plenty of compliments — and plenty of criticism. Hadassah received relatively less praise, but also much less criticism. After bringing the situation to light in a family discussion, Noam and Hadassah were offered to trade places. They both refused.*
>
> *Noam and Hadassah realized they were being treated in a way that suited their personalities. Hadassah could not stomach criticism. She kept a low profile and was generally obedient. Noam craved action and risk. He was boisterous and outspoken, drawing more attention to himself, sometimes positive and sometimes negative.*

You can hope that your children will love each other — and they might, over time. But you cannot legislate that children love each other. You cannot squash your child's animosity, either. Personal feelings have to develop on their own. You can encourage them to work out perceived injustices. But above all, expect and demand that your children respect each other and treat each other well. Good feelings will follow.

21

Teaching Sensitivity

Dear Feuermans,
I am an eighth grade rebbe of an academically advanced
and well-behaved class. However, there is one point that
really bothers me about my students. They seem to be
self-centered and ungenerous. For example, when we
recently were discussing how we might celebrate a siyum
(celebration upon completion of studying a Torah unit),
no one was willing to concede, compromise or otherwise
show respect for another classmate's opinion. Do you
have any suggestions on how I might teach them to
become more sensitive without just lecturing (which
hasn't worked anyway)?

OUR RESPONSE

Of course we are familiar with the story of Rabbi Akiva's students who were presumably the most promising Talmudists of their generation, yet they were lacking in respect for each other, and ultimately met an unpleasant fate. (*Yevamos* 62b)

The strategies that can be used to successfully navigate marital disputes (see section one, *How To Argue with Your Spouse*) can be implemented among children with equal effectiveness. Here we'll explore how to introduce these concepts in a classroom setting.

As academically advanced students, perhaps you can try to engage their hearts via their minds. Consider discussing the famous Gemara regarding Bais Shammai and Bais Hillel.

Why was the *halacha* ruled in accordance with the opinion of Bais Hillel? Because they were gentle and forgiving in nature, and they studied their opinion as well as Bais Shammai's opinion. Furthermore, they would state Bais Shammai's opinion first. (*Eruvin* 13b).

Why, in a matter of *halacha* and intellect, is the decisive factor the character traits and humility of the protagonists? The *halacha* should be decided based on their intellectual acumen and prowess, for which Bais Shammai was known. (*Yevamos* 14a) There are many possible interpretations to this Gemara, but a logical answer is that the one who shows respect for both opinions is most likely to arrive at the more accurate answer. Hence the *halacha* is in accordance with Bais Hillel.

After your students have studied this piece, you can implement an exercise based on Bais Hillel's practice. Propose the following rule for all classroom discussions, even about matters not related to Torah study. Any time someone expresses an opinion, he must first explain someone else's opinion and what he thinks the feelings are behind it.

To illustrate, when the class has to decide about how to celebrate a *siyum*, before a child puts forth his own suggestion, he must present the counter-opinion. "Someone in this room may not prefer to go for pizza because he is allergic to dairy products. However, my vote is that we go for pizza." Once the child is forced to contemplate the other viewpoint, he will feel at least partially compelled to compromise — and that's the whole point!

Parents and spouses should realize that this same sensitivity building exercise can be utilized to tone down and ameliorate sibling rivalry and other relationship conflicts. Following the path of Bais Hillel makes it a lot harder to be selfish and argumentative.

22

Promoting Appreciation and Gratitude

Malkie prepared an elaborate supper for her family. Though it was obvious that everyone enjoyed the food, no one bothered to say thank you. The closest thing to a compliment was when one child mentioned, "The soup was good, but needed a little salt." Malkie was not very happy. And it upset her even more when, on top of all this, her children grumbled over bentching and bickered about cleaning up.

Aaron was happy that this year's chol hamoed (intermediate days of holiday) was a great success. He took off from work the whole week. One day, the family went to an amusement park. It was expensive, but well worth the quality time they spent together.

On the last day of chol hamoed, Aaron planned to go bicycle riding with the whole family. But when they took the bikes out, Dovid's was broken. The best last minute solution was to take turns. Yisroel and Dovid were close enough in height to share a bicycle. Yisroel was bitter and sullen about letting Dovid use his bike "because he will break it."

Aaron was infuriated to find that after all the time and money spent, Yisroel just moped. If only his kids could appreciate that he took all this time off work to spend with the family. He could have bought ten bikes with all that salary he happily lost!

Do these scenarios sound familiar? Are your children petty, selfish and unappreciative? Some parents feel that children should be automatically grateful, that it's not something that has to be taught. But children need to be taught everything! It's possible to promote your children's *hakaras hatov* (gratitude).

Some parents have difficulty insisting on concrete expressions of gratitude from their children, out of a misplaced sense of modesty. Most people are trained to be kind and generous without ulterior motives and without expecting gratitude. Surely it is considered rude to insist on gratitude. But this should not be so.

Every parent is also a human being, entitled to respect and gratitude. Parents have an obligation to insist on a thank you, for our children *need* to learn to say thank you. Parents should not feel bashful demanding that children show gratitude — as long as it is with the intent of developing their characters.

Of course, there are parents who depend on their children to satisfy their need to be recognized. But these emotionally needy parents place an unbearable burden on their children. After all, Rambam teaches, "One should always be careful not to place a heavy burden on his children" (*Mishneh Torah, Hilchos Mamrim* 6:8).

Parents must model appropriate behavior and say thank you to each other as well as to others — including their own children! But this alone is not always enough. Children have a way of tuning things out. Perhaps it will work in the long run, but there are other interventions with more immediate results.

THE "BORUCH HASHEM" INTERVENTION

Every Friday night when the family is together, encourage each family member to share one thing from the past week that he is grateful to Hashem for. It helps children feel more comfortable sharing their feelings and sets an optimistic and grateful atmosphere for the whole family. (*Mishna Berurah* 166:3 provides *halachic* support for this idea.) During the course of the week, as problems and issues arise, family members are trained to first focus on something positive.

- ‣ Perform this exercise before singing *Shalom Aleichem*. There is no greater motivator than hunger. Everyone is seated and focused and it sets the tone for the rest of the meal. If everyone is unusually hungry or tired, don't be too rigid about it.
- ‣ Don't spring this new exercise suddenly on your starving family. Warn your children ahead of time about the new routine to forestall tantrums and resentment.

- Parents also participate.

- An unwilling or unable child should not be forced to say something. If he's just not ready, tell him, "If you're too tired/upset/hungry right now, that's okay. But the first thing you should say when you are ready to speak should be a 'Boruch Hashem.'"

Before Shabbos morning *kiddush*, you can institute a similar exercise. Everyone in the family must thank each member for something that he or she did for him that week.

This concept can be adapted for any time of the year. On Rosh Hashanah, family members recite a *"Boruch Hashem"* for the whole year. And on Yom Kippur, you can share requests for forgiveness. On Purim, you and your family can share the funniest thing that happened all year. The possibilities are endless, and they give the holiday table a positive structure.

Some people object, claiming that these interventions merely enforce external displays of gratitude, but do not guarantee any internal feelings. It is true that a brother may thank his older sister while inside he hates her thoroughly. But we can never really control what our children are thinking and feeling. We can only lead them in the right direction.

After all, *Mesilas Yesharim* teaches us, "By route of external actions one may arouse the internal feelings." Though there are extreme situations to which this dictum would not apply, in raising normal children teaching proper behavior will help shape healthy emotions.

Pushkas and Pedagogy

Tzedaka, charity, is a principle tenet of Jewish practice. In fact, one of the three essential character attributes of a Jewish person is to engage in acts of kindness. (*Yevamos* 79a) Jewish parents strive to inculcate their children with an appreciation for the *mitzvah* of *tzedaka*. Even young toddlers are entrusted with loose change to place in the *pushka* (charity box) at home, in school, or at *shul*.

COLLECTING FOR OTHERS

Many community organizations, foundations, *shuls* and schools send our children out with *pushkas* to collect money for their respective causes — and reward children in measure. Years back, we used to receive little trinkets for every ten dollars we collected, trinkets that fell apart in a few days.

Today the prize system in much more expansive, with colorful pictures and enticing descriptions. As children mature, they can begin to comprehend that the prizes are mere tokens. They learn from their Torah teachers that the main thing is the *mitzvah* of *tzedaka*, not the reward.

And then there are the organizations that entice our children with major prizes, such as electronic devices, a set of Talmud, or even a trip to Israel. Today's children — who in some ways are less mature than we were, but in other ways worldly beyond their years — raise hundreds of dollars for these organizations.

This generation has more financial resources — parents well established in their careers, grandparents with fortunes built off the hard work and aspirations of the previous generation of immigrants. Who hasn't been approached by their children or called by a niece or nephew to contribute $25, $50 or even $100 to a cause on their behalf?

Charitable foundations that use this child-based method of fundraising may indeed provide much needed services to those who are in despair, and are certainly worthy of our generous support. It is not our intention to criticize or question their legitimacy.

But there are *chinuch* implications that we need to pay close attention to. We cannot afford to be naïve about anything that can potentially affect our children's character development.

- ▸ Is it harmful to have our children perform a *mitzvah* — such as collecting *tzedaka* — in order to receive a large prize?
- ▸ Is it proper for children to impose on relatives by asking them to contribute major sums of money?
- ▸ Since we are dealing with adult-sized sums of money, will this be too much for child-sized personalities to handle?

The pressure to raise large funds can induce children to engage in dishonest methods, such as stealing cash from a mother's purse. They also may be enticed to "borrow" some of the money collected for the organization to buy a new Game Boy cartridge. Some of the prizes offered in certain campaigns are so significant, a child might even rationalize that he is just taking his payment up front!

In sponsored marathons, friends and relatives pledge a certain dollar amount per lap the child swims or bikes. Sometimes children inflate the number of laps they swam. It's dishonesty for a good cause, but it still is dishonesty. It can be financially damaging to an unsuspecting relative who pledges a few dollars per lap and then is told the child swam two hundred and fifty laps!

SETTING PARAMETERS

There are some advantages to these types of programs. Collecting *tzedaka* from adults exposes children to this *mitzvah* in a grand way. Compared to the mere pennies of toddlerhood, adult role models donate hundreds of dollars.

Jewish law endorses the coercion of others to give *tzedaka*, as long as they can afford it. (See *Bava Basra* 8b; *Mishneh Torah, Hilchos Matnos Aniyim* 9:5; *Shulchan Aruch, Yoreh Deah* 256:3.) Using prizes as an incentive for children also has support in our tradition. (See Rambam, *Perek Chelek*, Introduction.)

But parents need to take charge of the situation. The following are some guidelines you may want to implement.

- ▸ Have a discussion with your child about the *mitzvah* of *tzedaka*. Instead of lecturing, ask your child to tell you why *tzedaka* is important, and what is important specifically about the organization he is collecting for. After you hear what your child has to say, you might want to add in some points of your own.

- ▸ You may want to limit the prizes that your child is allowed to choose from. But do warn your child in advance, before he raises the money.

- ▸ Review which relatives your child plans to call, and how the solicitations will be made.

- ▸ If your child collects cash, have him turn it over to you every day so you can keep temptation at bay.

- ▸ If you are asked to pledge an amount of money based on a certain goal such as swimming laps, enforce an upper limit in order to discourage exaggeration. For example, you might pledge a dollar a lap, but only up to twenty-five laps.

- ▸ If your child has access to his own funds, allowance or babysitting money, you can require she match all money raised with a personal contribution, five or ten percent of the total.

24

Creating a Boundary of Responsibility

Dear Feuermans,
Recently my six-year-old daughter was invited to her
classmate's birthday party. At first she was very excited
to go. At the last minute, she chickened out and refused
to attend. We think it is because she is a bit shy. Our
question is — should we have forced her to go, or at least
should we have forced her to call and say she is not
coming? On the one hand, we think the birthday party
would be good for her socially. (We recently moved to a
new neighborhood.) On the other hand, maybe this is
normal behavior for a six-year-old and we should just
leave her alone. What do you think?

OUR RESPONSE

Before we discuss your particular concerns about your child's
social life, it is important to discuss parenting in general. You cannot force your child to have a social life, but at the same time it is
not your job to protect her from feeling bad, conflicted or bored if
in fact she regrets deciding not to go to the party.

A rule of thumb for all parenting — avoid demanding behavior
that you cannot force your children to do. How can you realistically force your child to attend the birthday party? If you drag her
kicking and screaming to the birthday party, you'll either dump

her on the host's parents or have her spend the whole time sniffling on your lap. This is hardly constructive.

So how can you be an effective disciplinarian if you don't force your children to do anything?

> *Sarah begs and whines for a second sandwich. Her mother asks her repeatedly, "You're still hungry? Are you sure you can eat the whole thing?" Lo and behold, Sarah doesn't want to finish the second sandwich. Though her mother feels infuriated and would like to shove the food down Sarah's throat, she knows that's a bad idea. What are the helpful disciplinary options available? Sometimes it feels as if there are none, and that is when there is an urge to become physically or verbally aggressive.*

The key is to create a boundary of responsibility. Enforce a consequence that is not as intrusive as forcing the child to eat, but still guides the child. You might tell Sarah, "I can't make you eat this, but a minute ago you said you were still hungry. So you must stay at the table for the next few minutes just to see if you don't change your mind."

This intervention is effective for several reasons. First, on a practical level, many children are fickle and really do change their mind several times. If Sarah has to stare at the food for a couple of minutes, it will give her time to solidify her decision. Sarah may very likely opt to eat the food in the end. But in case she is not hungry, she will not be forced to eat the food. Of course, you have to be firm that Sarah remains in her seat, but at the same time be totally relaxed about whether or not she eat the food.

Second, creating a boundary of responsibility is important for the child's development. It is much better for Sarah to make the choice on her own than being forced into something. You fence her in with an appropriate restriction, but she still has the freedom to choose whether or not to eat.

With the birthday party, forcing your daughter to attend would only create more shyness and insecurity. But you feel that it would be beneficial for your child to socialize. You have to set up a boundary of responsibility that guides her but does not force her.

If this party is scheduled for a Sunday afternoon, tell your child, "We planned on taking you to the birthday party this Sunday, but you changed your mind at the last minute. We think it still is a good idea for you to go and make friends, but we can't force you. But remember, this is the activity that we planned for today, so if you are bored later or want to do something else, we won't be going anywhere special."

You allow her to make up her own mind. If she chooses to go to the party — good and well. If she chooses not to go to the party, she'll remember next time how bored she was the last time she turned down an invitation. This dynamic mimics the natural way children develop from their environment, through experiencing normal consequences.

ANOTHER CASE STUDY

Your teenager refuses to join you at the Shabbos table, or she eats quickly and then leaves. Either you are drawn into bitter confrontation or you resign to tolerating this rude and disrespectful behavior. The older the child is, the less likely you will succeed in forcing a child to conform.

To more effectively deal with the situation, parents can set up a boundary of responsibility. You can tell your independent-thinking teenager, "The Shabbos table is important to the family and we put effort into making it special. We want it to be special for you too, and if there is some way that you want it to change we are open to suggestions. If you are in a bad mood, you do not have to come to the table. You will certainly be missed! But if you do come, you must stay for the entire meal and be pleasant and helpful throughout."

You are placing the choice in her hands — either the child participates at the Shabbos table respectfully or does not attend at all.

GROWING FROM DISCOMFORT

Children — and all people — only grow as a result of feeling some discomfort. A child struggles to walk or talk because of certain frustrations he experiences in not having his needs met. If his parents could read his mind and always gave him everything exactly the way he wanted, he would never bother to learn how to speak. Many parents today have difficulty tolerating their children's discomfort. They often try to protect them from struggles that are necessary for normal development, depriving them of growth opportunities.

Yishai is ten years old. He likes to play chess with his father. But his father always lets him win since Yishai can't tolerate losing. "When I win, he gets all frustrated and angry. I'll deliberately lose a few games to boost his self confidence," the father justifies.

This parenting strategy will backfire in the long run because Yishai will not develop the capacity to tolerate loss. He will display poor sportsmanship with his friends and in other life situations.

Children are very perceptive. Likely Yishai will detect that his father is losing purposefully. Instead of building self-esteem, Yishai's is being undermined. His father's cover-up proves to him that he is indeed as incompetent as he thinks he is.

You might benefit from a heart to heart talk with your son about his abilities and good sportsmanship before playing a game. Maybe he'd appreciate ongoing pointers throughout the game, or that you should play with a handicap, perhaps without a Queen. This way, you guide the child in making a realistic assessment of his ability and encourage him to take responsibility for it in a way he can tolerate.

Your younger child watches an older sibling open a special birthday present — and boy is he jealous! Hearing the child wail in despair is emotionally painful, or maybe frustrating or annoying. You try to calm your child, promising him another present. Or even worse, you run roughshod over the older child's feelings and force him to immediately share the toy with his younger brother.

Though there may be occasions when it is appropriate to be sensitive to the needs of the younger child, parents' automatic response should not be to protect a child from feelings of anger or jealousy. Parents need not step in and make it instantly better. Your younger child is experiencing discomfort; he will eventually learn to grow from it.

Yes, children should be taught to share. But the birthday boy is entitled to basic respect. How would you like to receive a gift, and even before you get a few moments to savor it, be forced to share it with someone else? As everything in life, this too is an opportunity for growth.

25

A Trip to the Grocery Store

I saw you having a terrible time with your son yesterday in the local grocery store. I wanted to say something, but of course it was none of my business. Perhaps you are so used to being disrespected that you think it is simply a part of parenting. But just as a musician cannot bear to hear a song sung out of tune, it was excruciating for me to watch you struggle and be defeated so needlessly by your toddler.

So just to make myself feel better, I am going to convey my observations to you, the mother, and include my play-by-play commentary. Who knows? Maybe you will read it, maybe you will not. At least it will give strength to others who feel trapped in the daily pattern of their lives.

Your three-year-old is certainly an energetic boy; Yossi seemed both bright and happy. He stood on top of the cartons in the store and jumped off. Clever for him to find a way to entertain himself — but it was dangerous and disruptive. You were concerned, weren't you?

"Yossi, get off the boxes. Get off the boxes, Yossi. It's dangerous."

Yossi took absolutely no notice of your warnings. He did not even turn around or slow down.

"Yossi, I am counting. One … Yossi, I am counting. One … Yossi! I am counting!"

Then a customer passed and complimented Yossi, "Hey, you really are a good jumper!" Now Yossi received praise from outsiders for disrespecting his mother and store property!

Yossi was having fun, he was feeling very competent in his physical ability. All this reinforced Yossi's behavior. And since you were completely ineffectual, Yossi was not the slightest bit concerned about any punishment.

Yossi wasn't paying much attention to you otherwise, but he noticed when you picked up those bags of potato chips. "Can I have one, Mommy?" Of course, he didn't say please. But at least he asked.

"I can't give you potato chips! You have not listened to me at all so far. Yossi, I think I won't be able to take you shopping because you cannot listen to me."

That was the way to go, Mom! But Yossi continued to disobey. You gave up. The next minute, I saw him holding a bag of candy. I wished I could yank it out of his hand.

You were probably afraid to take his candy away, afraid he would make a scene. But he is supposed to be afraid of you, not the other way around. Are you afraid of a tantrum or that he will get out of control? Watch and see. With your method of discipline, his behavior will only deteriorate.

"Yossi, please. Please, Yossi. Yossi, please. It's not right to not listen to Mommy. Please, Yossi. It's dangerous, can't you see?"

That was so pitiful. You, the mother, begging your three-year-old child for mercy. If you only knew. If you only saw and heard yourself. I know you must be tired and overwhelmed. But believe me, you can get your son under control. It's not as hard as it seems. Just a little planning and courage — planning what to say, and courage to put up with a few tantrums until he learns that you mean business. You are suffering needlessly. Yossi can be proud and confident in his abilities, and still learn to listen.

Then Yossi moved on. "I want a lollipop! I want a lollipop! Lollipop!" You didn't respond at all to this outburst, but you looked completely exasperated.

Then the storeowner came over. "Here you go, young fella!" And he handed him a lollipop. Of course Yossi didn't say thank you.

Mom, what you really need to do is to take charge. You need to have the guts to know what's best for your son. You should have told the storeowner firmly, "Yossi does not deserve this lollipop. He needs to apologize to you for standing on your boxes, and to me for his misbehavior. I will hold the lollipop for him until he is ready to do that."

But you didn't. Yossi got his lollipop, compliments from everyone, and not a peep from you. So then he went looking for some other way to entertain himself, to attract more positive attention.

He opened the door of the store, stuck his head out and started roaring like a lion. Customers going in and out of the store tripped over him. But there he stayed until you completed your purchases.

By the way, Yossi's prognosis for success in life is good. Perhaps he will grow up to be slightly narcissistic, and perhaps will not respect women as much as he should, but probably he will be fairly confident in himself. Who knows? Maybe one day he will become President. (Come to think of it, haven't we had presidents like that?)

Yossi will need internal structures and boundaries. If his teacher is organized and effective, he will perform adequately in school. But if his teachers are not organized, he'll get a little out of control and might be labeled a "behavior problem."

Mom, you had one tough day. I wish you the best.

Many people think that psychotherapy is for crazy people, but that's not true. The mentally ill need medication and various long-term treatments, sometimes psychotherapy. But psychotherapy is helpful for functioning, resourceful, and intelligent people who have problems in living. It is for people who need to sort through issues with someone who is trained to be an objective and non-judgmental observer. Many people benefit greatly from just one or two sessions, especially when it comes to parenting issues. Why not give it a try?

26

Self-Esteem
Without Arrogance

A plethora of school curriculum, therapeutic programs and self-help books focus on building and enhancing self-esteem. Our pop-psychology culture has adopted this label as its most desirable brand name. But self-esteem is overrated.

Self-esteem is not a means unto itself. As Hillel states, "If I am not for myself, who am I? And when I am only for myself, what am I?" (*Avos* 1:14) Secular society has erred — it has taken the concept of self-esteem and elevated it as a goal in itself, instead of a means toward achieving something higher.

What is self-esteem really? And what can it help a person accomplish?

DEFINING SELF-ESTEEM

All boys who are tall wear long pants, but if you give a short boy long pants, he won't necessarily grow into them. We want our children to be successful — but giving them self-esteem doesn't necessarily mean they'll "grow into it." High self-esteem may be a positive indicator of success, but not a cause.

Success and self-esteem are subjective — it all depends how the person feels about it. A student who gets grades in the low ninety's is objectively successful, but if she is a perfectionist from a family of talented overachievers, she feels badly about "getting only a ninety." Her self-esteem is low, despite her relative success. This young woman will do just fine in life, even if she does-n't get a sixteen hundred on the SAT's, but that's not how she looks at it.

Or consider a child who is very bright, but doesn't make any effort to study. This child happily coasts through school with C+'s and B-'s, perfectly satisfied with himself. He thinks his friends are foolish for spending hours studying just to get a higher grade. Does this child have a self-esteem problem? If anything, he holds himself in too much esteem!

Self-esteem stems from each person's view of himself, his self-image. We want our children to be happy with themselves. Not stubborn and complacent, but comfortable with who they are. How can we convince our children to change the way they look at themselves — without becoming full of themselves?

THE TORAH VIEW

We want to give our children enough self-esteem to say, "It is better for me to be called a fool my entire life than be considered evil for even one moment in the eyes of G-d" (*Eiduyos* 5:6). Only someone very confident in himself, yet willing to be utterly humiliated for the sake of G-d, could ever make a statement like that.

Many ancient societies scarcely acknowledged the individual. When a pharaoh died, all his servants were killed and buried with the king, to keep him company on his voyage to the afterlife. The ancient Egyptians believed the servants belonged to the king much as we believe that cattle belongs to the farmer.

Today there still are cultures and countries where the rights of the individual are scarcely acknowledged. One cruel despot can exterminate millions of his countrymen — and they tolerate it because deep down, they accept this as the natural order of things.

The Torah impacted the world at large with its emphasis and acknowledgment of each individual. The Torah requires caring for the poor and needy, both in terms of charity and in terms of equal treatment in the eyes of the law. (*Shemos* 23:1-9)

The Torah denounces suicide. (*Bereishis* 9:5) A single human being is considered like an entire world. (*Sanhedrin* 37a) These ideas fueled humanity's awareness and respect for the individual. Even the United States Constitution composed by the Founding Fathers was written with the influence of Jewish ethics. Personal correspondence of the Founding Fathers testifies to this.

The Torah's respect for the individual's rights and concerns teaches us that everything we do counts. Each person has a task to fulfill — and the tools needed to fulfill it. While Western civilization values identity for the sake of its own well being, Torah promotes a person for the sake of fulfilling a mission.

Yet for the most part, the Torah emphasizes the diminishment of self; it does not promote self-esteem as a goal in itself. "One should be exceedingly humble" (*Avos* 4:4). And even Rambam, who generally endorses the moderate path, in the case of humility versus arrogance exhorts that one be extremely humble. (*Mishneh Torah, Hilchos Deos* 1-2)

The Torah does not endorse promoting our own selves. The Torah view believes in esteem for others. Through esteem for others, self-esteem will be promoted in society at large.

NARCISSISM

The term narcissism comes from the Greek legend of Narcissus. Narcissus fell hopelessly in love with his own reflection, which he saw in a pool of water. Narcissus was unable to move from the spot; he was so bound by his love with his appearance that he died of starvation.

The Talmud relates a story about a person who was moved to change due to his perception of self. A man once came to Shimon HaTzaddik. He had "beautiful eyes, good looks, and curly locks of hair." Shimon HaTzaddik could not contemplate how he could destroy his beautiful hair by taking a Nazirite vow of abstention. The man replied,

> I worked as a shepherd for my father in my hometown, and one time I went to draw water from the spring and I caught sight of my reflection. My evil inclination quickly overtook me and attempted to drive me out of this world. [He was overcome with temptation to sin with his extraordinary handsome looks.] I said to him [the evil inclination], "Empty one, why do you make yourself haughty in a world that does not belong to you and your end will be worms." By the holy sacrifices, I will shave my hair off in G-d's honor! (*Nazir* 4b)

The Torah's concern is that even true and accurate awareness of one's great qualities can be dangerous and promote sin.

According to the Diagnostic and Statistical Manual for Mental Disorders, a person suffers from narcissistic personality disorder when he or she exhibits these attitudes or behaviors:

- Grandiose sense of self-importance
- A need for admiration
- Lack of empathy
- Exploits others
- Believes he or she is special and unique and can only be understood by or associate with other special or high status people

How does a child become narcissistic? Children learn to treat others based on how their parents treat them. If a child is respected and well-cared for, he is less likely to be selfish and narcissistic. If a child is indulged and not taught to share, then he will likely show narcissistic behavior.

Many parents mistakenly apply this concept. Parents try to teach a child to share by forcing him to share. But children learn more from their experience than from teaching. When a child is forced to share, he develops a bad taste for sharing, a taste he will always remember. The parents demand too much; they are insensitive to the child's feelings — and that's the behavior the child picks up, to be insensitive and harsh, instead of patient and kind.

Freud observed that any time an instinct is under- or over-gratified a delay in development will occur. Overindulging a child will lead to selfishness — he does not get an opportunity to develop a capacity to share and empathize with others. Forcing a child to share is under-gratifying. This emotionally starved child is unable to grow into a sharing and empathic individual because his own emotional needs were never met.

Jewish philosophy supports treating children with extra sensitivity. The Talmud acknowledged that some young children have a strong emotional bond with their fathers. If a child is crying for his father to hold him, it is permitted for the father to pick him up on Shabbos even if the child is holding a *muktza* object (item that cannot be handled).

This is fascinating. The father could first demand that his child put down the object, and only pick him up afterwards. But the Talmud favors indulging the child. Though the child's cries and anguish are not life-threatening, they are enough of a threat to the child's health to override a rabbinic prohibition. (*Shabbos* 141b)

Parents must achieve a balance between tolerating age-appropriate selfish behaviors while gently encouraging sharing behaviors. Toddlers are not too young to learn how to share toys, to say please and thank you, to ask an older sibling who has a cold how he is feeling. But parents should use positive reinforcements — praise and extra attention — instead of being punitive.

Older children are expected to show more sensitivity. They should be rebuked and disciplined for insensitive or selfish behavior. But even here, parents should focus on the positive. Parents can ask questions that help the child understand what being narcissistic is. "How does it feel when someone hurts your feelings or ignores you?" Instead of an arbitrary punishment, parents can punish the offending child by making him ask the offended sibling to describe how it felt when he was treated that way. Then he can be required to devise a plan to rectify the hurt he caused.

PRACTICAL SUGGESTIONS

We would like our children and ourselves to feel emotionally secure, be successful in personal and professional spheres, but at the same time not be arrogant or grandiose. How can we do this?

Number one, love yourself. Be a model of self-esteem. Okay, so if we must love ourselves, what is love really?

Love is accepting another person as is. We do not have to like or be fond of every single character trait of our loved ones. But we do have to see them as they are, love them as they are, and not love them for what we wish they could be.

To have healthy self-love, we have to understand and accept who we are, not who we dream to be.

We don't have to be complacent and self-satisfied. We can and should have goals for self-improvement in the areas we are lacking. But it is unhealthy to spend every conscious moment internally criticizing ourselves. This is common sense when it comes to relationships with significant others such as a spouse or a child, but somehow people do not treat themselves with the same courtesy. We should be patient and gently encouraging with others and with ourselves.

To foster self-esteem in our children, we need honesty. Deep down, every child has a pretty good idea about her abilities. If a child shows you work that is way below standard, even if it represents an improvement for her, it is dishonest to offer ecstatic praise. The child knows you are being false and this only reinforces a belief that she is inferior.

The correct way to praise is to accurately reflect the child's own feeling about the work, and to perhaps amplify it slightly, if you feel that it is being underestimated.

Shlomo normally fails in Talmud studies, but this time comes home with a seventy on his test. If you tell him, "Wow, great job!" Shlomo thinks, "Big deal, I improved from being a moron to just plain stupid." Your praise was not in tune with the objective facts — or with Shlomo's thinking.

But the test score really does represent progress, and you do want to encourage Shlomo. Be honest, specific and balanced in your praise. "Shlomo, this is the best grade you have gotten yet. It shows real improvement. When I see you improving, it makes me happy and proud." Now the praise is accurate. You express pride in the improvement and not the grade itself, which is objectively poor.

Or you could ask Shlomo what he thinks about the grade. Shlomo himself might offer several meaningful remarks such as he is happy that he is doing better but still frustrated at his relatively low academic standing. Of course, Shlomo may exaggerate his failure and express feelings of hopelessness and despair.

But still be honest and specific. "It's true you have a long way to go to be on par with your classmates, but that is not the only thing we should focus on. Forget the grade for a moment and let's look at the test. For example, I really liked the clear analysis you made in question five. You knew nine out of ten words on the vocabulary section of the test. You didn't get just a plain seventy throughout the test. There were some areas where you showed real knowledge and strength."

Being honest in our assessment of our children and ourselves ultimately leads to a healthy confidence in our ability to succeed.

SECTION THREE
Torah, Chinuch and Psychology

*P*sychology, like any other area of modern science, provides us with valuable tools to understand and improve our lives — many of which seem to contradict the traditional Torah outlook. But these apparent incompatibilities may result from misunderstanding either the psychological concept or the Torah principles. Those ideas that are not consonant with Torah can still be adapted to a Torah parenting approach. In this section we will look at some of these areas where Torah, chinuch and psychology intersect and supply the reader with insight to make the best use of these ideas.

Transformative Learning

We want our children to learn more than just the facts we teach them. We want the learning process to change our children, to refine their character, to transform them. "People whose intelligence exceeds their character are compared to a tree whose branches are larger than its roots" (*Avos* 3:13). As the branches stretch further and further into the sky, the roots should be digging deeper and deeper.

THE DISORIENTING DILEMMA

The essential ingredient for transformative learning, learning that develops character, is a disorienting dilemma. A person is faced with a disorienting dilemma when he confronts a situation that forces him to challenge his perception of reality. Suddenly he has to find a new rationale to set the world right again. A disorienting dilemma can be a major event or a minor incident, but it is always dramatic for the protagonist.

> David believes in G-d. He has faith that He will always protect him from harm and misfortune. But one day David is mugged and beaten. Now David has to adjust to a new reality to resolve this conflict. David might revise his understanding of G-d's providence or come up with a different approach, but he must deal with it somehow.

> Eli is prejudiced. He believes all people of a certain ethnicity are not intelligent. But one day, Eli is forced to work with such a person — and much to Eli's surprise, he is smart! Eli's experience is disorienting. It challenges his assumptions about reality, and he has to find a new way to account for this.

When people are confronted with a disorienting dilemma, they do not always choose to adjust themselves to the truthful reality. Some might engage in self-deception and denial.

After the World Trade Center attacks, members of the Islamic world had to reconcile how practitioners of their "peace loving" religion could perpetrate such a barbaric act. Instead of turning this into an opportunity to re-evaluate some of their rhetoric and the role it plays in fostering global terrorism, many chose to buy the concocted libel that the bombing was a Mossad plot.

When a person is confronted with a dilemma he is ripe for growth. This is the moment when he can choose to accept the truth — or devise a lie to believe in. At this crucial juncture, David and Eli can develop and change their characters, or ignore the opportunity.

TRANSFORMATION IN JEWISH LIFE

In many ways, the *seder* on Pesach models Jewish education. Our sages designed this multidimensional, multimedia tool for teaching children a fundamental facet of the Torah. Via taste, song, vision, emotions and much more, our children learn about G-d's miraculous hand.

The *seder* is a prime example of transformative learning. As we sit down to the *seder*, the children's curiosity is immediately aroused. Daddy is dressed in white, the whole family recites *kiddush* aloud, we wash our hands without a blessing, dip a vegetable in salt water …

Every action we do at the *seder* is designed to pique the children's interest. Before the Four Questions, before reciting the story of the Exodus, the children watch and wonder, "Why is this night different?"

Why is it so important to get the children to ask? Our customs and traditions create a disorienting dilemma so the participants will be thirsty to know. Suddenly the child's world stopped being predictable. "Have all the adults gone crazy? Will someone please explain the new reality to me?"

Educators, parents — if we want our children to be transformed by their learning into moral and responsible adults, learning must take place in an educational environment that orchestrates disorienting dilemmas. With a little creative forethought and planning, any lesson of Gemara, Mishna, or Tanach can be framed in this manner. Before asking the familiar question, "What's bothering Rashi?" we must get the child to be bothered, to ask Rashi's question of his own accord.

28

Punishments versus Consequences

To enforce rules or maintain discipline all parents punish their children at some time or another. But not all disciplinary actions are equal. Certain consequences encourage psychological growth and maturity, while others retard development and breed hostility. The key factor lies in the distinction between a punishment and a consequence. Though they are in many ways synonymous, we will clarify important psychological nuances.

DEFINING THE TERMS

A punishment is a penalty that one inflicts upon another in order to make him change his behavior; it is a way of forcing a person to comply. A punishment may have no relation to the offense, just an arbitrary linking of two events. For example, "Shmuly, you did poorly on your math test so now you may not sleep over at David's house." Or, "Malkie, stop teasing your brother or you won't get dessert!"

A consequence is something that occurs, or is engineered to occur, as a result of the action taken. Consequences can be positive or negative, depending on what the action causes. Because consequences are more neutral, they will be less likely to provoke power struggles and create resentment. They also help children develop personal responsibility and self-control because they become aware of how their actions can directly affect their fate.

Since we want our children to grow up to become responsible adults, our choice of disciplinary responses should mimic real life as much as possible. And in real life, as adults, we are constantly motivated by consequences. When we feel tired and lazy we don't force ourselves out of bed because we fear punishment. We get up because we know we will suffer consequences — we might fall behind at work or miss an opportunity.

TURNING PUNISHMENT INTO CONSEQUENCE

Whether a disciplinary action is a punishment or a consequence depends on how it is framed within the context of the child's life, and the emotion with which it is conveyed.

If Shmuly is doing poorly in math, his parents can explain to him in advance the following consequences: "Shmuly, we have seen your math grades are suffering. We would like for you to enjoy yourself on weekends by sleeping over at friends, but your schoolwork must come first. If you aren't doing well in math, you need to set aside time on the weekend to study. Once your grades return to eighty or higher, we would be happy for you to go on sleepovers." Of course, parents can offer assistance, and set any standard they feel is appropriate.

Or with Malkie, her parents can say, "Malkie, we want to enjoy dinner with a degree of peace and quiet. If you keep teasing your brother, we will have to ask you to leave the table."

In both of these cases, the children are obviously being punished. But they also understand that whatever happens is a direct result of their own choices. Shmuly can choose to study and improve his math performance, thereby earning a sleepover — or he can choose not to. Malkie can either control her behavior at the table and remain for the entire meal, or she can tease her brother and miss dessert.

Parents should discuss the consequence in advance, without any hostility or anger, giving the child a chance to digest and comprehend the situation. Then, if the child misbehaves, parents can simply remind the child of the consequence and even be sympathetic by saying, "I am sorry we have to do this, but this is our agreement and we warned you."

It is important for parents to choose a consequence that is fair and comes as close as possible to real life. Sometimes parents choose overly harsh punishments because they are obsessed with compliance. If a child doesn't obey, parents might be drawn into an escalating series of punishments that become ridiculous and devalue their authority. Governments create inflation by printing too much money; parents create "punishment inflation" if they impose too many overly harsh punishments.

A consequence does not demand immediate compliance. It exacts a fair and reasonable price from those who disobey, so they can eventually decide to behave differently. The worst thing parents can do is become furious and demand immediate change.

If Malkie's and Shmuly's parents play it cool, they do not have to get angry if Malkie continues to tease her brother for the next week. There is no reason to get upset if Shmuly's grades do not improve over the month. Shmuly and Malkie simply suffer the consequences. Eventually, Shmuly and Malkie will be motivated on their own to change their behavior. Consequences create a real-life framework for children to develop their decision-making capacities and self-control.

Emotional Freedom versus Repression

29

Your son is angry. He is screaming insensibly, banging his fist on the wall, the table, and the counter. He's not disrespectful *per se*, but he is venting his frustration in a very visible way. What do you do? Do you overlook this outburst, or do you demand that your son maintain his composure no matter what he is feeling?

The secular world places so much emphasis on emotional freedom, allowing children and adults alike to express themselves as they wish. But this idea presents a conflict for religious parents. We want to provide an environment for our children that is emotionally wholesome while morally wholesome as well.

REPRESSION WITH HARMFUL RESULTS

At the turn of the previous century, Sigmund Freud fathered revolutionary psychological discoveries that had a tremendous influence on Western culture until this day — such as the existence of the unconscious.

Freud, who originally was a neurologist, encountered many patients with an assortment of neurological ills such as partial paralysis, depression, nervousness and anxiety. No one was able to find any physical cause for their symptoms. Together with a few like-minded colleagues, including Joseph Breuer, he began to investigate what psychological mechanisms might be at the root of these illnesses.

First through hypnosis, and later through a special method called free-association, Freud discovered that these symptoms often were the expression of unconscious defenses or conflicts within a person.

One woman came to see Dr. Freud because of paralysis in her hand, which seemed to have no physical basis. Eventually, Freud discovered that the psychological origin was from a hostile wish to hurt her child. Since such a wish was very fearful and troubling to the woman, part of her mind repressed this wish from her conscious thoughts. As a defense against its troubling nature, she became paralyzed in that arm. After this unconscious conflict was brought out into the open, the woman's paralysis was relieved.

Repressed thoughts rarely disappear or stay completely repressed. They usually find a way to express themselves through symbolic thoughts or actions. Imagine a crowded speaking hall where one person starts heckling the speaker. The ushers jump up to silence the person and escort him outside. But even after he is locked out, he still pounds the door and accosts people on the way inside.

When the mind silences an intolerable thought or feeling, it finds other ways to express itself. The woman whose arm was paralyzed still had the angry urge to harm her child. Freud cured this woman, and others like her, by making the unconscious conflict conscious. The patient learned to accept and handle the harmful urge in a more constructive manner.

In this case, the woman perhaps needed to recognize that even a loving mother can have angry impulses at times, but she is not necessarily compelled to act upon them. People who try to shut feelings out, to completely repress them instead of channeling them constructively, can cause much more severe problems.

THE TORAH PERSPECTIVE

If we look to our tradition, there is both support and opposition for repressing feelings. The Talmud states, "Whoever breaks objects out of anger, it is as if he has worshipped idols" (*Shabbos* 105b). Acting out on anger in a destructive manner is expressly forbidden.

But it seems there is a special allowance made for children. The great sage Rabbah bought cheap vessels specifically for his children to break. (*Yoma* 78b) Perhaps they were for his children to play with, and he bought them cheap because he knew they would inadvertently break them.

However, Rashi goes out of the way to indicate that Rabbah bought these vessels because he knew it gave his children pleasure to break them. This implies that children have a greater need to express themselves by breaking and smashing things.

MERGING BOTH VIEWS

The wide arc between expression of feeling and repression ranges from the violent discharge of physical activity to the verbal rational expression of feeling to total squelching. Though it can be harmful to bottle feelings inside, it is not necessarily beneficial to bang, yell and scream.

The healthiest and most helpful approach is to train children to become aware of how they are feeling, while at the same time guiding them in how to express these feelings in an appropriate way. Their capacity to contain and manage their feelings is less developed, so parents need to make allowances.

For example, you can tell a child, "You may be angry at your brother and want to hurt him, but instead of hitting him or banging the wall, you can talk about why you are so upset." But the child may not be ready for that degree of control. If a parent is too strict and controlling, the child may repress his feelings and incur serious damage to his character.

Use common sense. Over time, guide your child toward more mature forms of emotional expression. Angry outbursts should not be overly repressed or overly indulged. And as always, a most important aspect of good parenting is good modeling. You must always set an example by identifying and expressing your own feelings in a calm and clear manner.

Understanding a Child

30

The king had a beloved son, the apple of his eye. But one day the prince became convinced that he was a rooster. He refused to wear clothes and he spent all his time under the table, eating from the floor. The king sought help from all the wise men in the land, but none could cure the prince of his outrageous notion.

One day a fellow came to the kingdom. Upon hearing of the prince's situation, he presented himself at the palace, claiming he had a solution.

The visitor took off his clothes and got down on the floor near the prince. "How are you, my friend?" he asked the prince.

The prince replied, "I am a rooster."

"You are a rooster? What a coincidence, so am I! Pleased to meet you." And they began to talk.

The next day, the man came in dressed and sat down next to the prince. The prince said, "I thought you were a rooster?"

"I am," said the man.

"So why are you wearing those clothes?" asked the prince.

"Who says a rooster can't wear clothes?" said the man. So the prince too donned clothes.

The next day, the man sat down under the table and began eating with a fork. Seeing the prince's puzzled look, the man said, "Who says a rooster can't eat with a fork?" So the prince too began eating with a fork.

These interchanges continued in a similar manner until the prince was acting like a completely normal person.

But he was still convinced he was a rooster. (Rav Nachman of Breslov)

The interpretations of this parable are many, but there is a special meaning for parents and teachers. The prince is a metaphor for every child who feels that he does not quite fit in. Who has not experienced a sulky child who sits under the Shabbos table or pulls away from the family in some other way?

All the wise men in the kingdom talked themselves blue in the face — with no results. In order to reach the prince, the visiting man did not preach or lecture. He joined the prince, on his level. The prince needed someone to see things from his perspective first, and then slowly bring him back to reality.

If you want to help someone, merely preaching or giving advice is not enough. You must really empathize and join that person in his troubles. Once he feels understood, he is more open to listening.

Often it takes only an extra sentence or two to make the difference. "I see you really are upset about such and such. I guess if I were in your shoes I might do the same thing. But there is another way of looking at things which I can share with you that I think will be helpful ..."

We also can gain some chinuch insight along these lines from our family's personal experience in its encounter with a Godol baTorah, Rav Avigdor Miller ZT"L.

One of the great *zechusim* of our family was being related to Rabbi Avigdor Miller. Although he was extremely busy, and planned and calculated every minute of his life, his practice was to always make himself available to family. When we would come to see him, which was rare because we didn't want to abuse the privilege, he would heartily exclaim in his trademark singsong voice, "R-E-L-A-T-I-V-E-S!"

At the time, our daughter was about six years old and our son four and half.

> *Planning to receive a blessing from him, we anxiously prepped our children to be on their best behavior — make blessings over food out loud, be respectful, say please and thank you, and of course, to sit quietly and not whine or complain.*
>
> *We informed Rabbi Miller in advance of our planned visit; he knew the occasion was intended for the children, not the adults. And so when we arrived, he directed himself toward the children. "Make noise! Make noise!" Rabbi Miller enjoined them.*

As he extracted two whistles from a drawer, he explained, "It says that the seas, the mountains and the forests give praise to Hashem. How can they give praise if they have no voices? Their very existence praise Hashem. The wind's blowing or the crashes of the waves are a song. So, too, with children. Children were meant to make noise, and when they do, this is praise to Hashem." He spent a few moments explaining this concept to the children and showed them how to use the whistles.

The Chazon Ish used to tell children to jump around from furniture to furniture. "Just like you are jumping now on the furniture, in the future you will jump from the Ketzos to the Rashba to Tosafos."

Two great Torah leaders employed the same method of *chinuch*. They met the children on their own level. Family therapists call this joining. Instead of forcing silence upon them, Rabbi Miller encouraged the children to do what they do naturally — and showed them how even this can be *avodas Hashem* (service of G-d).

We cannot hope to really reach our children unless we can teach them in a way that connects to their perspective. To whatever extent a parent or teacher can make learning a part of their child's world, the more likely the child will remember and integrate the knowledge — and the loving warmth that comes along with it.

31

Fostering a Motivating Environment

Children like to make their own choices. They like to take charge of their own future. It is an empowering feeling. Constant parental surveillance undermines a child's sense of independence. So when it comes to schoolwork, how do we find the correct balance? When do we oversee the child's study and progress, and when do we leave the choice in his hands?

INDEPENDENCE

Setting up a rigid study schedule for your child to follow removes control from his hands. Capitalize on your child's natural desire for independence. Ask him to set up his own personal study goals and methods, subject to your approval. Then lay off his case. Let him handle his own affairs, provided he meets an agreed upon standard, such as a grade point average.

Finding this balance is difficult and requires keen judgment as well as the emotional flexibility to accept that your child's goals and visions may not always be in complete agreement with your own. You have to tolerate some degree of variation, risk and uncertainty. But if you remain patient and calm, you will be surprised by your children's innate capacity to solve their own problems.

It might be disturbing to see a child go through a whole weekend without once studying for a test. But he wakes up early, or he crams during recess — and he gets a good mark anyway. It may not be the recommended method, but at a certain age, the choice of how to study should be in the child's hands if he can maintain his grades.

SETTING GOALS

The Netziv, Rabbi Naftoli Tzvi Yehuda Berlin, Rosh Yeshiva of the Volozhin Yeshiva (1817-1893), upon the completion of his commentary *Sheiltos D'rav Achai*, invited friends and family to a feast to mark the occasion. At the celebration, he related a key incident in his childhood, the turning point in influencing him to become a great Torah sage.

> *As a young boy, the Netziv was uninterested in learning and scholarship. How his parents wished he would study seriously! Once when he was supposed to be asleep he overhead his parents talking.*
>
> *"I think we should give up," his father said to his mother. "This child is not inclined to be a scholar. Maybe he should develop a trade instead. We should look into apprenticing him with a tailor or a shoemaker."*
>
> *When the Netziv heard that candid conversation, he turned over a new leaf, studying Torah seriously and ultimately developing into an outstanding talmid chacham.*

What changed for the Netziv after overhearing this exchange? Surely he already knew that he was disappointing his parents. But that moment made a great impression on the young child. A *baal mussar* might say he had a sudden *hisorerus*, a religious awakening, an inspiration. No doubt this is true. But there was something unique in his parents' aspirations for him that made him emotionally open to this sudden change.

In light of the psychodynamics of parental over-involvement, perhaps the Netziv was a highly independent and stubborn lad. As long as his father was so invested in his child's scholarship, the Netziv lacked a sense of independence and control.

But then his father gave up. And then the Netziv was free to develop his scholarship. He could even show his father that he was wrong about his nature, that he could become a Torah scholar!

Too Low?

Sometimes parents can set the standards too low, especially for children with learning disabilities. Out of compassion, parents may "sell a child short" and reduce his challenges to such an extent that he gives up. If parents are not involved enough in communicating expectations and setting goals, a child may become bored, apathetic and depressed.

In such a case, parents really should step in and be supportive but firm in setting realistic goals that this child can achieve. Despite some initial protest, a child will usually respond and even develop greater self-esteem. With realistic goal setting, his parents send him the message, "You are capable of doing more, and we believe in your ability."

In real life, outside school, there is no resource room. Even a child with a disability must learn to adapt, compensate, and possibly overcome his disability to succeed as an adult.

32

Why Some Boys Hate to Learn Gemara

Talmud mastery is the crowning achievement of a male Torah Jew. Adults who did not have the opportunity to master Talmud sometimes feel they are missing a basic rite of passage and a credential of Jewish manhood. The study of Gemara is a major part of yeshiva curricula. Students who cannot unlock its secrets are doomed to academic disaster and failure. One well-known yeshiva principal refers to these cases of failed learners as "Gemara casualties."

THE SKILL SET

Though Gemara study requires mastery of many discrete skills and serious concentration, the subject is introduced at a relatively early age. It requires language arts skills: reading Hebrew and Rashi print — without vowels. Reading comprehension — a student needs a command of Aramaic vocabulary and grammar. In the area of thinking skills, the child must draw inferences, compare and contrast, and apply abstract concepts and *halachic* rulings to different hypothetical and actual situations.

The students must memorize dozens of facts and premises for each *sugya* (topic). No page of Gemara exists in isolation — to understand a single page, a student has to be familiar with several other references throughout the Talmud. Feuerman's First Talmud Postulate: "Any given *daf* (page) and any given Tosafos assumes that the reader knows every single other *daf* or Tosafos in the entire Talmud except the one being studied."

Throughout a child's learning career, he will encounter many teachers — some more talented and some less so in their ability to bring the material alive. And this will significantly impact the child's success in his studies.

But in the final analysis, a child must have personal motivation. He has to dedicate years to become truly proficient in Talmud study. Most yeshiva students are able to develop a basic proficiency in Gemara, and some go on to reach even higher levels as they mature intellectually and emotionally.

CHILDREN WITH OBSTACLES

But what about a child at risk? Consider a child with an emotional disturbance or learning disability. He will encounter special challenges learning Gemara. The nature of his difficulties will cause him to be distracted and interfere with the sustained commitment required for the mastery of Talmud.

Each year's work builds on the previous year. So if a child had a troubled year or series of years, he may be at a permanent disadvantage even if his emotional and academic problems have otherwise been resolved. Lacking competence in this key curriculum, the child will be alienated and marginalized in the yeshiva world. He'll align himself with practices, social activities, and other peer groups where he feels more accepted.

Sometimes, these children feel that the Gemara's abstractions and intricate details have no relevance to daily life, which may make it even more difficult for him to focus. "Of what use is it to me that one guy's ox gored another guy's cow? I am depressed, unpopular, and resentful. I'm not getting along with my parents, and I don't really care."

Some might argue that Gemara study provides the basic blueprint and rationale for many of the rituals and halachic rulings that encompass an observant person's daily life. But an alienated and unhappy adolescent will not be likely to see this.

A TALMUD CURRICULUM

It is possible to create a carefully crafted curriculum of Gemara study, including meticulously selected portions and a plan for the study process. What are the goals for such a curriculum?

1. To master reading, vocabulary, and grammar of the Talmud
2. To master the reasoning process of the Talmud (See *Mishneh Torah, Hilchos Talmud Torah* 1:13)
   A. Comparing contradictory texts and rulings
   B. Resolving contradictory texts and rulings
   C. Understanding the derivation of abstract concepts from particular halachic rulings
   D. Understanding the derivation of rulings from abstract concepts
3. To become familiar with the philosophical and moral tenets of Judaism as expressed in the Talmud and learn how to apply them to everyday life
4. To enhance a sense of commitment, involvement, and connection to Judaism and halachic practice

Items one and two belong in the logical and intellectual spheres — their goal is intellectual attainment and mastery. Items three and four are part of the affective or emotional spheres; morality and personal development are the aim.

For an average youth, these goals should be achieved in the aforementioned order. But with kids at risk, prioritization is necessary. Though a child needs to master the technical skills so he can eventually study on his own, the ultimate purpose of all Torah study is the development and enhancement of moral character.

"People whose intelligence exceeds their character are compared to a tree whose branches are larger than its roots" (*Avos* 3:13). A tree with weak roots will fall. For kids at risk, the roots must be properly tended before the tree branches out too far. The moral benefits of Gemara should be stressed first, followed by Talmudic reasoning skills. Once students are properly rooted and secure in their Torah values, the curriculum can concentrate on the technical textual aspects.

A Lesson Plan

This small segment demonstrates how moral, emotional, and intellectual goals can be incorporated into a traditional Gemara lesson. Though it may be ideal for a child at risk to be in a class or school that applies this curriculum, a parent can set up a program with a tutor or mentor to accomplish the same purpose.

Perek Elu Metzios (*Bava Metzia*, chapter 2) is traditionally taught as a primer to most Gemara beginners. But the myriad moral and character-building lessons can go by unnoticed. These lessons not only help the student develop character, but also help him better understand the material and build up his skills by keeping the complex details of *halachic* analysis relevant and interesting.

Overview: *Elu Metzios* discusses the *halachic* obligations regarding an object lost by the owner and found in the street by a passerby. The Gemara requires the finder to return a lost object with an identifiable feature to its rightful owner. The finder is forbidden to keep the object for himself. He may not ignore it. He must actively seek out the owner through various public announcements. The relevant verses can be found in *Devarim* 22:1-4.

Detail: Circumstances where one is permitted to leave a lost object on the ground

Concepts and Skills: Respect for rabbis and teachers, respect for self, judgment and decision making, *lefnim meshuras hadin* (beyond the letter of the law), understanding the meaning of *mitzvos*

Challenge: You come across a possession of yours and a friend's possession at the same time. There is only enough time to save one — a hurricane, for example, is about to strike. What do you do?

Answer: The Talmud (*Bava Metzia* 33a) rules that in all cases you may save your possession first.

Questions to Explore:

‣ What if the other object belongs to a parent or teacher? [Yours takes precedence]

‣ Why is the above ruling true?

‣ Isn't this disrespectful to parents or teachers?

‣ What if you come across a possession of your rebbe's and your parent's and there is only enough time to save one of them, which one goes first? Who should be honored more? [The rebbe's object is saved first, because "his parents brought him into this world, but his rebbe brings him into the World to Come" (ibid).]

‣ What if your parent is also your rebbe?

‣ Read and translate the passage.

33

Gemara for a Different Type of Yeshiva Student

Jewish education in America has come a long way over the past fifty years. Among the general population, literacy in *halacha* and Gemara has surpassed that of many eras in Jewish history. But despite the abundance of Torah education and knowledge, many of our children are lacking in certain character qualities.

Not that our Torah children are faring poorly next to their secular counterparts. Their carefully chosen Torah curriculum positively impacts their character development in a major way. But we must analyze our educational system so our children can learn and grow even more.

THE PROBLEMS

The Talmud advocates Torah study as the preferred method for overcoming the evil inclination. (*Sukkah* 52b) So why aren't our children developing good *midos* (character traits) that are worthy of their level of Torah knowledge? Some children behave so poorly. They are nasty to each other and disrespectful toward their elders. Certainly this doesn't behoove children of their stature.

And this is not something that these children outgrow. They graduate from fighting and name-calling to reckless driving. How can a young yeshiva student ignore an elderly person crossing the street? Why does he fail time and again to replace the volume he finished studying on the shelf? Our children — young and old — are missing some of the simplest traits of decency.

Why are more and more yeshiva children prescribed medication to allow them to conform with the school environment — instead of the school environment conforming to them? Some "at risk" yeshiva boys show exceptional intelligence and adaptability when it comes to scheming ways to make money in business ventures. But when it comes to Torah study, their skills are poor and motivation is lacking.

The yeshiva system places heavy emphasis on avoiding *bitul* Torah (wasting time from Torah study). But many graduating yeshiva students do not fill their free time exclusively with Torah study. Yes, they establish regular times for study, but when they need to relax, they read the newspaper. As a product of the yeshiva system, they should be inculcated with an unquenchable love and thirst for Torah. Why doesn't it last?

CHANGING THE FOCUS

Yeshiva boys are trained to think that the only type of Torah study is in-depth Talmud study. For the majority of Yeshiva students, this is ideal — and it works. There are some students, however, who do not find fulfillment in this type of study. For these students, Torah has become an activity — and certainly not for relaxation and pleasure.

Because of the heavy emphasis on in-depth analysis, yeshiva students are often deficient in their mastery of Hebrew. They do not have the appropriate skills to enjoy reading various Torah texts as a pleasurable activity. They are not trained to easily read and comprehend Tanach or any other worthwhile forms of study from our vast array of Torah literature.

And so they are in constant violation of the commandment, "And you shall ponder it day and night" (*Yehoshua* 1:8). Radak underlines this point. "You shall study it day and night whenever you have free time."

What is the solution for those students who do not have the right combination of intellect and temperament to spend every free moment studying Talmud? They, too, need a model that demonstrates how Torah can realistically be a part of every facet of their lives.

Here's a simple illustration of this problem. Take the Shabbos table *dvar Torah* (Torah thought), a hallowed institution of observant life. Our sages admonished, "Any table where no Torah was spoken is considered as if people ate from idolatrous sacrifices" (Avos 3:3, *Mishna Berurah* 170:1). Clearly it is important for Torah to be spoken at a meal.

But what actually occurs in most homes? Somewhere in the middle of the conversation about sports or politics, the host announces, "We need to say a *dvar Torah!*" Then perhaps one or more children, or even an adult, will dutifully say a Torah thought, usually from a pre-arranged script brought home from school or a book designed for this purpose.

Perhaps in more *halachically* scrupulous homes these scripted and prepared Torah thoughts will take up the entire meal. Certainly admirable. But, we submit, this is not enough. Torah has become an external activity thrown in as an adjunct to the meal, but it is not the meal in and of itself.

We suggest the following: Converse about anything that seems to be on the children's and/or the guests' minds. But because we are interested in Torah, the issue itself can become a Torah discussion.

A child might relate an incident that occurred in school. Such incidents are never without numerous possibilities for Torah discussion — ethical and *halachic* quandaries, tie-ins to the weekly Torah portion. The parents, the Torah guides for the family, can raise some possible issues, and before long a lively debate will ensue. Even small children can bring proofs from stories of the sages that they have heard.

Torah study and thought are blended into real life, not just a practiced ritual. We never have to interrupt a conversation to say a *dvar Torah*, because the entire conversation is Torah!

MOLDING TO THE TIMES

If we want more of our children to internalize Torah and live Torah, we need to find a new way to teach them. Part of the solution lies in becoming more sensitized to the idea of broadening what is considered Torah study for those students who we have identified as not thriving in the current curriculum. Through this, Gemara will not be experienced as a merely rote and formulaic activity.

Admittedly, de-emphasizing Gemara study is not ideal. In-depth study of Talmud is considered the highest level of Torah study for the advanced student. (See *Mishneh Torah, Hilchos Talmud Torah* 1:12.)

But different times require different chinuch responses. For example, originally Torah instruction was performed by the father. There was no such thing as a *cheder*. Why should a father appoint a proxy if he can fulfill the commandment himself? (*Kiddushin* 41a) But our sages observed that many children were not getting a proper education, either because their fathers were weak in Torah or perhaps because their fathers did not have sufficient time. So they created educational institutions to teach children Torah. (*Bava Basra* 21a)

The father-son system was ideal; each child received individualized education. But since the times called for it, our sages intervened and modified the *chinuch* system, even though the modifications made *chinuch* inferior in certain ways.

Jumping approximately two millennia ahead in time, the Bais Yaakov movement was necessitated by similar circumstances. Originally, Jewish communities were not subject to secular influences. Girls didn't need to be taught Torah. Mothers lovingly bequeathed their daughters with all the necessary knowledge about the faith and practice of Judaism. But due to encroaching secular influences, great numbers of Jewish girls began to stray from the path of Torah. Then formal instruction for Jewish girls was founded.

Rav Yisroel Salanter's *mussar* movement was founded in response to a general spiritual crisis. He emphasized the study of Jewish ethical texts, encouraging people to take a deep look into their souls. Otherwise, Rav Yisroel felt, they were doomed to lose the war against assimilation.

The movement was initially greeted with suspicion and hostility. The Lithuanian Torah leaders feared he would create a new religious sect and diminish the prominence of Talmud study. (Weinberg, *Lefrakim*, 104-112) One of the stories about the tensions between the mussarists and the hard-line *Litvacks* puts our current problems in perspective:

> Reb Itzele Peterberger met with Rav Chaim Soloveitchik in the hope of convincing him to introduce the systematic

study of mussar into the Volozhin Yeshiva curriculum. Rav Chaim replied, "Mussar is medicine for the soul. One only gives medicine to a sick man. If you give medicine to a healthy person you can even do harm. Our students in the yeshiva are spiritually healthy and therefore only need Torah study." (Ibid, 60)

Are all our children "healthy" today? Are we missing an opportunity to give some of them the educational nutrition they need?

THE ELITIST MODEL

In the yeshivas in Europe, by and large, only the best and brightest students would enter to be trained to become even better and brighter. A select few would be able to continue to study Torah — the social and economic conditions made sure of that.

American yeshivas have been modeled after this elitist system. In fact, however, they serve the entire population of observant Jews, not just the top students. Because we live in a comfortable and affluent society, all children from observant families are expected to spend many years studying Torah. There are few socially sanctioned options within the mainstream yeshiva system for lighter or more diverse forms of study.

This is the beginning of how we can lose many of the children. Those with learning disabilities are a given. There are some gifted children who do not have the disposition that allows them to sit for hours in class. And we also lose many unconventional bright children, who find that our current Torah curriculum is not broad enough to offer stimulation that can compete with secular forms of study.

These children may indeed be studious in Torah and do well in school, but how many of them see it as a way of life? Given a choice between reading an interesting book or studying Torah, would these children choose to study Torah? Perhaps not. Because to this unconventional child, the current system portrays Torah in a one-dimensional manner.

This is not the first time in history that such problems have been considered. Indeed, the introduction to *Mesilas Yesharim* laments that though there are many who spend time in in-depth study, few devote time to studying aspects of the Torah which focus on character development.

Rabbi Samson Raphael Hirsch offers some chilling words in his commentary on the upbringing of Yaakov and Esav.

> An observation made by our sages indicates that the sharp contrast between the two grandsons of Avraham was caused not only by their natural tendencies but also by mistakes in their upbringing. (*Bereishis Rabbah* 63:10) As long as they were little, no one paid attention to the differences in their hidden natures (C.V. 24); they were given the same upbringing and the same education. Their parents overlooked the cardinal principle of education, "Educate each child in accordance with his own way" (*Mishlei* 22:6).
>
> Each child should be guided in accordance with the path intended especially for him, the path that suits the qualities and tendencies latent in the depths of his personality, and thus he should be educated ...
>
> Precisely for this reason, each child must be brought up ... according to his own unique way, in keeping with his potential. To attempt to educate a Yaakov and an Esav together in the same classroom, in the same routines, and in the same manner ... will inevitably mean to ruin one of the two. A Yaakov will draw from the well of wisdom with ever increasing interest and desire, whereas an Esav will hardly be able to wait for the day when he can throw away the old books ...
>
> Had Yitzchak and Rivka delved deeply into Esav's nature; had they asked themselves at an early stage how even an Esav — with the strength, skills, and courage latent within him — could be harnessed for G-d's service, then the future *gibor* [strong one] would not have become a *gibor tzayid* [strong hunter] but a true *gibor lifnei Hashem* [strong in the service of Hashem] (*Hirsch Chumash*, 558-559).

The Torah curriculum itself should have been made more appealing to Esav — with a form of Torah study that he could relate to. In the same way, Torah study has to appeal to all children, not just those who are gifted and temperamentally suited to intensive study. Our *chinuch* approach has to be individualized within the school curriculum, from gifted to learning disabled.

In order for a person to be successful in Torah study, the Talmud advises that a person "always study an area that his heart desires, *ma shelibo chafetz*" (*Avoda Zara* 19a). This is common sense, but how can we apply it in our schools? Sometimes our children don't want to study certain subjects, or accept responsibility. But we push them to do these things anyway because in the long run, it is in their best interest. It may not be enjoyable now, but it pays off down the road.

To assure that Torah study becomes a part of the lives of all our children, we need to become more attuned to what it takes to reach each child in his own world. We have to connect to their perspective so they learn and apply what they learn to their everyday lives, instead of just memorizing facts. This will affect their retention of the material and their *midos*.

A New Method

Taking into account these social and *chinuch* concerns, we have developed some fundamental principles for the "*Libo Chafetz* Method," a new way of learning for children who do not seem to be thriving in the mainstream system.

▸ All Torah learning is to be valued and encouraged, no matter what area of study.
▸ The definition of Torah study is any inquiry that leads to greater practical and ethical fulfillment of the commandments.
▸ Each child should be encouraged to study in areas where he shows a natural interest.
▸ Academic success in Torah study should be de-emphasized when appropriate. Torah study is for its own sake.
▸ As age and maturity allow, parents create a framework of choices for their children, so they can exercise independence and control over their lives.

Some of these goals can be achieved within a school framework, some at home. Schools can offer elective courses of study. Parents can provide extra-curricular learning, where the child has input in the subject of study. With the encouragement of a one-on-one tutor outside the school curriculum, a child who is failing in Talmud might blossom in Tanach or another branch of Torah.

34

Risks at Summer Camp

Every year thousands of Jewish boys and girls spend their summer days away from their parents under circumstances far less supervised and structured than those that exist during the school year. Parents trust the leadership and staff of the camp to keep things safe and under control, and in most instances, this trust is appropriately placed. However, parents still must keep their eyes and ears open, remaining on the lookout for dangerous and harmful influences.

THE ENVIRONMENT

There are some key differences between the summer time and the school year:

- If your child is in sleep-away camp, you only see him on visiting day, perhaps talking on the phone twice a week. This makes subtle signs of trouble easy to miss.
- Authority figures such as counselors and other staff are not much older than the campers, and often are unmarried teenagers. The behavior, judgment and *midos* of the counselors are not much more mature than the campers.
- While camp's more heterogeneous mix of kids from varied religious levels of observance may serve as an excellent opportunity to broaden your child's horizons, it also can expose your child to behaviors and practices you feel they are not yet ready to learn about.

Two areas of most serious concern are that of sexual abuse and drugs. Our sages did not turn a blind eye to such things. *"Ein apotropus learayos*, there can be no sure guarantee to protect from sexual temptation" (Kesubos 13b).

Bais Shmuel (*Shulchan Aruch, Even Haezer* 24:1) strongly suggests that two single males should avoid being alone together, particularly those who live in areas where immorality abounds.

In the time of our sages, drug abuse was not a major problem. But they did link intoxication and promiscuity. "Why does the Torah place the law of the *nazir* following that of the *sotah* (unfaithful wife)? In order to teach you that whoever sees a sotah in her degradation, will react by vowing as a *nazir* to abstain from wine" (*Sotah* 2a).

Boys are generally more at risk than girls, but from anecdotal evidence gathered from other therapists, it seems that the gender gap is closing. Women can be predators too.

TAKING PRECAUTIONS

What are you supposed to do as a parent? We do not suggest that you never let your child out of your sight or send him away from home. The overwhelming majority of children have positive experiences in summer camp.

Look for a camp that has a high degree of structure and supervision. No child should be allowed to loaf around for extended periods on the sidelines. Socially marginal children are at the greatest risk. The lonely child in search of friends is easy prey for those who seek to take advantage of them.

And talk to your children in advance — on more than one occasion — about Torah values, sexuality, and drug abuse. Some parents are afraid to expose their children prematurely to ideas and issues. But nature abhors a vacuum. If you don't fill this role, your children are vulnerable to others who might prey on their naiveté. So share your wisdom and guidance when it comes to these matters. Encourage continuous dialogue throughout their formative years.

You might remember from your own childhood what you learned at a particular age. But kids today, with unprecedented exposure to images and ideas from the media, must know certain things years earlier than we learned them. There's plenty of literature to guide parents about how to speak to children, but your best guide is basic decency, love and common sense. Think back to what you would have wished to hear or have been told when your were their age, and you will know what to say.

SECTION FOUR
Transition to Adulthood

F ive years in the life of an adult is a relatively small amount of time. But in the life of an adolescent, five years is a very long time. Parents have to adjust their attitudes to their young adults, who not too long ago were immature children. These newly minted adults bring a fresh perspective to the family, albeit with various challenges. And there are healthy ways for parents to respond.

35

Unconditional Love

Your son is totally disrespectful. Your daughter is verbally abusive. Your teenager is simply unmanageable. How can you show love and affection for a child when she is completely undeserving of it? This is not the child who misbehaves occasionally — this is the kid who is a constant source of heartache. Aside from the immediate professional guidance these children require, parents must address this issue — how to show love, especially when they feel none.

DEFINING PARENTAL LOVE

Some experts strongly advocate that children receive unconditional love. No matter what a child does wrong, he or she should still feel loved. A child needs parental support and affection in order to grow and develop self-confidence. Whether he behaves or misbehaves, he still must receive love.

Though it sounds good in theory, the more you think about it, the more difficult this problem becomes. What does "loving unconditionally" really mean? Imagine a child who is insolent toward his parents and misbehaves at school. What are his parents supposed to feel? What is there left to love — his good looks or his talents? Must parents search for an aspect of their child to love when he is acting obnoxious in so many ways? Perhaps parents can muster a sense of pity — but is it realistic to expect love?

The Torah commands us to love our neighbor, which Ramban (Vayikra 19:17-18) interprets as to be loving toward our neighbors. Parents can't force themselves to love their unruly child, but they can outwardly act in a loving manner.

Poets and philosophers have been pondering love for eons, but psychology also has some thoughts on this matter. Psychology defines love as the acceptance and understanding of another person's uniqueness and differences. To love a person is to see him as he really is.

APPLYING LOVE

Using this more subtle and sophisticated definition of love, parents of an obnoxious and very unlovable child can be unconditional in their willingness to understand and accept their child's emotional and inner states, thereby showing "love."

Loving does not condone the behavior. Parents are entitled to be honestly angry and irritated. They also can continue to work with the child on changing his behavior in the future. However, parents should not distort or try to change what they see or know about their child right now, whether it is good or bad. This is the type of love and acceptance everyone needs.

If a child is expelled from school for some horrible deed, parents have the right to be upset with the child. But they also have to face up to who their child really is, which will help the child face up to who he is, too.

A parent can say, "You have done a terrible thing. It makes me angry and it's going to cause a lot of problems." This reaction is better than yelling and screaming. It is not a fake or forced effort to show love. And the parent does not jump too quickly to excuses, solutions, or punishments, although these might be appropriate in a later stage.

By reacting to this child's behavior in a realistic and honest manner, parents show acceptance. The child sees love and support — someone else knows about what he has done and is sharing the experience with him. This child may be troubled, he may be obnoxious, but if parents can follow through with this realistic form of love and acceptance, the child will not feel alone.

36

Encouraging Respectful Behavior from Teenagers

Teenagers are typically difficult.

Many parents tolerate disrespect because they want to avoid rocking the boat or alienating their teen. But during the emotionally difficult years when adolescents are evolving into grownups, it is important to maintain some constant standards that promote stability of the household, despite teenagers' quarrelsome attitude and general moodiness. A few basic rules can go a long way toward building respect and trust, a critical component for the tentative relationships between parents and teens.

Most parents of teens already know, or will inevitably discover on the battlefield, that they must pick and choose which issues are most worthwhile going to war over. Basic human decency among family members, including teenagers, is very much worth the war. The type of clothing she wears or the music he listens to — these are passing phases. But interpersonal relationships — this is the very basis of how you influence your child. No parent should allow disrespect to pervade the home for any length of time. It could lead to further breakdown in communication and more serious problems in the future.

FROM THEIR PERSPECTIVE

Teenagers go through a period of emotional growing pains, when they seek to form their identities. This involves separating psychologically from their parents in order to develop independent personalities and values. In this process, many teenage children seek their independence through negative means such as being rude to parents and siblings, testing their limits.

Parents need not and should not tolerate rude behavior from their children. One prevalent attitude condones that "it's healthy to let it all out," but from a psychological perspective, it is not conducive to teens' development. Allowing teenagers to tyrannize their families through moodiness, rudeness and uncivil behaviors can retard emotional growth. It fosters a chaotic helplessness in the household.

> Daniel comes home from school in a bad mood. He had a difficult day. He is rude and disrespectful to his mother. But his mother does not react or reprimand him. Daniel feels lonely and helpless. He needs to express his feelings. But Daniel does not yet possess the character to tolerate his own weakness. He is afraid of his desire for nurturing. Therefore, he lashes out with rude behavior.

Parents who think they are being accepting when they allow their child to yell, "Shut up," are being terrorized. These parents fear their teenager. Will he test their limits further? Will he destroy family property?

Teenagers need their parents to set limits, they need to be loved and nurtured. Allowing a teenager to persistently storm into the house and head toward his room without saying hello calcifies the emotional walls that sometimes go up between parents and their growing children.

Teenagers legitimately need space to grow and individuate from parents, to develop their independent personalities. But this does not legitimize a pattern of rude behaviors toward parents and siblings.

How to Help Yourself and Your Teen

If you have been the subject of verbal abuse or disrespect, you have a difficult dilemma on your hands. Respect must be maintained both from a Torah perspective and a developmental perspective. Yet you fear World War III will break out if you challenge the unruly adolescent.

Anger is contagious, so first you must keep your own feelings of anger or hurt in check for the moment. A constructive response can be a message of love together with the message of expectation for respect.

"It sounds like you're really upset about something today. Though I certainly can understand how you feel, you must know that being rude to your parents is not acceptable." You are thus criticizing the rude behavior but at the same time letting him know that you care and are interested in him.

An impatient and angry teenager can be told even more bluntly, "We can talk about this, but it must be with respect." Do not expect absolute or immediate compliance — after all, you are not dealing with a small child anymore. However, you should still persist in enforcing these boundaries of respect, without losing your patience.

As far as your personal anger is concerned, take care of your own feelings by seeking a spouse or friend. Talking about it with someone else can keep your views in perspective and provide emotional strength and support to properly handle the next attack.

You might conclude, "My fifteen-year old just needs some space. I prefer to let him be and I'll try to overlook his constant rudeness." But what happens when this young man or woman, who is still very much a child, needs a loving and attentive adult to talk to? Will you, tolerant as you are, have the ability and patience to really listen wholeheartedly after being repeatedly abused? After all, you have resentments too.

When communication is eventually reestablished with a teenager who has been hostile and uncommunicative in the past, there needs to be a basic foundation of respect and trust between parent and child so the parent can serve in his or her role of authority.

What if communication has stopped months or even years ago? This, coupled with daily negative interactions, totally rules out honest conversation, no matter how much your teenager might feel the need for it. In fact, a child who has not had limits set regarding his acceptable behavior will likely have intense unconscious guilt feelings that may prevent him from approaching a parent for that help.

If you are firm in your expectations for at least minimal civility in your home, the door is open for your teenager to approach you.

These minimum limitations prevent accumulated guilt feelings and the resulting embarrassment a teenager might feel in seeking guidance, understanding and help from his parents.

SETTING THE RULES

Rule should be established at a quiet time, before communication disintegrates within the family. They should be simple and easy to follow. You should make it clear that though the teenager may not feel like talking or is not in a good mood, he or she must still be civil to others in the household.

Minimum standards might include saying goodbye before leaving home in the morning, greeting those who are home upon returning in the evening, and saying please and thank you for food that has been cooked, prepared or bought. Though these rules may seem simple, it is surprising how the daily grind can wear many parents down and allow them to tolerate absurd levels of disrespect.

Since teenagers are halfway adults, these rules should not be enforced with hostility, no matter how annoying and obnoxious your teen may be. You should instead appeal to their sense of reason and firmly but politely insist they be kept. If you establish some simple and not overly burdensome rules for respectful behavior and consistently remind family members of them, over time most adolescents will comply — for their own benefit and their family's.

37

I Can't Stand
the Music He Listens To!

What can parents do when their children listen to distasteful music? Choice of music is just one way teenagers assert their identities and independence. You have to pick and choose which behaviors to overlook and which should be absolutely forbidden. Is music an issue worth going to war over? Every family has different priorities and values. But some of the following psychological insights and parenting strategies will help you choose the approach that's right for your family.

PUTTING THINGS IN PERSPECTIVE

The fact that teenagers' music is distasteful is not unique to the religious world. Many parents will confess that they too listened to music in their youth that their parents found objectionable. While the average American parent fears the harmful moral impact of the lyrics or the way certain musical groups dress, *frum* parents are suspect of any non-Jewish cultural influence.

The Torah forbids the influence of secular culture even in regard to modes of dress. (See *Shulchan Aruch, Yoreh Deah* 178. Note the difference between immoral customs versus civil customs.) Certainly music written and sung by a machine-gun toting or hedonistic pop icon should be unwelcome in a Torah home. Parents who enjoyed non-Jewish music in their youth may feel that their children should be given the opportunity to have a more religious upbringing, or that today's music is more harmful.

Adolescents, in their efforts to form their own identities, are quick to point out flaws or hypocrisy in parental logic, so it is important to identify exactly what is objectionable in their music.

Music written and sung by non-Jews, or irreligious Jews, may be forbidden because it is a custom of the gentiles. Even when singers put Jewish words and messages into non-Jewish songs — "Jewish rock" — the tunes and beats are of non-Jewish origin. But according to this reasoning, classical music would also be forbidden since the melodies were written by non-Jews. Some of the melodies were even written specifically as church music!

Some contemporary music is wanton, suggestive and immoral, not because of the lyrics or the composer's morality, but because the beat itself seems to encourage sensuality. According to this line of reasoning, some of today's Jewish tunes written and performed by sincerely observant Jews could be off limits. One could argue: Many of these songs are clearly inspired by rock music tunes and styles. Tunes in the end are just music, but if the singer on stage is sporting a beard and a black frock, but his hips undulate in a suggestive manner, is this really kosher?

When talking to children about this topic, it is important for parents to avoid a knee jerk reaction. Think about the issues first to crystallize your philosophy — or you run the risk of being unwittingly hypocritical, which your teenager will almost certainly pounce on!

TRADITIONAL JEWISH PERSPECTIVES ON NON-JEWISH MUSIC

Elisha ben Avuya, a great Torah sage from the time of the Mishna, became a heretic, renamed Acher. The Talmud attributes the cause of Acher's defection from Judaism to the fact that "a Greek song was constantly on his lips" (*Chagigah* 15b).

How did the Greek song cause Acher to stray? Rashi explains Acher disregarded the prohibition of enjoying song subsequent to the destruction of the Temple, and so the song caused him to stray. Interestingly, Rashi omits any reference to the immoral influence of the words in the song, though the Maharsha adds this factor.

Mishna Berurah quotes the Shelah, warning Jewish mothers not to sing love songs to their children as lullabies.

One should not sing love songs to the baby as it develops an evil nature in the child. Furthermore, such songs are forbidden because they contain profane language and incite the evil inclination. One who wants to protect his soul should distance himself from this and also warn his family about such matters. (*Mishna Berurah* 560, *Shaar Tzion* 25)

Rambam presents a Jewish perspective on the value of music in general and how it can be of psychological benefit to a person:

If one is overcome by bitter bile [depression], one can cause it to lift by listening to melodies and various songs and by strolling in gardens or viewing beautiful structures and the like, which helps calm the soul and remove the mental confusion that the bitter bile causes. In all this his intention should be to keep his body healthy so that he can continue his study of the ways of G-d. (*Shemonah Perakim* 5)

Rambam recognizes the value music has in lifting depression and bitter moods. He points out that the listener's intention should not be solely for empty pleasure but to restore physical and mental balance so as to allow a person to further his development and growth in Torah.

Before cutting off music from a teenager who is at that stage in life when he is particularly prone to moodiness and depression, parents should consider how the teenager uses music to stabilize his mood and cope with stress. If parents feel the music is forbidden but is somehow helpful in calming the child's nerves, perhaps a rabbi should be consulted before taking any action.

Regarding non-Jewish music, Rambam observes:

You should know that the preferred and appropriate songs, in whatever language they may be, are only determined by their content … I must explain this point even though it is obvious because I have seen great and conscientious people amongst our nation who, if invited to a party or a wedding or the like, and someone wants to sing in Arabic [the spoken language of the time] even something that is very worthy and inspiring, these people object in every possible manner. They do not permit anyone to listen to such songs. Yet, if the singer wants to sing a song that is in Hebrew, they have no objection and no difficulty with that, even though such songs have content that is either forbidden or unworthy. This is absolute foolishness, for speech is not permitted or forbidden, worthy or unworthy, based on the language but rather based on the content. For if the song has in it a worthy intent, then it is an obligation to sing it in whatever language it is written in. And if the song's content is base then one is obligated to abstain from it no matter what language it is written in. However, I will add one more thought. If there are two songs, both of which have a purpose of stimulating desire and to arouse the [animal] soul to it, which ... one should distance himself from because it arouses one to be drawn toward low character traits, and one of these songs is in Hebrew and the other is in Arabic or another foreign language, the song in Hebrew is even worse because it desecrates the holiness of the language. One should only use Hebrew for high purposes. And surely, it is even worse if the song uses a verse from the Torah or from *Shir Hashirim* because then the song is no longer merely inappropriate but also forbidden, for the *halacha* forbids using the words of the prophets as assorted base and low songs. [See *Sanhedrin* 100a] (*Shemonah Perakim* 1:16)

Rambam essentially mentions three categories of music: (1) Forbidden music, (2) inappropriate music which is not forbidden but not conducive to the development of proper character traits, and (3) music that a person should listen to. Aside from these, Rambam refers to the prohibition against degrading verses of the Scriptures by turning them into songs of low morality.

What might Rambam think of today's Jewish music, that puts Hebrew verses to non-Jewish tunes? Rambam does identify emotional and inspirational potential in music, not based on the language but on its use of content. This does leave an opening for at least considering non-Jewish music acceptable if it helps soothe a person's mood and provides inspiration, though obviously it cannot contain obscenity or lewd content.

LET'S BE REALISTIC

When parents are locked in a battle with a teenager it is important to be realistic about the issue. Victory is broader than immediate, one-hundred-percent compliance. A resentful teenager forced to obey today may escape your grasp as soon as he is old enough and do whatever he wants. It is far more worthwhile to work with your teenager today so when he matures, he will ultimately emulate your values and way of life.

Most parents fear that if they do not force compliance and instill good character traits now, they will never have a chance to influence their children in the future. There is merit to this concern, particularly with younger children. But the older the child is, the less ability the parent has to enforce rules.

No one can force anyone to do anything, especially not a mature young adult. But along with increased maturity there are increasing opportunities for logical discussion. Instead of relying exclusively on brute parental force and punishment, add more tricks to your repertoire to get your child to comply.

One way to help your child live up to the standards of morality you espouse is by showing a willingness to fully understand his side of the story. Ask your child what he likes about the music he listens to. Listen to this music together and ask what he thinks of the lyrics.

Sometimes teenagers are oblivious to the deeper meanings of the songs they like, and they just enjoy the beat or one particular concept in the song. By being fair-minded and asking your son to comment on the song, you just might motivate him to really pay attention to the offensive content. At least then he will understand why you wish to forbid it.

Using this method, you can work out a compromise with your teenager. He or she can listen to the music, as long as you review the content at set intervals to explore the possible harmful messages contained in it. It doesn't solve the problem instantly, but by using real respect, the teenager becomes partially vaccinated from the influence of the music. He develops critical thinking skills to combat other cultural influences or fads. The battle may not be fully won — but there is hope for the war.

38

Maintaining
Your Relationship

Parents of a severely rebellious teenager have gone through so many fights that they fear continued strife will tear apart the family. Sometimes they adopt a strategy of pulling back in their criticism and disciplinary efforts. Professionals often advise parents to "give their child some space," to avoid harping upon every behavior.

If a child from a very religious home wishes to wear clothes that are not modest or see movies, parents might consider backing off and accepting this behavior as part of adolescent experimentation and identity seeking. In a more modern Orthodox home the objectionable behavior may be different, such as flirting with violating Shabbos or laws of kashrus — but the process is the same.

"Do whatever you want — just not at home or in front of your siblings." While this approach may be necessary at times, it also has a potential pitfall. Parents may inadvertently send the message that they have given up on their son or daughter.

Teenagers still need their parents' involvement, concern and love. A sudden absence of criticism and arguing can be perceived as an absence of love. He or she may think, "At least before when we were fighting all the time I knew where I stood. Now all I get is cold looks. It's as if I don't exist." The parents are trying their best to control their anger, to tolerate their child's differences, but the child perceives the tense silence as evidence of the parents' disregard.

So what are you to do? If you get involved in your child's behavior, terrible and damaging family arguments occur. If you try to hold back criticism and judgment, they become cold and aloof. Your success or failure is dependent upon the emotional process.

If you are backing off because of respect for your child's need for individuality, and you communicate your confidence in your child's ability to learn about the world and ultimately make good decisions, then doing this during certain stages of a teenager's life may be helpful. But if you are backing off because you are exhausted from all the quarreling, because you have given up — then you are sending the message that your once precious child is not worth bothering with. While in certain cases parents should stop trying to control their teenager, nevertheless, you should never stop being involved in your teenager's life and activities he or she chooses.

You might find this very painful. After a certain point, some parents don't want to know what their rebellious child is up to — it hurts too much. The more they know, the more likely they will get angry and start fighting with their teenager. But it is worthwhile to tolerate this pain and still stay involved in the child's life.

If you are a parent in this situation, communicate your willingness to conduct a "cease fire" and allow your child more autonomy. But also indicate that you would like to hear about what he or she is doing, even if it is behaviors that you have forbidden or not approved of in the past. The message is, "Although we do not approve of all the things you do, we are your parents, still love you and are interested in hearing about your life."

Asking your child to tell you about what he and his friends enjoy doing and what their personal goals are does not mean you are condoning them. This keeps the door open and allows an opportunity for parents to remain involved. Once your rebellious teenager is truly convinced that you respect his right to choose, there will certainly be times where he will seek out your advice. But this will only occur if the respect is real, and not merely a form of giving up.

Why Doesn't My Child Talk to Me Anymore?

Sometimes during the teen years, sometimes earlier, we suddenly realize that our children are not talking to us anymore. Suddenly we don't know what's going on in their lives. Much to our frustration, a question like, "How was your day at school?" is met with shrugs and monosyllabic answers. Thankfully, there are methods and tips to facilitate meaningful conversation between parent and child.

SEPARATION

A child is fighting against two opposite forces — on the one hand, unconsciously the child deeply yearns to return to the blissful state of infancy where he was completely enveloped by his mother's embrace. Yet the child knows that he cannot return to that state, and with every passing phase he must become more self-reliant to survive.

When a child goes off to school, he is terrified to leave the protection and love of his mother. So he develops a psychological defense — he begins to despise that part of himself that wishes to be a baby. The most insulting school yard taunt one child can give another is "Mama's boy!"

The mother-son relationship poses the most unconscious conflict. Fathers do not provide the same level of nurture and intimacy that mothers do. A daughter can comfort herself with the fact that one day she will grow up to be just like her mother. But a young boy knows he can never become his mother. He sees his role in life is different, and identifies more with his father, but doesn't feel that same level of closeness. He will always miss his mother to some extent because he cannot fully return to her, or ever find a way to fully identify with her.

Children and young adults — boys and girls — will turn to their peers as a surrogate family. Their peers provide emotional support without the conflict that staying close to mother and father evokes. Since his peers are really like family, it is at this time that peer pressure is the most difficult.

INITIATING CONVERSATION

You are suddenly irrelevant in your child's life — except to chauffeur him from one friend's house to another. But if you realize how difficult this separation is for your child, it will be easier to deal with these feelings of rejection.

As a parent, you still need to know what's going on in your child's life, even if he is uninterested in sharing. Trying to force your child to talk will only lead to frustration and resentment. But you still need to tune into possible emotional disturbances and dangerous or harmful behaviors.

When a child, especially a teen, is in the mood to talk, make yourself available. If you try to reinitiate the conversation later with, "Did you want to talk about something before?" most likely the response will be something like, "Oh, nothing. Forget it."

Sometimes parents really are too busy to talk. In such a case, try to give your child two or three minutes of real concentration to hear the basic points, and then you will have enough material to go back and start a discussion later.

Children seem to have a knack for choosing the worst times to speak, such as when you are rushing off to a meeting, or just before midnight, when both of you are exhausted and past ready for bed. While it may be a manipulative delay tactic to avoid bedtime, perhaps it is a unique opportunity to speak. When children are sleepy and ready for bed, they feel more vulnerable and in need of nurture.

EMPLOY ACTIVE LISTENING

Teenagers hate to be told what to do. If your teenager is talking, let her say everything on her mind, even if you disagree. A parent does need to provide guidance, a firm and confident moral perspective, so the child develops into a secure adult. But there is a time and place for everything. When your child is talking to you, it is not the time to lecture.

Your teenager needs to think out loud. She hopes for your approval, but at the same time is hypersensitive to your criticism. So even if a child seems to be asking for advice, help her generate her own thoughts on the matter. "What would you advise a friend about that?" "What does your teacher say?" "If my opinion was such and such, how would you react?"

Yes, it is a parent's responsibility to tell a child what to do — but wait until your child has expressed himself completely before you step in and offer your wisdom. Once your child has a chance to fully explore her own thoughts, she will be more receptive and more likely to heed your words.

40

Does the Apple Fall Far from the Tree?

Many parents would like to take exception to the famous adage, "The apple does not fall far from the tree." And rightfully so. We all know at least one truly fine and upstanding family whose child diverged from the path. Or a child from a broken home who grew into a great leader.

But these are the exceptions to the general rule. A child's home environment is a key influence on his development. Nevertheless, every individual makes his own choices in life. You can't place too much blame on parents of a bad child, nor can you give too much credit for a good child.

The Talmud points to a priestly family, a family with illustrious ancestry, whose daughter became an apostate, "because of her poor upbringing" (*Sukkah* 56b). Parents, good as they may be as people, sometimes exercise bad judgment when it comes to raising children.

There are well-meaning parents who try their best. You can never know for certain if a child's upbringing caused his decline, or if some other factors came into play. But parents have subtle influences on their children, and despite the best intentions, some parents may be unconsciously guiding their children down an undesired path.

WHAT CHILDREN LEARN

Your behavior and your actions are the most important model for your children. Children will not comply with, "Do as I say, not as I do." But even beyond that — children learn the most not from what their parents say or do, but from how their parents feel.

An honest, dedicated family man devotes many of his free hours to Torah study and is scrupulous in his observance of the commandments. If the home environment is a decisive influence on a child's moral development, by all rights his sons should become great scholars and supporters of Torah.

The *eishes chayil* (valiant wife) makes great sacrifices to support and maintain a Torah home. Logically, her daughters should grow up to emulate her lifestyle. In many cases, this is exactly what occurs.

But how do we account for children who rebel, opting for the path directly opposing the values of their upbringing? What about the situation where several siblings do follow in their parents' footsteps, and just one black sheep in the family wanders astray? If this child's behavior is due to his upbringing, how could he have experienced a different upbringing from that of his siblings?

FEELINGS COMMUNICATE

People have many conflicting emotions. Children are very adept at tuning into an adult's feelings, even if they are not explicitly verbalized or even fully conscious. When a father goes off to study Torah, is he excited about it, or does he show a grim determination? When he returns, is he grumpy or does he come back feeling satisfied and accomplished?

Does the mother show she is happy about her choice in life, or does she have an air of bitterness and resentment? A child's biological and psychological tasks are to absorb and learn from all the cues in his environment. He will surely pick up on these non-verbal messages and make decisions accordingly.

The overall tone and emotional climate of the home critically influence a child's moral development. Parents can be scrupulous in their dedication to their values and morals, but if they go about their lives with a grim or bitter feeling — even if they never verbally utter a complaint — they should not be surprised if a child does not want to follow in their footsteps.

No one is perfect. We all have mixed feelings, even about those matters that we recognize are important. Hard working, honorable parents do not deserve to suffer for periodic lapses! On the contrary — because at times we struggle to live in accordance with our moral standards, we should be rewarded for doing the best we can. If children are as perceptive as we claim, why can't they learn from the positive aspects of their parents' dedication?

Children are not prophets or mind readers, so while they are highly perceptive, what they perceive may not be the reality — or at least not the whole reality. A father who makes great sacrifices for Torah clearly is a good role model in one aspect. Based on their own temperaments and learned behaviors, one child may be impressed by his father's steadfast determination, while another sibling is turned off by his father's subtle feelings of resentment and dissatisfaction.

FAMILY DYNAMICS

Sometimes a parent may have conflicting feelings about Torah observance, feelings he may not be fully aware of. This can have a significant impact on the child.

> Thirteen-year-old Shalom does not want to join the family in the sukkah because it's too cold. His father consulted with a rabbi and the rabbi ruled that given the mild climate and his son's good health, he is obligated to eat in the sukkah. Shalom's parents engage in various forms of disciplinary measures to enforce the values of the family. Shalom's parents are not abusive; they just take whatever measures parents must take to impose standards of behavior.

Let us consider for a moment the possibility that deep down, Shalom's father shares some of his son's ambivalence about eating in the *sukkah*. Even though many times it is a great pleasure, sometimes eating in the *sukkah* can be uncomfortable and a major inconvenience.

His father, fighting his own unrecognized feelings of resentment about the *sukkah*, projects his uncertainties onto Shalom, responding with an inappropriate measure of impatience and harshness. His own mixed feelings psychologically block him from disciplining with more empathy.

Our sages recognized that a person tends to criticize others who have his own flaws (*Kiddushin* 70a). Shalom's parents rightfully enforce their expectations, but his father does not show enough compassion because, deep down, he has the same flawed attitude.

A parent who finds his child misbehaving in a way similar to the way he used to act as a child, or even in the way he sometimes still feels as an adult, should pay careful attention to this dynamic and make sure he is not overly harsh.

DIFFERENT MANIFESTATIONS

Parents may think their problem child is a "bad seed" and has nothing in common with them, but if they dig deeper they may find that in fact their core values are alive and well within this child's personality, albeit expressed in a different form. When dealing with a rebellious child, parents should search for ways their child expresses parental values, even if it comes from a different perspective.

> Malkie comes from a family of high academic achievers where scholarship and study is encouraged. Malkie is the black sheep because she is "lazy and proud of it." She never studies and does poorly in school. Malkie's parents are disappointed and befuddled because they have always worked to make learning fun and foster intellectual growth in the family. Why is Malkie so different from everyone else in the family?

But is Malkie really so different? What is the core value behind all this study? Malkie's parents claim, "We value scholarship because it helps humans serve Hashem better by being able to appreciate the world around them. Scholarship also elevates people above their animal natures by strengthening the intellect so it can have mastery over the base instincts."

While this may be one aspect of the family's values, they are also influenced by deeper, more problematic values. Constant striving for intellectual achievement may be a defense mechanism against certain insecurities. This "intellect over instinct" attitude may evolve out of a fear of trusting their emotions and intimacy with others. Or perhaps this constant striving for perfection is a defense against deeper feelings of inadequacy.

So Malkie's problem can be interpreted differently. When Malkie says, "I am lazy and proud of it," she is insecure, just like her parents and the rest of the family. Fearing she may not perform up to the highest standards of her family, Malkie chooses to be successful at failing, instead of trying to succeed and then failing despite her best efforts.

Both she and her parents share these core values: (1) we must be perfect and in control at all times, and (2) we cannot trust our own feelings.

Malkie does not trust herself to endure the disappointment and failure she would feel if she tried but did not do well. Malkie's parents do not trust their feelings ("base instincts," as they refer to them). They fear inadequacy, so they make achievement and success the highest priority.

CONCLUDING THOUGHTS

The good news is that children are impressionable and are very likely to become like their parents. The bad news is that children are impressionable and are very likely to become like their parents! Parents cannot afford to be naïve about the emotional climate and currents in their families. Children will do as parents feel. And since feelings are very powerful and honest, we must acknowledge the tremendous impact they have on our children.

41

When the
Rabbi's Children Misbehave

What does the principal do when his son misbehaves in class? What does the rebbetzin do if her daughter is spotted on a motorcycle with a boy — a *shanda* on a Honda?

It's difficult enough to be a parent of a problem child; if the parent happens to be a prominent community leader, the experience can be excruciating and humiliating. For parents in the limelight, personal and public life are stressfully intertwined, interfering with parents' ability to give their children the attention, discipline and love they need.

There surely are many spiritual and emotional benefits to being in a prominent rabbinic family. The potential negative effects mentioned below are not to dissuade parents from choosing this lifestyle, but to help parents inoculate themselves and their children in advance against some of these risk factors.

INFRINGEMENT ON FAMILY TIME

Parents in chinuch, the rabbinate or other forms of community *chessed* tend to be extremely busy, even at times traditionally reserved for family. The most obsessed workaholic father has to stop working on Shabbos and Yom Tov. But if you happen to be the rabbi, you are busy and stressed at a time when other families draw closer to each other.

Having guests for Shabbos and Yom Tov is wonderful, but sometimes children can get lost in the shuffle. Parents may miss important cues about how their children really are doing. Children don't show obvious signs that they are in trouble until problems have gone on for too long.

Parents may learn that a child has questions or doubts about religion after the problem festered for years and has already made a lasting dent in the child's spiritual and emotional development. This is especially true in a family where expectations are high, since the children will naturally feel reluctant to discuss their shortcomings and difficulties.

LIFE IN THE FISHBOWL

Savvy parents of adolescents realize it is a natural part of development for teens to experiment, question authority, and even rebel as part of their efforts to form separate identities. For prominent families, these rebellions become unnecessarily magnified.

Parents may feel scrutinized by others in the community and therefore lose their objectivity when trying to discipline their children. Some parents may feel their children's misbehavior jeopardizes their career, but overreacting will only cause further rebellion.

Adolescents are obsessed with being treated fairly and have keen noses for hypocrisy. If a teenager senses his parents are upset about his misdeeds because of their fear of what others will say — instead of from moral conviction — he will reject his parents' message.

Even when a parent strives to be fair and understanding, the community may not be. Surreptitious murmurs and disapproving frowns on the part of interfering others exacerbate a child's feelings of rebellion, adding fuel to the fire. No one wants to be controlled; the more controlling the environment, the more extreme the rebellion.

BEHIND THE SCENES LOOK

In the elegant dining room of a world-class restaurant, wealthy patrons dine on sumptuous gourmet dishes prepared by an expert chef. Behind the doors of the kitchen, a foul-mouthed chef verbally abuses the underpaid illegal workers who scurry about in unsanitary working conditions.

The most pleasant experience of dining in style would be ruined if the customers actually saw what goes on in the kitchen. Children of clergy are deprived of enjoying the experience of religion precisely because they see "what goes on in the kitchen." To the outsider, the prayer service is inspiring and uplifting. But the child of the rabbi might know that the chazzan's amazing voice is not matched by the quality of his character. He may have overheard his father or mother grumbling about some political or personal matter that implicated the chazzan.

Often children overhear parents' criticism of other rabbis or teachers. Even if the criticisms are legitimate, not just idle evil talk, a child can become disillusioned from such a revelation and lose respect for all rabbis or teachers, and possibly for the whole concept of organized religion.

THE DRAW OF THE RABBINATE

Although persons who dedicate their lives to community and religious service are likely to be highly altruistic, there still may be particular psychological reasons why they have chosen this career. Some teachers choose their profession because they themselves had a difficult time in school when they were children. They enjoy a personal satisfaction giving the next generation a better experience than they had.

A rabbi might be drawn to guiding others about religion because in his youth he had many doubts and challenges. Now he wants to share the wisdom of his experiences to help guide others onto the correct path.

A child of a rabbi or teacher may be at greater risk of running into conflict with his parents over these very same matters because of two possible reasons. First, there may be a genetic or culturally transmitted disposition toward these issues, which the children then develop, since one or both parents has a similar personality.

And second, when the parents see these problems in their children which they fought so hard to overcome themselves, they may be horrified — and overreact. Consider a parent who had a problem with lying as a youth. Many children experiment with lying, but this parent will be horrified when he catches his child lying and will be tempted to deliver an inappropriately harsh punishment, instead of providing gentle guidance.

What can clergy do to protect their children from the detrimental effects of life in public and religious service?

› Create boundaries where family time is sacred. Obviously, the rabbi has to be available to community members in times of crisis. But that does not mean he must live a life without boundaries, where his family life is constantly interrupted for every person's whim. The rabbi needs to work with his lay leaders to help establish reasonable boundaries for his work. For example, callers with questions might be told the rabbi is available for questions for one hour in the evening. If there is an emergency, there should always be someone who screens the call first to determine if it truly is an emergency.

› Give children a chance to express their feelings about their lives in the public eye. Listen to and validate your children's feelings without being apologetic for the lifestyle you have chosen to lead. You should be proud of your good work, but at the same time, show genuine sympathy and concern for some of the difficulties it causes.

› Share your positive feelings about your work. Encourage your children by showing them that they have a share in your good deeds when they are forced to give up something of themselves. Don't share your negative feelings and resentments about your work. When your children are grown and need sincere advice about a profession, you can be honest about the potential drawbacks. Until then, if you are negative about what you are doing, your children will wonder why you inflicted this life upon the family, with the result that you inspire their resentment instead of the admiration you deserve.

How to Parent
a Twenty-Five-Year-Old

Dear Feuermans,

I'm having a really difficult time with my twenty-five-year-old son, who has always been considered a model citizen. After years away in yeshiva, he moved back home. He is now working and learning. I know that being home after all these years of freedom must be hard on him.

He has suddenly become very disrespectful toward me and is resisting more and more helping around the house. Since my husband and I have always stressed derech eretz at home, it was unusual when recently our son became very belligerent, yelling and screaming at me with disrespectful language and tone.

After thinking about the incident overnight (since I didn't want to do anything hotheaded that I'd be sorry about) and since he didn't seem to be remorseful, I decided I had no choice but to punish him by taking away privileges. Well, now he's angry with me, and there is all out war in the house. No matter how much my husband has tried to talk to him, my son will not deign to apologize for his disrespectful outburst. My husband, incidentally, agrees that the disrespectful behavior is unacceptable, but he feels that since our son is too insecure to admit he is wrong, that I should be more flexible and less angry.

What is sad is that of all my children, he was the one I had the best rapport with. We always had a special relationship, so this situation is especially painful (and inexplicable). Do you have any suggestions on how we should proceed without losing the benefit of the current punishment so he learns a lesson that will impel him to exercise more self control, yet still be able to repair the relationship?

Our Response

You appear to be organized and thoughtful about your parenting style and philosophy so we do not see a need to directly advise you on how to settle your argument with your son. We are sure you will come up with a way to make peace without surrendering your authority. However, we do have two observations for you to consider that may help you in future dealings with your son.

First, dependence breeds hostility. The fact that you are very close only intensifies the issue — your child's dependence on you may be exacerbating the situation. After all, he is twenty-five and has spent many years living apart from you. If he is working, and he no longer wishes to assist in the household chores, perhaps he should move out on his own. At the very least he will gain an appreciation for what it takes to keep a home running. If this option is not appropriate for your family, perhaps he should use some of his money to pay for extra cleaning help around the house.

At twenty-five he is essentially an adult. You have a right to expect *derech eretz* (respect), but he is no child anymore! You cannot just scold him and send him to his room. When your husband does something wrong, you don't revoke his privileges. You discuss the issue and work together to resolve the problem.

Your son should be treated with dignity, while you demand and deserve respect — since he is still your son and you are not equals. The Talmud forbids a father from inflicting corporal punishment on his grown son, because it will tempt the son to wrongly hit his father back. A son is never allowed to strike his father, no matter how old he is. But at the same time, the father is expected to exercise his authority appropriately, not to treat his child in a way that will encourage rebellion.

The application of this principle varies, depending on current social expectations to determine what behavior at what age will lead to rebellion. Rambam codifies this principle much more broadly (*Mishneh Torah, Hilchos Mamrim* 6:8), advising parents to counterbalance their authority and power by being careful not to be overbearing upon their children, no matter what their age.

Healthy Parents, Healthy Children

The best way to promote mental health in our children is to keep ourselves mentally healthy. Children learn how to manage anxiety, stress and other character traits by watching how their parents handle themselves. We must strive not only to be moral models for our children but also to show them appropriate ways to manage our inner emotional lives.

43

An Emotionally Happy and Healthy New Year

Rosh Hashanah is a time for new beginnings. Aside from the Jewish new year, we also usher in a new academic year for our children. It is a grand time to recognize new opportunities and potential pitfalls in our personal and family life. The holidays and beginning of school can be a source of anxiety and stress. Instead of turning over a new leaf, it is easy to fall into our old bad habits — or even create some new ones! But one year older, one year wiser, we are capable of making great strides in our personal and character development.

Often we get so involved in the details of seasonal religious obligations that we forget to enjoy the holidays, to use it as a time to grow closer with our families.

> One husband was very concerned that everything on the Shabbos table be ritually correct. During kiddush every Friday night, in accordance with the custom, the challah is covered so it will not be "embarrassed" that the wine precedes it. One Shabbos in this particular home, the woman of the house forgot to cover the challah. The husband was furious over this lapse. Such disrespect to the Shabbos table! In front of all the guests that surrounded the table, the man accused his wife, "You forgot to cover the challah! Now you embarrassed the challah!" This man was more concerned with the challah's embarrassment than his own wife's!

Even though most people usually do not commit such obviously hypocritical offenses, on a more subtle level, at times, we might be found guilty of the same.

PREPARING FOR THE HOLIDAYS

Every year you send Rosh Hashanah cards to hordes of friends and far off relatives. But what about your own young children? Each child would be touched by the beauty and intimacy of a personal Rosh Hashanah greeting. This special gesture would build their confidence and offer them encouragement for the coming year.

You have a big and beautiful *sukkah* erected painstakingly every year, nail by nail. This year, your young and clumsy son wants to "help." Of course, this kind of "help" is more of a drain than assistance. Your choices — build a beautiful *sukkah* and have a mediocre relationship with your son, or have a mediocre *sukkah* and build a beautiful relationship with your son. Don't be such a perfectionist! Let a few nails go in crooked, but spend the precious time with your son, showing him how to build something and discussing the meaning of the holiday. You will come out ahead of the game.

Over in the kitchen, you are one of many women slaving over a hot stove preparing meals for the holiday. The family does not appreciate or thank you quite enough, but the sumptuous meals are a very important part of the holiday.

Yet these hours of preparations must be weighed against the bitterness and resentment that does not quite heal even when the holiday has started and the work is done. What dishes can be eliminated without too much loss? How can family members really help you? Perhaps you should sit down with your family and realistically delegate chores that each member is capable of completing.

GETTING READY FOR SCHOOL

Your child receives an impossibly long and detailed list of school supplies, loaded with costly and esoteric items. "Where am I supposed to find a purple highlighter? This teacher must own stock in a stationery store!"

Why are you bothering with all this stuff? Because you want your child to be well equipped for his first day at school. But the number one item on the supplies list is your patience and understanding. These are more important than any color highlighter.

If you are letting out your resentment against your children, if you are missing critical opportunities to spend time listening to them during the difficult first days of school, that purple highlighter inside your child's desk does not help very much.

Your children need to be emotionally well equipped for school, and that means they need your care, support and listening ear more than every last folder and pencil sharpener. School supplies are important, but do not let them interfere with more important things — hugs, smiles, and an atmosphere of genuine understanding in the home.

Children often complain about situations at school, suggesting various quick fixes. Most of the time it is less important to solve them than to show that you care and understand.

> Your daughter is devastated that she did not get the desk she wanted. "Mommy," she begs as soon as she arrives home, "can you please call the office and make them switch my seat?"

Good suggestion, but not always the best approach. She needs honest sympathy at this point, but don't jump to solve the problem. You might say, "That really is a hard thing. You wish you could have a better seat." Even a first grader can be very resourceful. Your child may adapt without your further involvement.

This time of year is especially designed to grow and develop our relationships with our children, our spouses and our families at large. But we can only use this opportunity if we respond to the demands and stresses of the new year in an emotionally balanced manner. In this way, we model for our children how to handle the challenges of life and respond to them in the most helpful and healthy ways.

44

In the Wake of a Catastrophe

Author's Note: The following selection is based on a column written immediately following the catastrophic events of September 11, 2001. There are references pertaining to the weeks following the World Trade Center disaster, but with the ongoing traumatic events in Israel, and G-d forbid, the possibility of continued terrorist strikes to Jews and all people across the world, the observations are relevant for every day.

SORT YOUR OWN FEELINGS OUT FIRST

Words fail us at a time like this. But parenting is a 24/7 job. We have a responsibility to guide our children past the horrific events of the day. First and foremost, in order to help our children, we have to sort out our own feelings first.

Our sages teach us, "A prisoner cannot free himself from jail" (*Berachos* 5b). He needs someone from the outside to help him escape. Before we hold out a hand to our children, we need to extricate ourselves from the disorienting quagmire of the times.

The Yom Kippur service describes various sacrifices of atonement that the High Priest brings on the holy day. "And he will obtain forgiveness for himself, his house, and all of Israel" (*Vayikra* 16:17). The Talmud points out (*Yoma* 44a) that the High Priest must first obtain forgiveness for himself and his family, then for the entire priestly family, and only then for all of Israel. As with all spiritual matters, the High Priest cannot help pardon others until he himself has been pardoned.

Of course, the reality of our current situation will dawn on us over weeks and months. This is not something we can recover from instantaneously. We will alternate from feeling numb to irritable to tearful without any logical order. Even when we feel this is all behind us, we may suddenly be overcome with a feeling of sadness, vague irritability or a touch of depression.

Nevertheless, when we talk — or better yet, when we listen — to our children, we should project an image of relative calm. Catastrophe represents a loss of control, and as adults, we must help our children re-establish a certain sense of security and stability.

THE TRUTH, IN MEASURED DOSES

We should not attempt to pacify our children with statements such as, "This will not happen again." First, we don't know that for a fact, and most children will be smart enough to realize that. They will only feel more insecure when they find adults lying to them. Second, if a child is gullible enough to believe you and something does go wrong, you have destroyed your credibility and further damaged their sense of trust.

The parent image of stability is based on honesty. If a child is afraid to go to school or afraid to let you go off to work in the city, you must honestly acknowledge the situation. "I know you are afraid that something bad will happen, but your teachers/parents/authorities have made the decision that it is safe enough. It is the right choice to go to work/school."

First, you validate the child's feelings. No attempt was made to deny that there is something to be afraid of. Quite the contrary! But we understand the child's fear.

The second part of the statement provides containment for the child's feelings. "You are afraid, but the adults feel it is safe enough or feel that it is the right thing to do."

Your role as a parent is to listen to your child's feelings, acknowledge them, but then provide a structure to contain them. To provide further structure, you might add, "We are all a little afraid. That is why we are all trying to do the right thing by praying, performing *mitzvos* and doing acts of kindness. Hashem wants us to live our lives and we need to go to work to help other people."

Some children will be thirsty for facts; others won't want to hear anything. Take your cues from your child and try to do less talking and more listening. Ask them what they have learned about what happened. Try to answer questions in a few simple words, and then see if they digested what you said. Let your child be the guide. If he or she is still curious to know more, further questions will follow. Be careful of overwhelming your child with more information or images than he or she can tolerate.

The dinner table might be a good setting to discuss the world situation. Bedtime is also a naturally conducive time for a discussion, when children are more relaxed and ready for nurture. Despite the inconvenient hour, try to make yourself available, emotionally and otherwise.

Encourage them to adopt the traits that have been identified in emotionally resilient people. Model these traits to your children — a religious value system, belief in G-d, network of family and friends, and flexibility in changing circumstances.

Symbolic Modes of Expression

Children rarely are so cooperative as to share their feelings directly. Many times they will express their feelings indirectly through play. We saw a toddler playing with toy airplanes and helicopters; a grade-schooler building Lego towers, then toppling them.

Another therapist worked with a nine-year-old child who was fidgeting with a toy frog. Feeling frustrated that the child was not saying much, the therapist asked, "What does Mr. Frog have to say about all this?"

The child responded, "Mr. Frog is very happy that he can jump. He is the only one who was able to jump out of the World Trade Center without getting killed."

Children often work through their feelings by expressing them through play. It is unnecessary to explicitly interpret the meaning of the play; it may even be harmful. Interpretation may puncture the child's defense mechanism, forcing him to deal with what he cannot.

Instead, parents can join the child in the play, and address the feelings metaphorically through the play. This way dangerous feelings are addressed from a safe distance. You may say, "I see you are building and knocking down the tower. What do you like about doing that?"

Or keep up the frog charade, mentioning details and specifics only as the child dictates. "I am happy Mr. Frog survived, but I am also sad about the others who did not."

Your child's choices of bedtime stories may also reflect his thoughts and feelings about current events. One child whose grandfather had passed away chose a story about a girl who builds a snowman in the winter and then watches the snowman melt as spring comes along. This is an obvious reference to death and loss. Even more telling, the title of the story was *Sadie and the Snowman*. Sadie sounds very much like Zaidy.

Children can also draw pictures or make other crafts that will allow them to work through their feelings.

Optimism versus Defeat

What is the difference between Tisha B'Av and Yom Kippur? Externally, they seem so similar — fasting for twenty-four hours or more, no leather shoes. But many people find Tisha B'Av so much harder to bear.

Tisha B'Av is about defeat. Yom Kippur is about optimism. On Tisha B'Av we mourn a loss. The Temple was destroyed because of our own sins; we blew it. But Yom Kippur — this is a once-a-year opportunity to influence our fate, to change the course of our own future.

We might want to explain to our children that perhaps this tragedy happened as a result of our collective or individual sins. But we should deliver the message as if it's Yom Kippur, not Tisha B'Av. Not that we blew it and it's all over, but that we can take our fate in our own hands and act to change our future with repentance, prayer and charity.

As need dictates, give everyone the opportunity to talk, or the privilege to remain silent. We are victims of brute violence. Great care should be taken to respect other people's feelings, not to force anyone into social or emotional situations that he cannot tolerate. Catastrophe and disaster shake our sense of control. We must try to bring back a sense of routine and stability in our own and our children's lives.

Everyone reacts differently. The process of adjustment will take some people weeks, months or even years, depending upon their personality and developmental level, previous psychological traumas and predisposition. Recovery is not a straight upward curve. There are ups and downs, good days and bad days.

Even several months later, perhaps you will look out the window and see an airplane passing by a building. This everyday sight can trigger a whole series of feelings ranging from anger and sadness to irritability and malaise. Let us all be patient and loving, to each other and ourselves.

45

When Parents Disagree About Discipline

You feel your spouse is too lenient and soft. But your spouse thinks you are cruel and harsh.

Parents often disagree about discipline.

In the worst case-scenario, they disagree right in front of the children, perhaps even insulting each other or making threats. No child can learn proper discipline in such an environment. If this sounds too much like your situation, it is time to make some changes so your children will not be deprived of a healthy and balanced upbringing.

IT'S NOT MY FAULT!

"Don't look at me. I'm the normal one. It's my spouse who has it all wrong! Maybe he should read this chapter!" Nice try, but finding fault is a very ineffective way of solving a problem.

Even if your parenting methods are one-hundred-percent correct and your spouse's one-hundred-percent incorrect, your children will not be able to survive in this inconsistent and tension filled atmosphere. Children need parents who are generally in agreement with each other so they can struggle with and internalize their values.

In the case of the *ben sorer umoreh*, the rebellious son, our sages rule that he is only liable for punishment when both parents, in complete agreement, bring him before the elders of the court for judgment. Interestingly enough, the *halacha* even requires that the parents be similar in appearance. (*Sanhedrin* 71a) Rav Samson Raphael Hirsch sees this as a lesson for all parents. The Torah only holds the child fully responsible for his actions when he experiences a high degree of consistency in his upbringing.

Healthy and well-behaved children are raised in a wide variety of homes and parenting styles, from rigid to informal. The key to successful parenting is not strict or lenient rules, but simply that rules must exist, and they are clear, consistent, and enforced in a humane but firm manner.

Every child will test the rules and the limits as part of the process of developing his own identity. He internalizes the rules and standards when he is appropriately disciplined for transgressions.

A child who does poorly on a test can be disciplined in many different ways. He may be denied a privilege, or encouraged to study the correct answers to prove that he does know the material. The child may simply be warned that he should take matters to heart and do better the next time.

What the resulting action is really doesn't matter as long as there is a clear expectation and a consequence. Even a warning is a consequence, as long as it is followed through with a punishment the next time he performs poorly on a test.

Most children will respond to any of these methods. But when mother and father present radically different standards and expectations, when one parent punishes the child while the other protects and defends, the child will become anxious and insecure.

So whether you are the strict one or the lenient one, realize that the greatest damage is caused by parental inconsistency and quarreling. Even a child who has unreasonably strict and demanding parents may accept their approach because he sees and feels that it is consistent. He may resent it and try to rebel, but he will probably be much less confused and less of a behavior problem than a child of parents who argue with each other and undermine one another.

CAN PARENTS EVER DISAGREE?

People are different, even if they are married to each other. They will not always have the same ideas and attitudes. Shouldn't children learn about healthy forms of disagreement?

This may be true in theory, but you should not expose children to something that they are incapable of tolerating. You would not feed an infant the same food you would give your school-age children, nor would you allow your small child to read a book intended for adults.

Young children are still developing their own internal sense of discipline. It is too confusing for them to be caught in the middle of two perspectives. Parents must present a unified front. As the child gets older, you may experiment with gradually showing multiple perspectives or even allowing a child limited choice on certain moral issues.

The proof is in the child's emotional and moral development. If his behavior shows that he can handle this exposure, then perhaps it is appropriate. But if the child becomes irritable, anxious, confused or rebellious, perhaps he needs more consistent parenting. It is best to err on the side of caution.

FIRM, NOT ANGRY; MERCIFUL, NOT LENIENT

Good discipline has nothing to do with being nice or cruel. Children should not be disciplined out of anger, nor should they be spared punishment out of leniency. The single most important factor is the well being of the child.

If you feel your child has already learned his lesson, perhaps mercy is in order. Perhaps it will teach him to be forgiving and accepting. But if your child is not taking matters to heart, he needs a firm punishment and consequence.

Punishment is not a personal power struggle between parent and child, and leniency should not be due to emotional weakness. You have to have the child's best interests in mind. Your child senses this. He will either accept and be inspired, or rebel and lose respect for you.

"But what if I really am angry at my child? How can I be expected to act as if I'm not?" Of course you should be angry. And you should show it. Children need to learn about relationships, about how their behavior impacts others.

But punishment is not the means to express your anger. This is a subtle but critical distinction. Express your anger in words first, without entering into an abusive and screaming rage. That's just an adult temper tantrum. After the controlled show of anger, punishment should be briefly explained and administered calmly and seriously. Rambam speaks of how a parent should externally display anger in order to discipline, while remaining calm internally (*Mishneh Torah, Deos*, 2:7)

Our children should learn to express their feelings in a respectful and civilized manner, and not act them out physically. If you punish out of anger, how is that different from Dovid taking revenge and beating up Shlomo for popping his toy balloon?

Finding the Right Balance

A parent who was brought up in a very strict home might overcompensate by not making any rules for his children. He may see himself as avoiding the mistakes of his parents and being quite heroic and selfless; but in fact, he is hurting his children and depriving them just as much as he had been deprived, albeit in a different way.

There are parents who are too strict because they are afraid their children might end up like them. Deep down, they mistrust their own morality and try to overcompensate by being cruel and punishing.

Such parents might be very moral and respectable in many ways, but they have secret weaknesses, inconsistencies or lapses — ranging from relatively harmless hypocrisy to downright criminal behavior. For example, a person might be rigid and intolerant of falsehood within his family but practice shady and unethical business dealings.

It is hard to view yourself objectively, but try to analyze if your discipline style incorporates the following elements. If not, you need to take a good look at the personal and emotional factors that may be interfering.

- Consistent, humane and fair
- Agreed upon by both parents
- Objective, not out of cruelty or the need to be perceived as nice
- For the sake of the child's growth and development

46

Telling Lies

Lying is something that almost everybody does but few admit doing. The fabric of society is dependent on truth — and ironically, on carefully placed lies, as well. For humans to survive and work together, we need to trust each other. But absolute truth can sometimes be hurtful, interfering with normal social functioning.

LYING IN THE JEWISH TRADITION

Lying is immoral. The Torah commands, "Distance yourself from falsehood" (*Shemos* 23:7) But lying for the sake of peace is permitted. When G-d informed Sarah that she would give birth to a son, she exclaimed, "But my husband is old!" When G-d repeated her words to her husband Avraham, He quoted, "I [Sarah] am old." (*Yevamos* 65b)

A scholar is permitted to lie out of modesty, to downplay his intellectual achievements. This may represent a separate category, or is possibly under the same rubric of maintaining the peace. (See *Bava Metzia* 23b, Tosafos and Ritvah.)

Shammai and Hillel dispute whether it is permitted to falsely praise a homely bride as beautiful. Hillel maintains that it is permitted, while Shammai requires she be praised only for the qualities she actually possesses.

The commentaries discuss the rationale for Hillel's ruling. Tosafos Rid says Hillel allowed this falsehood/exaggeration to create pleasant feelings for the groom and bride. But the Maharsha claims that every bride is beautiful in some way, so technically it is not a falsehood. Perisha, Taz and Shach (*Even Haezer* 65:1) agreed with this latter view, as they forbid outright falsehood about a bride's qualities. (*Kesubos* 16b-17a)

Shulchan Aruch (*Yoreh Deah* 344:1) permits mild exaggeration of the good deeds of a deceased person at a eulogy, as long as it is not an excessive exaggeration. We can plausibly assume that the deceased did more good deeds than we are aware of, even if they cannot be confirmed. (See Taz ibid.)

A striking example of permissible lying is found in a ritualized form of marketplace negotiation.

> A merchant bargains with a potential customer, "I swear I will not sell this item for less than four dinar!"
> But an equally stubborn customer swears, "I refuse to buy it for more than two dinar!"

According to the Mishna, if the object is sold at the midpoint, for three *dinar*, neither the customer nor the merchant has violated his oath. Both the buyer and seller expect a certain degree of inflation or deflation. Within limits, it's not considered lying.

The context is as important as the actual words you say. As long as your intention is clear, you may use words that are not necessarily one hundred percent truthful. But although the Talmud theoretically permits this form of lying, it is not encouraged from an ethical standpoint. The opposite is also true. If the words you choose are technically or literally true, if your intent is to deceive, then it also may be considered a lie.

THE ADULT MODEL

Children model their behavior after their parents. If parents want their children to be honest, it is important for them to set an example. Life often presents us with opportunities to model integrity for our children. Sometimes, even a five-minute interaction can leave an impression for life.

> Squeezing through a tight spot on a one-way street, you accidentally bump into a parked car. With the kids in the car, you stop to assess the damage. There's a small dent near the gas tank. You can hop back in to your car and drive off, comforting yourself with countless rationalizations. Or you can leave a note for the owner of the parked car.

Every child is faced with the awesome task of taking responsibility for his actions. Your son's ball sails through the neighbor's window, shattering the glass. Will he run away or own up? If your daughter sees a friend being wrongfully accused for something she actually did herself, will she keep quiet or admit the truth?

As children mature in their sophistication and knowledge of the world, it is equally important to teach them about when it is appropriate to be dishonest. If they see you engage in certain forms of justified lying, such as to maintain peace, you need to explain you intentions or your children might misinterpret your actions.

But you should never lie to your children. There are many issues that parents should not share with their children. If your child asks about one of these taboo subjects, you shouldn't lie, obfuscate or mislead. Simply say, "This is not something I can tell you."

For example, your child notices you reading a lab report that indicates something personal, or another child's progress report. "What's that about?" he asks. Don't tell him, "It's nothing important," because it is important. Tell him, "It's something personal."

The Talmud grapples with this pedagogical issue in regard to training a minor in the mitzvah of *lulav*. In order to fulfill the Torah commandment of shaking the *lulav* on the first day of Sukkos, a person must own the *lulav*; it may not be borrowed.

According to *halacha*, minors of a certain age can acquire objects but are intellectually incapable of relinquishing ownership. The act of taking requires less developmental sophistication than the act of giving. From a practical and mercantile perspective, children need to buy things, but not necessarily to sell them.

So how can you train your child in the proper observance of the *mitzvah* of *lulav*? If you give the *lulav* to your child as a gift, he can fulfill the *mitzvah*, but then no one else will be able to use the *lulav* afterwards since a child cannot relinquish ownership of it.

You could lie, tell your child you are giving him the *lulav*, but not actually intend to give it to him. This would seem reasonable, but the Talmud rejects this solution because, "It teaches them to speak falsehood" (*Yirmiyahu* 9:4). (See *Sukkah* 46b, Maharitz Chayes.)

When your toddler comes home from pre-school with a pretend *shofar* or *lulav*, tell him, "This is a pretend *lulav*, so you can practice doing the *mitzvah*, just like Daddy." Avoid perpetuating the illusion that his *lulav* is real.

THE LIE DETECTOR

Among other fascinating publications and research on the nature of deception and emotion, Paul Ekman, Professor of Psychology in the Department of Psychiatry at the University of California Medical School in San Francisco, conducted a controlled study using experts from various professions — law enforcement officers, mental health practitioners, nurses. These professionals were shown videos of people speaking. The professionals were asked to discern if the featured person was lying or telling the truth. The overwhelming majority of professionals were right only 50% of the time — no better than random guessing.

Many people think they can detect a lie because they can see the accused person's anxiety, and they confuse this anxiety with the fear of being caught. But many people become anxious under scrutiny even when they are telling the truth. And certain skillful liars betray no anxiety whatsoever, confident in their ability to fool people.

Ekman discovered a very small minority of people who were able to consistently detect lies over 90% of the time. Much of his research focused on categorizing exactly what these hyper-intuitive people perceived. Ekman asserted that when people lie they show micro-expressions, involuntary emotional expressions that may last for only a split second. Ekman has studied and catalogued these expressions in a database, which he calls the Facial Action Coding System.

But most people will not take the time to master this system, so, practically speaking, how can we detect a lie? For one, inconsistency is a good indicator. When someone confuses or changes even minor details of a firsthand account, there's reason for suspicion.

If a truthful person forgets a detail of something that happened to him, he will either say, "I don't remember," or he will unconsciously create a new memory that he accepts as his true account. He will not consciously falsify information. But a liar will need to fabricate many details, and then recall them each time he tells the story. His inconsistency may show through if the story is carefully examined.

The judges of the Jewish courts employed this method of ferreting out lies. There was a judicial policy of *derisha vechakira*, wherein each judge cross-examined the witnesses about even the non-essential details. (*Sanhedrin* 40a)

When confronting a child who you believe has lied, first be certain that you are correct. Our sages considered accusing an innocent person a serious sin. (*Shabbos* 97a) Aside from the hurt, Rav Yisroel Salanter said there is an additional spiritual danger of accusing an innocent person, which is especially pertinent to parents.

When you accuse a young man of stealing merchandise from your store, you demonstrate that you believe he is capable of stealing. If you unfairly accuse your child of lying, not only have you hurt his feelings, you also open the door for future falsehood. Until now, lying was out of the question. But you just told him you believe he could do it. Now it is within the realm of possibility.

In cases when you know your child is actually lying, it is important not to overreact. Agitation shows panic and a lack of control, encouraging further lying. Based on the child's age and ability, you need to show your child the harmful effects lying will have on your relationship. A family has to be built on trust.

If you catch your child lying about homework, you need to ask, "Do I need your teachers to fax me a copy of your homework every night? Is this the way we should operate?" Parents need to take the long view, to stay calm as they teach their child the consequences of lying and the advantages of maintaining trust.

For toddlers, lying has a very different meaning. Their understanding of the world is so limited that when they lie, they actually believe what they are saying.

From a toddler's perspective, words are almost as real as actions. Whatever they hear their parents say magically comes true. Mommy says it's going to rain tomorrow, and it does! The toddler doesn't realize her mother heard the weather report. "If you keep eating that cake your stomach will hurt," warns Daddy. And amazingly, it happens!

So the toddler thinks that when he asserts himself verbally, he can make it true by saying it emphatically enough — as the adults appear to be doing. When toddlers lie, simply point out, "That is not true," and leave it at that. Eventually, the child will grow to understand what truth and falsehood really mean.

New Baby Blues

"Why am I not ecstatic with my new baby? Why am I feeling sad, crying all the time and feeling horrible about myself? Why don't I want to spend time with my baby?"

Feelings of hopelessness and a sense of being overwhelmed that last for more than a few days indicate that this mother — whether it's you, your family member or your friend — may be experiencing postpartum depression.

Common symptoms of postpartum depression include not wanting to spend time with the baby, being scared to care for the baby, and persistent thoughts and wishes that the baby "would not be here with me right now." Mothers experiencing postpartum depression sometimes have horrific wishes to harm the baby — and then feelings of guilt compound the depression.

UNCOVERING THE PROBLEM

First and foremost, the mother needs to recognize that her problem is common for many women after childbirth, and that it is treatable.

Postpartum depression has existed for centuries, but it was not always recognized or understood. As with all human difficulties that involve feelings or mood, it has been, and remains to some degree, attached to stigma and a sense of shame. The great value our Jewish culture places on maternal competence adds to the difficulties.

As mood disorders become better known, this embarrassment will dissipate and women can more freely discuss their feelings with their doctors, spouses and others who can be helpful during this trying period. We hope this segment helps women who experience these symptoms feel less ashamed and free to pursue treatment.

A woman suffering from postpartum blues should not be left alone with the baby for any significant length of time. Often, respite for the new mother is sufficient intervention to chase away postpartum depression. Symptoms may completely subside shortly after receiving this type of support.

Some mothers do not have the support of their husband and family. Even worse, the father makes light of the new mother's symptoms, running off to work each morning without providing another means of support. These mothers tend to feel overwhelmed and helpless for longer periods of time.

Family members might make non-supportive statements, faulting the mother for feeling unable to care for the newborn or her other children. "Snap out of it! Your job is to care for this baby properly and make this a happy home." Or a new mother may impose these feelings upon herself. And then she feels guilty, on top of the depression.

The family needs to marshal support. A husband, mother-in-law, or mother should be available to relieve the new mother of some of the baby care. Someone to watch or hold the baby while the mother takes a shower can be a great relief. Someone around to take over even minimal tasks can relieve the horrible feelings that overwhelmed the new mother before help arrived.

THE PROGNOSIS

The most common version of postpartum depression is short-lived. Generally referred to as postpartum blues, it ranges in duration from a few days to several weeks. It manifests as mild nervousness and anxiety. It requires no medication, only family support and understanding.

Mothers who do not experience significant relief after receiving family support have more severe postpartum depression. This condition is often treated with a very low dosage of medication, such as Flouexetine (trade name Sarafem), a selective serotonin reuptake inhibitor. Flouexetine is also prescribed for women suffering from premenstrual dysphoric disorder, severe mood changes before menstruation.

To assure those who are reluctant to take psychotropic medication, these medications have an excellent record of relieving symptoms within two to four weeks and are usually used for no longer than six weeks to a few months. Women who take this medication report feeling less nervous, more calm and in a happier mood.

Medication can be helpful in many instances, particularly in stabilizing mood states. But medication is not a substitute for communication. Couples and parents need to work on relationship-building skills, in conjunction with medication if necessary.

A RELATED CONDITION

Postpartum psychosis is a related condition, much more serious than postpartum depression — and more rare. Psychosis may or may not be accompanied by depression, but it always involves losing touch with reality, hallucinations, delusional thinking or paranoia. It requires immediate psychiatric help. Postpartum psychosis severely impairs the mother's judgment, endangering the mother and child.

RESOURCES

- ‣ Postpartum Support, International
- ‣ Depression After Delivery, National
- ‣ Postpartum Depression, National: 800.994.WOMAN
- ‣ Postpartum Stress Center: 610.525.7527
- ‣ Online support group http://www.ppdsupportpage.com/

Author's Note: The medical information in this chapter was prepared collaboratively with our good friend and colleague Gary Greenstein, M.D., FACOG, an gynecologist in private practice in the New York metro area.

48

One-Minute Therapy
for Busy Parents

In our rapidly changing information-based society, people are always looking for quick solutions to their problems. Is it possible to provide an intervention that takes only a few sentences to read, which a person can successfully apply to a given psychological problem?

This idea is not as new as it seems. The great sages Shammai and Hillel were confronted with a similar dilemma, when a potential convert requested that they teach him the entire Torah while standing on one foot. Shammai turned the man away, so ridiculous and unreasonable was his request. But Hillel attempted to impart the essence of the Torah in one basic kernel of wisdom. (*Shabbos* 31a) Like a seed, one short but powerful lesson can flower and bear fruit.

Presented below are several psychological problems, followed by a recommended course of action and an explanatory discussion and commentary — our attempts at planting a seed. If you would like to apply these lessons to your everyday life, refrain from studying the explanation until two weeks after you apply the intervention. The less you know about how it works, the less chance there is that past resistances and patterns will interfere, allowing maximum benefit from your behaviors and interactions.

PROBLEM #1: I AM DEPRESSED AND HOPELESS ABOUT LIFE

Make three separate lists — one of things you feel you must do, one of all the things you think you should do, and one of all the things you would like to do. Every day, review each list and find the item that would give you the most pleasure from each list. Based on these criteria, do only one item from each list.

Although depression can be a serious and even life-threatening illness, and some people do require medication, research supports the effectiveness of certain cognitive behavioral techniques in treating depression.

What causes depression? Some might argue that depression has no psychological cause but rather is due to a random chemical imbalance. But we believe depression is rooted in psychological mechanisms, barring, of course, physical causes such as thyroid or hormonal disorders that can mimic depression. If you feel depressed, you should first get a complete medical check up to rule out physical causes.

Unquestionably, antidepressant medications have helped large numbers of people, giving credence to the idea that increasing the availability of key chemicals such as serotonin in the brain alleviates depression. This tells us that serotonin is an important factor in depression — but what causes decreased levels of serotonin to begin with? All our thoughts must take place on a chemical level in our brains; that's how our brains function. Which comes first, the depression or the serotonin problem? Perhaps your mental attitude influences serotonin levels in the brain, not vice versa!

The above intervention changes mental attitude, attacking depression at its root. How? Depression often results from Learned Helplessness:

> *A dog was placed in a box with a door. With the door unlocked, an electric shock was applied to the dog. The dog quickly learned that it could jump out the door to avoid the shock. Subsequently, the door was locked. The shock was applied and again, the dog tried the door. But he couldn't get out because it was locked. After several shocks and several attempts to open the door, the dog gave up and no longer bothered to even paw at the door when the shock was applied.*
>
> *After that, even when the door was unlocked again and the dog was shown the exit, it just stayed put while continuing to experience the shock. The dog had learned that it could not escape and that it was useless to bother.*

After many failed attempts in life you may "learn" to give up hope, just like our canine subject. None of your efforts are going to pay off, so why bother? The multitude of tasks and obligations that comprise daily life is overwhelming.

Choosing one item from each list breaks the cycle. It re-introduces the satisfaction of doing something well. At times we must all do things that we really would rather not do. But someone who is depressed has an overdose of tasks he abhors. First he must discover tasks that will bring pleasure and satisfaction.

Initial progress may be slow, and you may choose relatively unimportant items from your lists. This is okay as long as the chosen items truly bring a degree of pleasure. The main point is to re-arouse your desire to do anything. Over time, the repertoire of pleasure-giving activities automatically broadens, leading to eventual recovery.

PROBLEM #2: I HATE MY SPOUSE

Ask your spouse what it is that you are doing or not doing that annoys him or her. Put aside your own resentments and work hard to change yourself. After one week ask your spouse if he or she is satisfied. Keep doing this every week with a full heart. Wait until your spouse gets the idea and starts asking you the same questions. Never, ever imply or state that you expect reciprocal behavior, or act resentful about what you are doing — just wait until your spouse comes around to asking what your needs are.

We all would like to think we are right and our spouses are wrong, we are virtuous and our other half is being unfair. But this is not the right approach to solving problems. Most relationship problems are part of a self-reinforcing cycle, and each partner's dysfunctional behavior induces the other's dysfunctional behavior.

You may be irresponsible with money and frustrate your spouse, who is trying to save and balance the household budget. Why do you like to spend money? Perhaps because it makes you feel nurtured and cared for. But the more money you spend, the more resentful and controlling your spouse becomes. The more resentful and controlling your spouse is, the greater your need to spend.

Another example of this reciprocity can be found with nagging. Your spouse is passive aggressive. She avoids authority, perhaps because she has deep resentments from past relationships but is unable to express them. Every time you ask her to do something, she avoids it or procrastinates. It is so infuriating — so you constantly nag her. But the more you nag, the more passive aggressive she becomes.

In order to make progress in a stagnate relationship, you must break out of this self-reinforcing cycle. If you can change your behavior and do something different, you can break the cycle, putting into motion a series of events that will lead your spouse to behave differently. It may not work for a while, but be patient. After all, if this problem has been going on for some time and you have tried other solutions unsuccessfully, what do you have to lose?

PROBLEM #3: MY CHILD MISBEHAVES IN SCHOOL

> *A behavior modification system arranged with the teacher requires a substantial investment of time and effort. Instead, for one half-hour every day for one week, spend special individual attention with your child. You resent his misbehavior. You don't believe he deserves any reward. But for the purpose of this exercise, let go of those feelings for a week. Absolutely do not discuss the problem behavior until a week later. At that time, tell your child you want the behavior to improve, and if it does you will continue to make the special time available as a reward.*

Many impulsive children have difficulty controlling themselves even if they are promised a reward or threatened with punishment. Intellectually or emotionally, they are not mature enough to accept the reward or the punishment as a reality. It is too abstract. So if you give them a real taste of what the reward is like and what they have to lose, it will serve as a greater incentive.

Also, children crave attention. "The squeaky wheel gets the oil." Children who "squeak" misbehave in order to get the attention. A child who has difficulty controlling himself, but a high tolerance for anger or pain, may unconsciously decide that it is easier to misbehave and get angry attention than to work hard at behaving. By giving him a sample of quality attention, it helps the child make a different choice in the future.

A family is the main tool for learning socialization skills. We learn how to be people from our family. If you spend a half hour of specialized time every day with your problem child, he will learn a great deal about how to behave, just from the natural give and take of parent-child interactions.

Playing board games successfully requires listening to directions, planning ahead, impulse control and cooperation. These are the same skills a child needs to behave well in school. You can play with a child and patiently teach him proper behavior at the same time.

49

Tolerating Children with Differences

Dear Feuermans,

I traveled a long road to get to where I am today. I have suffered from extremely low self-esteem for many years, doubting my self-worth and having difficulty asserting myself. I have had the opportunity to reflect upon how I was treated as a child and the different way I want to treat my own children. If you think it will be helpful, please share some of my thoughts with your readers.

Throughout my childhood/teen years, I had a very difficult time in yeshiva, going from one yeshiva to another, never feeling comfortable in any place. I did not think well of myself. I am now in my mid-thirties and a few years ago was diagnosed with a learning disability.

Many of the difficulties I had in yeshiva were compounded by my parents' inability to deal with my being different, whether it was due to a learning disability or my personality. My parents had extreme and strict views on how to raise children, and if we did not completely conform we would suffer the harshest of punishments for relatively small infractions.

My parents experienced great frustration if their children did not follow exactly in their way. To this day,

they still firmly believe they were completely justified in
everything they have done. In fact, they view themselves
as very intelligent parents who had a responsibility to
knock sense into their son so he would grow up to be a
ben Torah — according to their mold.

Yes, I did cause a lot of trouble, but in my view this is
where parenting comes in. It is easy to be a parent to a
child who does not cause trouble, but children, like any-
thing in life, do not always come to us as we would like!

A few years ago, a former rebbe of mine told me he
once suggested to my father that I be evaluated for
learning disabilities. But my father would not hear of it.
How much pain, suffering and tears could have been
avoided had my parents not been too concerned with
their own pride! It is for this reason that I write, to alert
parents who have attitudes similar to that of my par-
ents, that they should try to be more tolerant of their
child's differences.

OUR RESPONSE

A common thread in your story appears to be the importance of
parents recognizing and preserving a child's individuality. This
seems to have been an area of injury for you in the past.

When parents have difficulty accepting a child's unique set of
needs and experiences, the child will lack self-esteem. How can a
child learn to value himself if his parents do not?

Why are some parents — and spouses — so intolerant of their
loved one's differences? The psychological origins of this problem
stretch back to our earliest years of development.

As infants, even before we are aware of anything else, we become aware of ourselves. At that early point, we are our entire
universe. When we are hungry, milk miraculously appears. When
we are wet, we are miraculously dried and changed. Through the
inevitable hardships of experience, however, we begin to get the
idea that others exist.

An infant wants to be held. But despite his protests, he is put
back down in the crib to sleep. He eventually develops the notion
that there are other forces at work in the world other than his own
will. This is the beginning of a maturation process known as sepa-

ration and individuation, which continues through childhood and for some, extends to adulthood.

Due to environmental factors as well as individual predisposition, some people are less successful than others in achieving separation and individuation. These people have difficulty tolerating other people's viewpoints, become easily frustrated and offended when others do not comply with their wishes, and lack the ability to empathize with others.

These personality characteristics quite naturally result from not truly believing that anyone else really exists. Intellectually, they know that other people exist, but on a deep emotional level they cannot fully accept the existence of others. Everyone else is just a prop or actor in the fantasy word they call life.

An extreme sociopath can commit cruel acts without feeling any remorse — because everything in the world is there for him to do as he pleases. Those only mildly impaired in their separation and individuation may end up narcissistic, intolerant and selfish.

Not coincidentally, the parents who will have the most difficulty understanding and tolerating their children's differences are those who have not fully developed their capacity for separation and individuation. Their children are an extension of themselves. But even a motivated adult can individuate later on in life via honest self-assessment and psychotherapy.

50

Non-Typical Solutions to Typical Marriage Problems

Nearly all marital conflicts fit into one of five categories: money, in-laws, religion, children, and intimacy. Written words cannot replace comprehensive psychotherapy, but the following is a sample scenario from each arena. The suggested exercises will help bridge the gap in perspectives, allowing each spouse to understand the other's viewpoint.

SCENARIO #1: MONEY PROBLEMS

> **Spouse A**: You are highly budget conscious. Your spouse just came home with some bargains bought on sale — again. You are enraged because you really can't afford these items now, even if they're cheap. How could s/he be so careless?

> **Spouse B**: You know your family is on a limited budget, but you can't live life always worrying about every penny. You saw something you liked in the store on sale that seemed like a good deal, so you bought it. Big deal. Yet, your spouse is so mad. You can't believe how controlling s/he can be!

Spouse A, when your spouse spends more than is prudent, is this a real danger to the family's finances or are you just panicking? There are some people who are truly reckless in creating unmanageable debt. But others like to spend money instead of save it, perhaps make impulse purchases, while still exercising a degree of control.

If your spouse fits the second category, are you willing to love your spouse even if s/he is careless with money? It may bother you and offend your sensibilities when you aren't saving money and accruing modest debt. But being constantly frustrated with your spouse has hidden economic costs as well.

Unhappy marriages tend to cost more money because there is a lack of cooperation which leads to more accidents, mishaps, academic problems with the children, impaired work performance and health problems. Over time, this adds up to real dollars.

If you can manage to let go of your resentment and allow your spouse the idiosyncrasy of spending more than feels comfortable to you, in the end you might come out ahead.

If your spouse belongs to the first category of over-spenders, putting the family in major financial risk, then this exercise will not be helpful. But keep in mind that people tend to see their spouses as unreasonable far more often than is actually the case. Unless your spouse is really suffering from a manic episode or bent on self-destruction, his or her spending should still be manageable, albeit not as conservative as you prefer.

Spouse B, many relationships problems rely on complementarity, which means that each person's hang-ups serve the needs of the relationship. Your spouse might complain when you spend money, but s/he often benefits from the things you buy. S/he may be too cheap to spend the money, but when you spend s/he can benefit from it and blame you.

"There is nothing more frightening than getting what you want." Put your spouse to the test and try to out-frugal him or her! Do not do it out of spite — hostility disables communication and growth. Rather, engage in this behavior as an experiment with a genuine open mind to see what occurs.

Many times, when people change roles, it forces the other party to confront his or her own behavior in ways that might otherwise never happen. If you switch roles and say, "Oh, we can't afford this dinner/vacation/clothing," your spouse may be relieved at first. But over time s/he might get increasingly frustrated and get in touch with his or her own need to spend money — since you are no longer spending it for him/her.

Spouse A: You and your spouse planned a special evening together — weeks in advance. You arranged babysitting and made reservations in a fancy restaurant. A few days before the big evening, your mother-in-law called to check if you and your spouse are going to some second cousin's bar mitzvah. Unfortunately, this event is slated for the same night as your special plans. Your spouse caves in to Mom's demands and cancels your special evening. You are fuming because s/he seems to always put Mom's needs over yours.

Spouse B: Can you ever get a break? Everyone is always hassling you and you never get time for yourself. Your spouse is angry because you do not spend enough time with him/her. Your mother is angry with you because she says you don't spend enough time with her. You wish they would all just leave you alone.

Spouse A, loyalty conflicts are extremely painful. You may be right. Maybe your spouse really is being spineless and avoiding, when s/he should set boundaries with his/her mother. But the more pressure you exert, the worse you make it. It's like a knotted rope in a tug-of-war — as both sides pull, the knot gets tighter and tighter. Nobody can think clearly when two important people are pulling him/her in different directions.

Eventually your spouse will have to mature and firmly set priorities in life. This will take some time and cause you some deprivation. Meanwhile, let go of your end of the rope. Stop pulling your spouse, or s/he will never get untied.

Consider joining your spouse in the middle, throwing all your energy into helping your spouse with his/her mother. In fact, outdo your spouse in your devotion to your mother-in-law. You should be the next one to interrupt a planned event with some need of hers. It may feel like a bitter pill to swallow, but try it for a period of time. Giving your spouse the extra slack will allow him/her to mull over the issue without feeling pressure from you. This may propel him/her to make some changes.

Spouse B, you need to get the pressure off yourself. Let your mother know that your *shalom bayis* is being affected because you do not have enough time to spend with your family. You don't want to criticize your mother and accuse her of being an imposing mother-in-law, and you also do not want to invite your mother into your personal life. You must achieve the right tone in your communication to her.

You need to sound firm and in control, not helpless. You also need to make it clear that you are not criticizing her — you are informing her about this so if a situation arises where you feel you must tend to your immediate family, she will be understanding and flexible. If your mother starts criticizing your spouse, gently remind her that you are requesting her help and understanding, and that you trust her to hold back her criticism.

Making your mother aware of your bind will direct her maternal instincts toward preserving your *shalom bayis*. This appeal might fall on deaf ears if your mother is more selfish than most. But most mothers will eventually respond to some extent, even if you have to repeat this message many times.

SCENARIO #3: RELIGION PROBLEMS

> **Spouse A**: Your spouse made a mistake about a matter of religious ritual. It's deeply troubling to you because it seems that this aspect of observance is not important to him/her. You don't feel comfortable when religion is taken lightly; it's not how you were brought up and it is not how you want to bring up your.

> **Spouse B**: Once again your spouse seems to be obsessing over minor details instead of seeing the big picture. There are dozens of priorities to attend to, and instead of appreciating everything you do correctly, all s/he can do is notice a small shortcoming. Anyhow, s/he is a bit of a hypocrite in conveniently overlooking the liberties s/he takes when it comes to religious issues that are inconvenient for him/her.

Spouse A, if your spouse has an issue with religion, you are not going to make any progress if he or she feels criticized. Often people who have difficulty with religious issues have already been criticized by authority figures. So you are in danger of joining a long line of rabbis, teachers and parents whom your spouse has learned to ignore long ago.

So what can you do? Forget about religion for the time being. Talk about feelings. Even though this is not how you truly feel, act as if your need for certain religious requirements are a personal idiosyncrasy instead of a cardinal sin.

If you needed your spouse to wear a certain style of shoe, what method would be more likely to engender his or her cooperation? Would it help to demand that he or she wear this shoe, or would it help more if you humbly asked your spouse to accommodate this request of yours, even though there is no rational reason for it?

The latter method is much less likely to arouse resistance or defiance. For example, you could say, "Look, I know this is not how you were brought up and perhaps there are other opinions, but would you indulge me in following this particular approach? When you do such and such it makes me feel very uncomfortable. If you accommodate me on this, I will be forever grateful."

Your spouse might refuse, but that's okay. Wait a few days and ask again. If this matter is important to you, don't give up. Keep asking, but always in a respectful and non-accusatory tone.

Spouse B, you're in a hard to win situation. What's common sense to you is a religious violation to your spouse. What you consider to be middle of the road might be heresy to your spouse. Swallow your pride and try to accommodate your spouse. But if your spouse's religious demands seem to be truly unreasonable, you may have to bring in a rabbi to arbitrate.

What if you suspect that what you do is religiously incorrect, but you feel you cannot meet the demand? The best approach is to find an area of religious observance you do feel strongly positive about. Share your limitations with your spouse and ask him/her to understand that for now you have committed yourself to growing in the area you have chosen. Show your spouse you can be passionate about your religious practices as well, though they may not be the same as his or hers.

If you are a person who is not passionate about any aspect of religion, but your spouse is, it may be possible to work out an arrangement in your relationship, but it would likely require marriage counseling to help bridge the dramatically different worldviews.

Spouse A: Your ten-year-old son needs to become more responsible. He is a bit of a baby. He hardly does any chores — and what a picky eater! He leaves half his supper on his plate. Your spouse is more laid back, but it is really starting to concern you because you fear the lax discipline is hurting your child. Every time you try to crack down on him, though, your spouse undermines you and intervenes, leaving you frustrated with your spouse and angry with your child.

Spouse B: You love your spouse, but s/he can be a bit of a tyrant. S/he overreacts to minor shortcomings of the children. You don't like to undermine him/her, but you can't see your children growing while being oppressed over small details.

Spouse A, it is impossible to discipline a child when parents give mixed messages. If you compromise and lower your standards and thereby gain your spouse's cooperation, your child will respond much better than if you insist on a higher standard your spouse is not comfortable enforcing.

There have been studies that show that strict parents and lenient parents essentially achieve the same goals, as long as they are consistent in their discipline. Lenient does not have to mean wishy-washy. You and your spouse need to find rules and consequences that you both can live with. It is worthwhile for you to be flexible about your spouse's concerns and allow for a more lenient approach, as long as you can agree that whatever rules you set will be clear and enforced with regularity.

Spouse B, if your spouse is really acting like a tyrant with your children, then remember that behind the façade of every tyrant is an insecure person. This is not for you to use as ammunition. Just keep in mind that it is worthwhile massaging your spouse's ego at every available opportunity and allow him/her some amount of control. If you conduct yourself with grace and class, you can defuse any difficult situation.

Don't cave in to ridiculous demands you feel would oppress your children. But join your spouse emotionally by showing you agree, in principle, that parents must be treated with respect and children must be disciplined. You need to show your absolute concern for this matter, so your spouse's ego will be sated enough to allow for a rational discussion.

Assure your spouse that once you come to an agreement on how to handle a certain situation, you will never undermine him or her. Once you have made this clear, you then need to try to get your ideas across. Don't allow your spouse to impose punishments and take disciplinary action unilaterally without allowing you to discuss the matter together and come up with a unified approach.

SCENARIO #5: WORKAHOLIC

> **Spouse A**: You understand your spouse has a demanding career/life, and you respect the dividends it brings for the family. But you are also starting to wonder if s/he is avoiding you. You can't remember when you last spent time together in a relaxed, intimate way. Even on vacation there are somehow interruptions that pop up, either with work or child care related emergencies. But whenever you try to bring this up, your spouse gets defensive and begins to list all of his/her responsibilities and burdens — as if you don't have any of your own!

> **Spouse B**: The honeymoon is over for you. No matter how hard you try to get on top of things, it seems that there are more pressures and burdens each year. You have almost made peace with this, figuring, "Thank G-d I have a beautiful and healthy family. I have a good, dependable job and income. So what if I have to work hard?" But then your spouse comes along and keeps hassling you about spending more time together. Sure, you would like to, but it's just unrealistic at this stage in your lives. Why is s/he being such a baby?

Spouse A, if your spouse is truly addicted to being busy, whether it's with work or family, you might benefit from learning how the addict's mind works. An addict is addicted to a substance or a behavior because it distracts them from emotional or physical pain. What pain in your relationship is your spouse avoiding? Are you ready to honestly face long standing areas of resentment and miscommunication?

You need to be honest with yourself. Temporarily forget about your resentments, no matter how justified they may be. Ask your spouse in a non-threatening tone what is not going right for him or her in the relationship. What could you do differently that would allow you to spend more time together, as a couple or a family?

At the same time, addicts hardly ever respond to a soft approach because their addiction is too strong. So aside from trying to address the underlying reasons, at some point, you may also need to draw a line in the sand. Tell your spouse that certain behaviors cannot be tolerated. Be clear about your expectations that s/he make specific times for spending together with a minimum of interruptions.

Spouse B, you feel under enormous pressure from both your work/family and your spouse. But if you build your career and ignore your spouse — you won't have a family to support. How do you balance the two?

Share your schedule with your spouse, share your concerns and demands. This is not a problem for you to shoulder on your own. Suppose you have a new opportunity at work that will involve several evenings of overtime. Instead of treating your spouse as the enemy, or someone to be handled so you can get back to work, why not involve him or her in the dilemma?

Lay out the potential financial benefit, the current financial needs of the family, and the loss of family time this new project will cost. Ask your spouse for input, instead of playing the role of trying to convince him or her to agree. You might be surprised to find that once you include your spouse in the process, he or she will feel more involved and invested in your work, and therefore be more accommodating.

Of course your spouse may not be so accommodating, especially if there are years of resentment and neglect. In that case, you need to put your marriage first. But that should only increase your chances of success when you try again in the future.

$\langle 51 \rangle$

Family Time
versus Couple Time

Which is more important — spending time with family or spending time with a spouse? Many couples grapple with this question. But this is like asking, "What is more important, air or water?" In order to survive, a person needs both! For a family to survive, parents must dedicate time and attention to their children, but still have a vital personal life with their spouse.

Parents cannot function at their best, providing love, nurture and attention, without getting some themselves. Just as older children require less attention than infants, adults require less attention than children. But if husband or wife feels deprived, resentment can leak out in the form of bitter and hostile behaviors that can hurt the entire family. Happy parents model relationship skills, empowering children to one day develop into loving and supportive spouses.

FROM COUPLE TO FAMILY

One of the early challenges of a successful marital relationship is the transition from newlyweds to parents. For many couples with newborns, it comes as a big shock when they no longer have their privacy and freedom.

Midnight scurries to Seven-Eleven for slurpies are replaced by midnight scurries for diapers and formula. Romantic evenings of idealistic and deep discussions about the future are replaced by the practical and mundane demands of daily life.

Of course, the daily (and nightly!) demands of raising a family are actually the enactment of the "future" the couple discussed in their idealized state. But it does not always feel as noble as it did when they imagined it. While this transition is a normal stage in life, it doesn't mean that parents should allow their personal life to be completely monopolized by their parental responsibilities.

TRIANGULATION

A parent with a dissatisfying personal life can become over-involved in his relationship with the children. This is known as triangulation: the child becomes the third point in a triangular relationship. For example, Sruli and Miriam fill their evenings by fretting, cajoling and arguing with Ruth about her behavior in school. Ruth is a discipline problem — and she never goes to sleep on time!

Sruli and Miriam don't have time to face their own discomfort, depression or resentments. By the time they have a chance to be alone in the evening they are too exhausted to talk about anything emotionally meaningful or share any intimacy.

Sruli and Miriam object to these accusations. "Ruth really has a behavior problem! This is not about us — it is about our child. We are not doing anything to evoke her terrible behavior!"

Couples in this situation should try setting aside a significant amount of time each week to spend together without any distractions — dining out, playing a game or just talking. But no talk about the kids! Sometimes, this alone helps improve a child's behavior. It's a worthwhile investment — babysitters and restaurants are a lot cheaper than therapy!

WORKING TOGETHER

For a healthy relationship, couples must work together to designate boundaries for married, parental and professional life. Some people need more vacation and some need less; some enjoy more time with the children, and some need more separation.

One couple may have no problem with their young children sleeping in their beds and even consider it to be ideal, while another couple finds it intrusive. Some couples have toys strewn all over their bedroom and others make it off-limits. Some couples go out together once a week while others go out much less often, if at all. There is no one specific way of doing things, but the critical criteria for a successful relationship is that these issues are discussed and mutually agreed upon.

What if spouses have widely divergent views on how much time to spend with each other versus spending time with children? This may indicate a deeper dissatisfaction in the relationship and be part of an unconscious avoidance mechanism. After all, if over the years a wife has experienced repeated disappointment with her husband, or vice versa, why spend time with him? Career or children would be a far more satisfying and fulfilling focus. The couple should make an honest, even painful, assessment of their feelings and constructively address any problems that are found.

SECTION SIX
Intergenerational
Issues

O ur current social context has changed dramatically from past generations. It was once routine
to be born, live, and die in the same town — even
in the same house. But today most people live in several
cities throughout their lifetime. This dramatic difference
affects our relationships with our parents, our children's
relationship with their grandparents, their chinuch in
formative years, and the transmittal of religious beliefs.
We can't turn back the clock, but we must take a sober
look at what we are missing in our modern lives, assess
its impact, and do our best to compensate so we can create a culture where Torah, ethics and personal growth
can flourish.

52

Avoiding Insult

Dear Feuermans,

I am in a bind between halacha and hurting another person's feelings. My father's father unfortunately passed away when my father was a young boy. My grandmother, a Holocaust survivor, remarried a wonderful man of similar background and has since produced a new family. We have all accepted her new husband as if he is our real father and grandfather.

This is where it gets sticky for me. Due to the geographical distance between us, we only see each other on special occasions and holidays. We are always very excited to see them and spend time with them. The problem is, when my grandparents come, everyone exchanges hugs and kisses.

Since I'm married it's become increasingly uncomfortable for me to participate in these exchanges with my grandfather as he is not halachically my grandfather. But I'm very concerned about hurting the feelings of both my father and my grandmother who may interpret this withholding of hugs and kisses as a cold gesture.

How can I fit in with everyone else around me? My sisters don't seem to find any problem with these exchanges. I want to make sure my grandfather feels I love him, yet at the same time abide by halacha.

There are different *halachic* opinions regarding this question. We are not going to issue a *halachic* ruling, and you should definitely consult a rabbi. Let us offer some ideas on how to ask your *halachic* question and what to do once you get an answer.

Sometimes when a person seeks *halachic* guidance, he tends to minimize his feelings, not disclosing the full degree of distress — or potential distress. Perhaps he is concerned that it will reflect badly upon his level of religious commitment. "Ideally the *halacha* should not take my personal feelings into account. Torah observance demands personal sacrifice on a daily basis. If I truly believe that the Torah is an expression of G-d's will, there's no excuse to avoid a commandment!"

But this is not true. The Torah has allowances for personal distress. A well-known Talmudic dictum rules that in cases of disabling pain, a person is exempt from a commandment of rabbinic origin. (*Kesubos* 60a) In certain circumstances, the Talmud even allows a person to passively commit a Torah prohibition in the face of human dignity. (See *Berachos* 19b, Rashi "*Shev.*")

The degree of distress can be a major factor in a *halachic* decision. Whether your situation merits such a dispensation or not still requires a *halachic* ruling. You need to be frank and honest with your rabbi about the degree of pain and suffering at stake in order to receive the most meaningful and accurate ruling as it pertains to your situation.

There will always be situations when you are torn between personal commitment to *halacha* and the possibility of damaging a relationship. Communicate your feelings of regard and concern for the other party. "It causes me a great deal of pain to know that I may be hurting your feelings, or in some way making you feel bad. I tried to explore all possible solutions by consulting expert *halachic* authorities whom I respect, but the situation does not allow me to be flexible in this regard."

Some people have a need to pick a fight, especially when they are angry about something but have nowhere to legitimately direct their anger. If your step-grandfather is offended, he will feel confused and guilty about his anger toward you, and goad you into a fight. But don't take the bait.

Allow him — or your father, or grandmother, or whoever is insulted — time to vent, perhaps to criticize you and/or your religious beliefs. As long as it's not too abusive, tolerate it, validating his feelings while gently indicating your inability to change your position on the matter. If you follow this method, over time your family will adjust and accept the new reality and you will be able to maintain your relationship on good terms.

53

Thoroughly
Un-Modern Moshe

Dear Feuermans,

My family is Modern Orthodox. I went to an "out-of-town" yeshiva and then learned in Eretz Yisroel. Slowly, over the years, I moved more and more to the right of my family's religious observance.

There is an incident from this phase of my life that I will never forget which shows the impact it still has on me. At my family seder, everyone received their token-sized piece of matzah. I took a comparatively large piece from the box so I could eat the shiur (full measurement required by halacha).

One relative quite innocently commented that I really must like matzah. My mother came in and when she saw me gobbling down the matzah, she was infuriated. She yelled how foolish I was to fill up on matzah before a meal. Ironic really — the mitzvah is to eat the matzah, not the meal. And in fact, the halacha requires one to leave room for the Afikoman to serve as dessert.

I will never forget the embarrassment I felt in front of all those relatives, and the anger on her face. Many years have passed since that incident. My mother has mellowed a bit, but even today, if I quote a rabbi, usually a rosh yeshiva, a rebbe, or an important rav, she will argue and invalidate daas Torah.

*Everyone wants their parents' approval and validation
— I am no exception. So though I realize my mother was
brought up in the forties and went to public schools, and
her own parents were modern, how should she know
better, etc., I am in conflict. After all, she is my mother.*

*I felt from a young age that I had to please her to gain
love and approval. I know intellectually that her philosophy of Yiddishkeit is wrong, but it is hard to undo the
emotional need for approval. Do you have any advice
about how to manage this situation?*

OUR RESPONSE

Though your situation is very painful for both you and your
mother, it also is quite common. To some extent you and your
mother are victims of sociological trends that go way beyond your
ability to control.

Hyam Soloveitchik, in his essay "Rupture and Reconstruction:
The Transformation of Contemporary Orthodoxy" (*Tradition*,
Volume 28, No. 4, 1994), provides us with valuable insights into
the roots of the conflict between the current yeshiva generation
and some of their more modern elder family members.

In the Jewish *shtetlach* of yesteryear, customs and traditions were
handed down from one generation to the next for hundreds of
years. The primary resource for *halacha* was within the family.

But our American yeshiva system is a reconstruction from the
destroyed remnants of European Jewry. So now we tend to rely
upon the Jewish text and *halachic* codes. Today, a yeshiva student
from a modern family feels he cannot trust his family's customs
because perhaps they are in error. Even assuming his family's customs are correct, the rapidly changing technological world we live
in brings in variables we cannot account for in the tradition.

For example, your mother has an ostensibly correct tradition
that she can adjust the stove on a holiday. But how can you be sure
that the new electronic ovens fit under the same *halachic* criteria as
the ancestral hearth? This causes a great deal of emotional pain for
both generations because it is quite natural in Judaism to respect
tradition, parents and customs.

Notwithstanding the sociological issues, there may be certain
psychological fault lines in your relationship with your mother,

which exacerbate the situation. Perhaps you and your mother are a bit too close emotionally. Your poignant wish for her approval and her hostile reaction to your differing opinions and practices testify to this.

You and your mother are in a constant struggle to be important in each other's lives. Every practice of yours that is different from hers is perceived as rejection. Your need for confirmation and acceptance may be driving you to accentuate your differences, only to once again experience a crushing rejection.

You need to find a way to show your mother that she is important to you, but leave religion out of it. Have a discussion about the values you share in common — perhaps being stubborn and strong-willed is one — instead of focusing on the areas of difference.

54

Every Day is Mother's Day?

Dear Feuermans,
I have always looked forward to Mother's Day and
Father's Day and found it to be a good opportunity to
teach children about honoring their parents. Recently,
my grandchildren who attend an ultra-orthodox yeshiva
informed me that it is against the Torah to celebrate
Mother's Day and Father's Day because according to the
Torah, we must honor parents every day, and therefore
every day should be Mother's Day and Father's Day.
Can you please explain this to me?

OUR RESPONSE

Though there may be some religious basis for not observing these holidays, the reason you convey seems misguided and in error. It's true that we are obligated to honor our parents every day. But the Torah makes concessions to human nature and sets aside specific times for heightened awareness and observance.

For example, a person is obligated to repent for sins every day of his life (*Shabbos* 153a), but we still have Yom Kippur, one special day a year set aside for everyone to pay extra attention to this matter.

Rashi teaches us that we should accept the Torah upon ourselves every day. (*Shemos* 19:1) Yet we observe Shavuos, commemorating the giving of the Torah.

The possible basis for rejecting the observance of a secular holiday such as Mother's Day stems from the general prohibition of adopting the customs of the gentile nations. (See *Shulchan Aruch*, *Yoreh Deah* 178:1) Rabbinic authorities dispute whether this prohibition applies only to immoral or lewd customs, or extends even to customs that promote moral behavior. (See *Iyun Yaakov*, *Berachos* 18b favoring that a moral gentile custom may be adopted by Jews.)

Those who oppose the adoption of even benign gentile customs fear that it will inevitably invite other alien values, leading to further levels of assimilation. "If we follow the secular culture's observance of Mother's Day," they argue, "we might unwittingly begin to adopt secular standards for treating parents in general, which are far below the Torah standard."

There is validity to this argument. Lamentably, even religious children today are raised to treat parents with a degree of casual disrespect that is not only wrong religiously, but damaging psychologically. To develop healthy personalities, children need parents who are comfortable with their own authority and make appropriate demands upon their children.

Rabbi Yitzchak Hutner ZT"L, revered Rosh Yeshiva of Mesivta Chaim Berlin, prohibited the observance of any holiday that follows the secular calendar. Today's calendar is based on the birth of Jesus, and any reference to it constitutes *"abizrayhu d'avoda zara,"* indirect idol worship. According to this view, the mere recording of a secular date is prohibited.

While there is *halachic* basis to not wholeheartedly endorse the observance of Mother's Day and Father's Day, however perhaps from other standpoints, these secular holidays are beneficial by heightening awareness of the *mitzvah* of honoring parents.

55

Letting Go

Dear Feuermans,

I'm sure I'm not the only one with this problem. As the child of Holocaust survivors, I grew up with what I realized early on were issues and problems that other children didn't have. Chief among these was the role reversal of educating and caring for the parent, rather than the other way around.

One way the Holocaust affected people was that those who lived through this horrific era are loath to throw anything out — they become collectors of everything. In the case of my parents' home, it became the children's job to organize and control the clutter.

Both my parents kept everything, everything. They put away old shirts with fraying collars, because one day they would replace the collars. Everything was held onto for "one day," one day when we would take care of all the things that weren't getting done. Things to fix, things to sell, things to give away — things just accumulated.

Ironically, while our parents kept all the mail, all the bills, and tons of useless items, they told us that it was our stuff that was making the house a mess! It took years for me to clearly see this pattern.

Now I live with one parent, who still collects every bit of paper, but also complains about how the house looks and messes up anything I do. So I have to clean and *organize, and then go back and clean and organize all over again.*

I realized a few years ago that part of this is a way of keeping us tied to them. If my sibling and I were working on one area of the house, our parents would complain about another part of the house. It was very frustrating. I realized they would never be satisfied, and would continue to do this.

What should I do? I cannot move out until I marry. How can I deal with this behavior? I know my parent will not change. The worst part is that whatever I do is messed up, so what's the point? It's enough that I am the caregiver, and have work responsibilities, and have to find a shidduch. All this mess keeps me from getting on with the rest of my life.

Our Response

It's a shame you chose to send your letter anonymously, because you would benefit from an extended discussion. We hope you are reading this and that what we say can be in some way helpful.

Though you may be looking for advice, psychotherapists try to act as a mirror, reflecting a person's words and actions so he can see them more objectively, instead of just telling a person what to do. The solution to your problem lies in your own words.

You acknowledge that your parents "will not change." You are probably right, unless they recognize their problem and the difficulty it brings. But if they have personality disorders, the difficulty is not for them — their loved ones suffer most.

You also mentioned that in your family there is a role reversal, where you, as the child, must act as the parent. You astutely observed that this behavior "is a way of keeping us tied to them." You also stated, "I cannot move out until I marry ... All this mess keeps me from getting on with the rest of my life."

As long as you see yourself as the parent, instead of the child, you probably will never feel free enough to get married. What parent ever abandons a child? So you will not allow yourself to leave your parent. The people who you date can sense your emotional unavailability, and will find you unattractive as a mate.

Is there any way you can free yourself from this role of caregiver for your parents? You can't move out until you marry — does this stem from a religious, cultural or emotional restriction?

Perhaps you should consult with a rabbi you trust to clarify your obligations to honor your parents in relation to your own need to marry and succeed in life. You need to achieve some degree of emotional separation. You need to be free to be a child. Then you will have room enough in your heart to marry and become a real parent, of your own children.

This may be difficult. Your parent may suffer from this change. But ultimately, it will bring your parents more joy and *nachas* than whatever suffering they experience from your separation.

56

The Son Who Was Too Good

Dear Feuermans,

My daughter is married to a son of Holocaust survivors. My son-in-law's parents are healthy and able to work and live alone. Despite this, their son has to know every detail of their life and manage when and where they are going. He has assumed the role of parent to his own parents, as you mentioned in another article. And it is causing problems in his marriage.

My son-in-law travels quite a bit and when he is in town, he comes home after eight in the evening. His children hardly see him. Even when he's not working, he is often at his parents' house. If he ever has any time left over after that for his wife and children, his usual complaint is that he is "too tired" to spend any time on family activities. No wonder he is too tired — he spends all his energy on his parents!

My daughter is probably not the only one with this problem. Perhaps you could address this subject in future articles. Thank you.

OUR RESPONSE

If your description of your son-in-law is accurate, he has distorted perceptions about relationships. Some of his personality and relationship issues may be attributed to family dynamics more prevalent among children of survivors. Children of survivors often have difficulty separating from their parents.

Your son-in-law's extensive involvement in his work and his parents' affairs to the exclusion of his children and wife can be categorized as avoidance behavior. This avoidance may be completely unconscious. He may express great frustration and regret that he is unable to spend time with his family, but his actions tell another story.

Your son-in-law may have been trained by his parents to repress the negative feelings and resentments he has about his own family — which is why he is avoiding them. His parents did not do this on purpose; it is a normal and healthy survival response for someone who suffered from unimaginable and unforgivable atrocities. They learn to quash negative feelings about the past in order to lead a relatively normal existence. These individuals are our heroes; many of us owe our very existence to them.

But as a consequence of this emotional response, the children of these same heroes never learn to constructively address their own feelings and resentments. Whereas there's no point to being angry with someone who doesn't care what you think, when someone you love hurts or insults you, you should address it and discuss it immediately, or risk damaging the relationship by acting out your resentment in an unconscious manner.

Your daughter will have to be extremely patient. Living with people who have difficulty expressing their negative feelings can be frustrating. If she asks, "Is anything bothering you?" your son-in-law will likely respond in the negative. Or he might have an unexpected and hostile response with a list of long-standing resentments.

And you can't blame your daughter if she's angry either — she has been the brunt of avoidance and other passive aggressive actions. But your daughter should not give up. Showing support all the while, she must calmly show her husband how his behavior hurts the family and encourage him to be more honest about his feelings. Your son-in-law's behavior can change over time.

57

A Matter of Perspective

The apartment was completely infested, the walls writhing with roaches. And the filth! A horrible stench emanated from that home, wafting its way to the lobby. Pipes leaked, but Reb Shaya didn't care.

At a spry one hundred years, Reb Shaya was quite content with his surroundings. "I live in a palace, a large apartment with two closets!" He was fiercely independent. He washed his own clothes in the kitchen sink. Once a month, he made a trip to the bank.

If he ever needed anything, he would call out of his ground floor apartment window. Eager, chessed-minded, neighborhood children would pick up grocery items for him at the store, anticipating Reb Shaya's monetary tip — and the cookies he distributed. There were several families from whom he accepted Shabbos food.

Money was not a problem. He had a monthly pension and sufficient savings. His apartment was rent-controlled, under three hundred dollars a month. Yet despite the efforts of various community volunteers, Reb Shaya refused to admit cleaning help or other medical professionals.

Reb Shaya was mistrustful of everyone, especially someone who did not have the appearance of a *heimishe Yid* (religious Jewish person). Doctors and government officials were the enemy.

Reb Shaya was a Holocaust survivor. His wife and family of three or five children, depending on whose account, were killed by the Nazis. But despite — or maybe because of — the horrors he experienced, Reb Shaya lived the life of a devout Jew. The words of

Torah commentaries were often on his lips. And he was generous in support of the *shul* where he davened.

As far as Reb Shaya was concerned, life was good; all his needs were taken care of. But this was not so for others who lived nearby. His landlord and other tenants were disgusted with the stench and dirt. Water leaking from Reb Shaya's apartment damaged the floor below.

Finally, the neighbors made a call to Protective Services for Adults (PSA).

The condition of his apartment plus Reb Shaya's general demeanor and hygiene warranted immediate attention. PSA petitioned the surrogate's court to declare Reb Shaya mentally incompetent. Then an outside agency or individual could become his legal guardian and take responsibility for Reb Shaya's personal care and finances.

Reb Shaya's friends from the community were very concerned that if a stranger would become his legal guardian, he would be forced into a nursing home, robbed of his dignity and independence. Fortunately, the court was convinced of the relevance of Reb Shaya's personal history as a Holocaust survivor. A Jewish foundation assumed legal guardianship and was empowered to ensure his needs as a religious Jew.

Caring for Reb Shaya was not an easy task. How do you provide care for someone who doesn't think he needs it? Although Reb Shaya had more than enough financial resources to take care of all his environmental and medical needs, he was absolutely adamant in not admitting strangers into his home to clean up his personal belongings. He trusted no one. Even if home care personnel were stalwart enough to withstand spending time in his apartment, Reb Shaya would fight tooth and nail to keep out the unwelcome interlopers.

Thanks to the cooperation and support of numerous community organizations and rabbis, doctors were brought in to treat and monitor his health. Occasionally, he would allow the admittance of an exterminator or a plumber. But on the whole, Reb Shaya continued to live happily and stubbornly in his palace, with all its amenities undisturbed.

Toward the end of his life, Reb Shaya's remarkably good health deteriorated. He became less mobile, although no less feisty. Aides were hired to check on him every few hours. He still would not allow them to stay and assist him for any length of time, but at least he was being monitored periodically.

One day he was weaker than usual, his breathing labored. Hatzalah (Jewish volunteer ambulance corps) was called, and very much against his will, Reb Shaya was transported to the hospital. He needed a pacemaker; the prognosis was good.

The procedure was scheduled. But meanwhile, he developed secondary complications. His kidneys began to fail and he suffered from a serious infection. His prognosis changed from optimistic to grim. No longer able to breathe on his own, Reb Shaya was put on a respirator. The doctors said he had days, maybe just hours, to live.

The situation was grave. Due to the complications of his condition, he had the status of a goses, a halachic term for a person in the death throes. To limit his suffering, we were permitted to limit the scope of medical interventions.

A survivor, fighting to the end, Reb Shaya's condition began to reverse itself. For about a week, there was a glimmer of hope. At one point, he even began to breathe independently. Ultimately, Reb Yeshaya Zev ben Mordechai Pinchas succumbed to his illness at the age of 102.

So who was Reb Shaya? Was he a victim of the Nazis — or a victor? As one eulogizer said, "The Germans cannot extinguish the spirit of a Jew." Was he a bitter and unfortunate man — or fortunate and successful? Was he an able person — or disabled? A receiver of charity — or a giver? It's really a matter of perspective.

To Interfere
or Not to Interfere

58

Dear Feuermans,

Is it appropriate for married children to get involved in their parents' marriage difficulties? We grew up in a loving family, but now that we are all out of the house, I think empty nest syndrome has made my parents' marriage very unhappy. I worry that if no one intervenes they might get divorced, or at least be miserable for the rest of their lives. Yet part of me wants to pretend there is no problem.

I find it extremely difficult to talk to my parents about this because it is very emotionally upsetting to me. I am reluctant to get involved, but should something terrible happen, I will always regret that I did not do anything about it. Would it be disrespectful to discuss it with them?

OUR RESPONSE

You come from a loving family and still seem to be very close to your parents. You observed that your parents are suffering from empty nest syndrome.

Your parents probably always had some measure of difficulty and dissatisfaction. They were able to hide it because they used their children as a buffer in their relationship. In other words, they derived more satisfaction and pleasure from the family than from each other.

Such a relationship dynamic may even have included many family activities and vacations together, but your parents probably rarely did anything as a couple. Perhaps this was the best adaptation your parents could make at the time, and they chose to focus on the good things you children gave them instead of their own personal unhappiness in the marriage. Now that the nest is empty, they are arguing more and showing their unhappiness and dissatisfaction. As their child, what can you do about it?

Your concerns are quite understandable, but your parents' marriage is none of your business — except in terms of how it affects you. If your parents fight in front of you and your children, you may say something like, "It makes me very uncomfortable when you do this and I worry that it is harmful to the children."

You have a right to respectfully talk about ways in which their difficulty hurts you or your children. You can take this opportunity to express your concern about their happiness and welfare. If they continue to fight, you can tell them how much it hurts you, urging them to find a way to solve the problem. But tread carefully. Only speak about how it makes you or your children feel, because that is the only part that is your business.

As a child, you provided the *nachas* that cemented your parents' relationship and distracted them from their unhappiness. Perhaps you and your siblings unconsciously still feel responsible for making them happy. So go ahead — continue to make them proud. But do not feel overly responsible for their life choices. Realize that it is not your affair.

59

Honoring Your Parents in Modern Times

Among the great and looming obligations of the Torah are the commandments to honor and fear parents. The Talmud compares the obligation to honor parents to the honor due to the A-lmighty. (*Kiddushin* 31b) The Talmud expounds on the commands to honor and fear parents.

What is the verse referring to when it says to fear one's parents? One should not stand in his place, sit in his place, contradict his statements, or [even] approve his statements. What is honor? One should serve his parents food and drink, help dress them, and escort them in and out of the house. (*Kiddushin* 31b)

Even to agree with a parent is disrespectful, as it implies equality. And age is irrelevant. A fully mature adult must honor and respect his parents according to the biblical directive.

The Talmud is replete with stories where Jews, and even gentiles, suffered great humiliation, pain or loss at the hand of their parents, and still did not dishonor or disrespect them. (See *Kiddushin* 31a; *Kiddushin* 31b, Tosafos "*Rabbi Tarfon.*") These are not just stories of exemplary individuals. It is representative of the *halachic* obligation. The *Shulchan Aruch* (*Yoreh Deah* 240:3) codifies this into law when it states:

[Even] if a son was dressed in finery, seated at the dais and his father and mother came along, ripped his clothes, hit him on the head, and spit in front of him, the son is forbidden to shame them.

Rather, he must remain quiet [and keep in mind] the fear of the King of Kings who thus commanded him to do so.

THE CHANGING TIMES

Western culture values the needs of the individual. Members of this modern society are expected to care for themselves first, then provide for the needs of the family and community. Self-fulfillment and personal autonomy are top priority. In part, this is why the United States has achieved so much in terms of its economy, productivity and ingenuity.

But this success comes at a price. While families, clans and entire villages used to grow up, live, get ill, age, and even die together, today many people feel lonely and isolated. Young married children live far from their parents, robbed of vital support and wisdom their parents and grandparents offer. As parents age, these geographic distances make it difficult for children to care for them. These situations can become burdensome and cause a great deal of stress, guilt and resentment.

How different it would be if an entire extended family all lived on the same farm! There would be de facto built-in day care for the younger children and skilled nursing facilities for the elders, all provided by different members of the family. Alas, there is no turning back. But it is important to understand the past and present cultural contexts to find realistic solutions to these clashes.

EMPOWERING THE CHILDREN

At first glance, the Torah seems to place no boundaries on how much parents may demand of their children. But this is not so. Even though a child must always treat a parent with respect, a parent is still independently obligated to refrain from unnecessarily burdening or making harsh demands upon his child. (See *Mishneh Torah, Hilchos Mamrim* 6:8.)

When the parent in the above example tore the grown child's clothing in public, the Shach (*Yoreh Deah* 240:3,4) adds that the child may pursue monetary compensation through a court of law. (See also *Yoreh Deah* 240:8, Remah.)

A married woman is freed from the obligation to honor her parents when it conflicts with her ability to honor her husband.

(*Shulchan Aruch, Yoreh Deah* 240:17; *Yoreh Deah* 240:19, Shach) Of course, this doesn't permit disrespectful behavior simply because her husband demands it. But when confronted with an actual conflict of time or available resources, a wife must honor her husband's needs before she can tend to her parents'. Obviously, both husband and parents should be generous and forgiving, doing their best to promote *shalom bayis* all around.

If a married man hosts his father at his own home, the host sits at the head of the table instead of his father. (*Aruch Hashulchan* 240:11) A close review of the context shows that this ruling is based on a technicality, and not on any modern idea of adult autonomy. The reason for the seating arrangement is to maintain modesty vis-à-vis the daughter-in-law.

PARENT PRIORITIES

▸ Mother-in-law and father-in-law are included in the *mitzvah* of honoring parents. (*Pischei Teshuva* 240:20)

▸ A stepparent should be honored as a parent. (*Shulchan Aruch, Yoreh Deah* 240:21)

▸ A father's wishes precede a mother's contradictory wishes, since she should defer to her husband's wishes. (*Shulchan Aruch, Yoreh Deah* 240:14)

▸ If one's parents are divorced, a child is free to choose between directives of mother or father. (*Shulchan Aruch, Yoreh Deah* 240:14)

▸ A son can opt to honor his stepmother even if it is against his mother's will. (Shaalos Uteshuvos Be'er Moshe Volume I, 60:1)

WHEN IT CONFLICTS TORAH

A child is granted complete autonomy when a parent's instruction conflicts with another Torah requirement. The Mishna states, "If one's fathers tells him to … refrain from returning a lost object [a Torah commandment], he should not heed his words" (*Bava Metzia* 32a).

Rambam expands this exemption to include a case where a parent's wish is in conflict with a rabbinic law. (*Mishneh Torah, Hilchos Mamerim* 6:12) For example, if a parent ordered a child to abstain from lighting the Chanukah *menorah*, the child should disobey the parent and light the *menorah* regardless.

Logically, the Torah commandment of honoring parents should override the rabbinically ordained commandment of *menorah*. But Kesef Mishna explains that the requirement to obey rabbinic decrees is itself based on the Torah commandment *"lo tasur"* (*Devarim* 17:11), not to turn away from the directives of the Jewish court.

Minhag, customs, are not a part of this category. Yet the Debrecen Rav (*Shaalos Uteshuvos Be'er Moshe* Volume I, 59-60) rules that a child is not obligated to heed a parental directive in regard to a matter of custom. If a parent commands his child to eat legumes on Pesach, he does not have to obey.

In the Torah, the commandment to honor parents ends with the statement, "I am Hashem," implying both the children and parents must defer to the honor of the Al-mighty. And even though a Jewish custom is neither a Torah nor a rabbinic directive, it is an expression of honor to G-d. (*Tur, Yoreh Deah* 240) Therefore, the Debrecen Rav rules, one is not required to heed a parental request that is in conflict with a custom.

ASSERTING AUTONOMY

Loyalty to Torah law and custom override parental wishes, allowing you to assert your needs, at least in regard to religious matters. This is not limited to a small area of your life — Torah requirements encompass a broad range of personal choices.

Which *yeshiva* should you study in? Where should you daven? A child may assert his right to choose the place he believes will foster his spiritual growth, even if it is in defiance of his parents. (*Pischei Teshuva, Yoreh Deah* 240:22) Similarly, when it comes to choice of marriage partner, a child is free to choose whomever his heart desires. (*Yoreh Deah* 240:25, Remah)

In addition, if a parent is blatantly and continuously hostile to Torah observance, there may be grounds to exempt the child from honoring this parent even in regard to requests that are not in conflict with Torah laws. (For more detail, see *Yoreh Deah* 240:18, Remah.)

Though sources permit these dramatic moves, you should always seek guidance before making major life decisions in opposition to parental wishes. Choosing a vocation or marriage partner against your parents' wishes is an invitation for battle. Without parental support, you may be forced to function in the absence of emotional and financial sustenance. This can be a recipe for failure.

Nevertheless, there are situations where you must stand up for what you believe in, even if it is in defiance of your family's wishes. When Rachel married Rabbi Akiva, a complete ignoramus in Torah, her wealthy father completely disowned her. Rachel and her husband spent years in poverty, a worthwhile investment for one of the greatest Torah scholars of all time. A certain quality Rachel saw in Rabbi Akiva made her confident enough to risk her entire future, against all odds — and everyone's advice. (*Kesubos* 62b; Nedarim 50a)

RESPECT FOR AGING PARENTS

Watching a parent grow older is hard for any child. What is your obligation toward your parents as they age? Some elderly people make impossible demands due to mental deterioration. And sometimes, elderly parents require physical care beyond your capabilities.

Although you are obligated to honor your parents, you do not have to use your own money when your parents have sufficient funds. You are only obligated to care for them out of your own pocket if your parents are impoverished. (*Shulchan Aruch, Yoreh Deah* 240:5)

If your mother or father requires some form of medical care or support, your parents' money may be used first to cover the expense. As to administration of the actual care, as a son or daughter, according to the strict letter of the law, you are obligated to personally attend to your parents. You are not initially allowed to hire substitutes, even if this causes financial loss, such as taking off from work. However, in real life there are practical concerns that may make this ideal counterproductive and non-sustainable.

Sometimes a parent's mental deterioration makes it nearly impossible for a child to adequately provide care — a father needs to be physically restrained, or a mother becomes intolerably abusive. You cannot safely care for a parent like that. This is similar to the case of Rabbi Asi's mother. (*Kiddushin* 31b)

Based on the case in the Talmud, Rambam (*Mishneh Torah, Hilchos Mamerim* 6:10) codifies the following halacha: "One whose father or mother becomes mentally confused should endeavor to treat them according to their will … If it becomes impossible to withstand because they have become excessively demented, he should leave them and appoint others to care for them appropriately." (Note: Ra'vad disagrees with Rambam's interpretation of the Talmud in *Kiddushin*. But to what degree he differs is disputable. See *Yoreh Deah* 240:14, Taz; *Shaalos Uteshuvos Be'er Moshe* Volume I, 60:10.)

Care giving decisions are fraught with guilt and resentment, and people often feel torn between loyalty to their parents and loyalty to their children and spouse. Always seek guidance from a rabbi. An objective opinion, coupled with spiritual guidance, is invaluable, not merely to insure correct observance of the laws, but also to help forestall and mitigate guilt and stress.

There can be conflict with a parent about health matters without any dementia involved, too. A parent might ask for assistance in disobeying a physician's recommendations, such as discharge from a hospital against medical advice. A smoker asks his son to buy him a pack of cigarettes, or an alcoholic asks her daughter to buy her liquor.

The Debrecen Rav (*Shaalos Uteshuvos Be'er Moshe* Volume I, 60:7) rules that when there is a known health risk, even if it is not a potentially fatal risk, you should not comply with the parent's demand. A father is permitted to forgive his own honor. But even after he has done so, a child is forbidden to actively disrespect him. (See *Mishneh Torah, Hilchos Talmud Torah* 7:13, Kesef Mishna.) According to the formulation of the Debrecen Rav, causing damage to your parent's health is on par with disrespect. Your father asked you to buy him cigarettes; he has forgiven the concerns about his health. But you may not actively disrespect him by purchasing the cigarettes.

Similarly, the Debrecen Rav (*Shaalos Uteshuvos Be'er Moshe* Volume I, 60:11) discusses that sad case when a parent with a terminal illness demands the truth. If this information is harmful and damaging to the parent's health, the child is forbidden to obey the parent. However, personal circumstances and temperament are important factors here; we don't believe there is a "one size fits all" rule.

HANDLING THE CHALLENGE

Even with the strict requirements to show honor and respect, there are feasible approaches to resolving relationship problems with your parents. You do not have to tolerate and overlook hurtful parental remarks. It is possible to share constructive criticism with your parents within the guidelines of *halacha*.

Though a parent may be crossing over your line and the line of the Torah, you may not retaliate against a parent who is being verbally abusive to you, an adult. Children suffering from verbal, or G-d forbid physical, abuse at the hands of a parent may constitute *pikuach nefesh* (endangerment) on many different levels. A competent *halachic* authority should be consulted immediately. Some poskim consider consistent, unrepentant and willful abuse as enough to place a parent in the category of *rasha*, which may limit the scope of obligations placed upon the child.

But as an adult, if there's a way to respectfully bring this problem to your parent's attention, it is even a *mitzvah* to do so. And there is a way. You can enter into a constructive and corrective dialogue with your parents while remaining within the parameters of respect.

According to the *halacha*, it is disrespectful to tell your parents that they are wrong. But there is no prohibition against telling your parents how their actions make you feel. To a verbally abusive or hurtful parent, you can *halachically* say, "When you say that it makes me feel small." Or, "Ouch, that really hurts my feelings." Or, "I am very sad that you don't seem to be happy with what I am doing."

- Always stay calm, and speak in a respectful tone.
- Make no judgments, criticisms, or suggestions about whether your parent has done anything wrong.
- Use passive feelings such as, hurt, sad, and ashamed, instead of aggressive feelings such as angry, mad, or disgusted.
- Not every statement beginning with the words "I feel" are feelings. "I feel you are being unfair," is criticism, not feeling.
- For the greatest impact, state your feelings immediately when you are being hurt, as long as you can speak calmly and respectfully.

If you consistently and persistently let your mother or father know s/he is hurting you, s/he will eventually stop. Be patient and repeat this procedure, over months if need be, as many times as it takes. Almost everyone will achieve results with this method eventually. You can apply these guidelines in any relationship to encourage change while avoiding major confrontation.

60

The Sandwich Generation

Dad: Steven, that woman you sent over yesterday — she's stealing, so I threw her out!

Son: Dad, how do you know she was stealing?

Dad: It was obvious. I didn't like the joke she was making on the phone with her friend, so I began to suspect. I left $1.78 on my night table, and when I came back from the bathroom, there was only seventy-eight cents. You see, I caught her red-handed!

Son: But Dad, this is the third person you've thrown out. The manager at the agency said that soon he won't be able to find anyone to work for you.

Dad: Ach … Steven, I don't need any help. I got along just fine all these years since your mother, the good woman, passed away. This home help is really just a waste of money anyway. By the way, the light blew out in the kitchen. Do you think you can come by after work and put in a new bulb? Last night, I stubbed my toe when I tried to get a drink.

Son: Why didn't you call the aide to bring you a drink?

Dad: I didn't want to bother her in the middle of the night.

Son: Dad, sometimes I don't understand your thinking. First you complain that she steals, then you don't want to waste the money, and now you don't want to bother her?

Dad: Like I said, Steven, this whole home care business is a waste of money. The main thing is, I am lucky to have such a good son who comes by and helps out from time to time.

Son: But that's the point. I am stressed at work these days with several deadlines approaching. I love to come by and visit, but when you fight with the help instead of working with them, it makes it so much harder for me. Even if the aide stole a dollar or two, you have over two hundred grand in the bank. You worked hard all your life. Why not use a little of that money now to help make things easier? Give the lady a tip and ask her to put in the bulb.

Dad: Steven, I agree that it is good to spend money on worthwhile things, like your children, but I can't see wasting it and giving it away to these lazy no-goodniks.

[Phone conversation is interrupted with the BEEP! of the intercom]

Secretary: Mr. Goodson, your son's principal is on line two. He says David was fighting again and he wants you to come down to the school to pick him up …

Steven, the hapless hero, belongs to the sandwich generation. Many parents in their forties and fifties find themselves sandwiched between the demands of their growing family and the needs of their aging parents. Just at the time when the financial crunch gets tough — with bar mitzvahs, tuition, weddings, home improvements — these homemakers and breadwinners are heavily involved in caring for their own parents.

SORTING OUT THE NEEDS

In a moment of crisis, Steven has to try his best to be a good son. But in the long run, Steven can be proactive in addressing some of the complex family dynamics and how they interplay with his father's social and psychological needs.

Aside from providing physical care — nursing and home health aides — Steven could arrange a program of social and emotional support for his father and the family members involved as caretakers. There are agencies and social workers in private practice that specialize in working with the elderly and their families. A sandwich generation child such as Steven can gain relief by consulting with a professional in geriatric social work to resolve some of the issues.

Families often designate one sibling as the caretaker. The choice may have to do with geography or birth order, but usually there are other psychological reasons that are difficult to see and deal with objectively.

When one sibling becomes overly responsible, it can have catastrophic consequences on his/her personal life. It can strain — and even prevent — marriages. Guilt and resentment build to the point where a person feels helpless and overwhelmed.

A plan needs to be implemented where other siblings can provide support as well. If the siblings are unable to or refuse to help, this must be resolved, whether the cause is psychological — old resentments and fears, or environmental — distance and time constraints. Even if a sibling lives far away, he or she can be recruited to assist by making more frequent phone calls, or offering to assist the caretaker sibling in some other way.

DIFFUSING THE LONELINESS

Phone calls and visits are critical. An elderly parent's physical needs are increased by loneliness. This was a generation that grew up under harsh environmental conditions. In times of poverty and stress, who received the most nurture and attention? The physically ill — for if someone was ill or in danger of dying, personal ethics and community mores called for immediate attention. But when someone felt lonely or sad, there was no such imperative. Thus they were socialized to get their emotional needs met through physical ailments — real or imagined!

Some children report the weekend syndrome, where elderly parents experience more emergencies and crises on weekends than on other days. They are expressing their emotional needs with physical ailments. Weekends especially, a time usually spent with family and close friends, can be lonely and difficult for a person who has memories of a spouse, friends and neighbors who are no longer in this world.

STEVEN'S ISSUES

Steven's father has two needs. First, he really enjoys and loves his son. He wants to see him frequently. Second, he needs some physical assistance in maintaining his home and his health.

Steven's father is using concrete physical demands to ensure Steven's emotional involvement in his life. Subconsciously, Steven's father may be sabotaging his relationship with the aides as way of keeping close to Steven.

Of course, the moral and emotional obligations of honoring one's parents make it difficult to confront this matter directly, but Steven can address the matter indirectly. He could ask himself and his siblings if they visit their father often enough. If they only respond when there is a crisis, psychologically speaking, his father will unconsciously learn to create "emergencies" whenever he misses Steven!

With a combination of expert therapeutic guidance and environmental support, there are ways to change a family's psychological assumptions, sharing the burden among parents and all the siblings together.

61

Grandparenting

Grandparents enjoy their grandchildren in a way parents do not. You know what they say: "If I had known grandchildren were going to be so much fun, I would've had them first!" Without the day-to-day responsibilities of parenting, grandparents *shep nachas*, enjoying unstructured time with their grandchildren. Behavior problems that drive parents crazy are overlooked by Bubby and Zaidy, or even found endearing.

THE TORAH PERSPECTIVE

Are we obligated to honor our grandparents as we honor our parents? According to the Talmudic dictum, "Grandchildren are considered as children" (*Yevamos* 62b). This formula indicates that grandparents can fulfill the obligation to have progeny through the birth of grandchildren. So grandchildren are considered as children, but grandparents are not necessarily considered as parents.

The Remah (*Shulchan Aruch, Orach Chaim* 240:22) concludes that you are obligated to honor grandparents. But the Vilna Gaon (*Shulchan Aruch, Orach Chaim* 240:34) favors the opinion that you are not obligated.

The Yad Avrohom (*Shulchan Aruch, Orach Chaim* 240:34) indicates that according to both opinions, you are obligated to honor your grandparents at least while your parents are alive. Since you are obligated to honor your parents, and your parents are obligated to honor their parents, you are obligated to honor their parents — your grandparents — as well.

Primarily, your relationship with your grandparents should be with the spirit and intent of honoring your own parents. In support of this, the Remah implies that in case of a conflict between your parents' wishes and your grandparents', your obligation is to follow the parental wishes.

SPECIAL ATTENTION

An ever-doting grandparent can be a lifesaver for the self-esteem of a problem child. Often troubled children do not feel successful within the immediate family. They need an alternative venue where they can succeed. Children who are terrors at home can be quite helpful to their grandparents. When a child falls out of grace with his parents for poor behavior, he can still find comfort and security in his grandparents' love.

For the grandparents, there is a fine line between providing additional support and undermining parental authority. Grandparents have every right to dictate the terms of their relationship with their grandchild. They are free to enjoy and be proud of their grandchild even if his parents are not. But grandparents must ensure that this interaction does not directly undermine the parent's efforts.

> Leora's parents instituted an allowance system based on achieving certain grades at school, or some other behavioral objectives. For Leora and her siblings, five to ten dollars spending money is a lot. But one day, Leora's grandparents take her shopping. And they allow Leora to choose whatever toy she wishes, and " loan" her some cash as well.

Grandparents should try to tune in to the parents' *chinuch* objectives to make sure that they are not inadvertently undermining them. Grandparents are different — their values are never exactly the same as their children's. For example, a grandparent's financial burden is usually considerably smaller. But grandparents still have to be sensitive to the values their children are trying to instill as parents.

At the same time, however, grandparents should not be overly controlled by the parenting objectives of their children. To a limited extent, it is healthy for young children to be exposed to alternative role models.

Sometimes parents put too much pressure on their children, and grandparents can serve as an important safety valve in family relationships. With rebellious teenagers, grandparents are enough outside the family system that they can forge a helping relationship with the teenager and serve as a vital link to the family. Teenagers are often fascinated to learn about what their parents were like as children.

How can healthy alternatives be discerned from that which is undermining? The litmus check is intention. Grandparents should take an honest look at their motivations. Are they trying to control their children, to override their children's parenting techniques because they disagree? Such meddling will be damaging instead of helpful. Grandparents should have a frank and open discussion with their children, not manipulate behind the scenes.

But when grandparents simply want to enjoy time spent with the grandchildren, not become a substitute parent, such interactions can only be beneficial.

Future Care Planning for a Special Needs Child

At some point, every parent of a disabled child is faced with the difficult and frightening question: "Who will take care of my child when I am no longer alive?" None of us wants to think about our eventual demise. Caring for a disabled child involves so many emotional and practical challenges in the present that overburdened parents instinctively push off dealing with problems that may occur in the future.

Parents of a disabled child have a natural tendency to minimize the extent of their child's disability. Such coping mechanisms foster an optimistic approach to the present, but they hinder realistic planning for the future.

Planning for the care of a special needs child does not only protect his interests and ensure adequate care for his lifetime, but is also a fulfillment of the *mitzvah* of *tzedaka*. As it states in *Shulchan Aruch*, the obligation to give *tzedaka* to needy relatives takes precedence over giving to other poor persons. (*Yoreh Deah* 251:3)

Many complex issues and problems can arise in planning for the welfare of special needs children. It is vital to be aware of them, to be knowledgeable about the current options and care programs that are available to deal with them.

Parents need to ask:

▸ Who would be willing to accept responsibility and care for my child as well as I do?

- Who truly understands my child's needs?
- Who can best advocate for my child?
- Who will love my child?

CASE STUDIES

Mr. and Mrs. Goldfarb's youngest son, Yossi, was born with a developmental disability. The Goldfarbs want Yossi to live with them, and for the most part, it is a good arrangement. Yossi travels on his own to a day program where he volunteers in a local yeshiva kitchen.

Yossi is thirty-two years old and his parents are in their seventies. Yossi has two married siblings, an older sister who lives in Israel and a brother who lives about two hours away.

Recently, Yossi's father was hospitalized, and his mother was torn between caring for Yossi and caring for her husband. Fortunately, Yossi's brother Dovid came to the rescue and brought him home for the week. It wasn't so easy for Dovid with two young children and a newborn in the house, but under the circumstances, how could he not help out?

As a result of this experience, Dovid started to wonder what would happen to Yossi if their parents were unable to care for his disabled brother. He certainly can't assume the responsibility. Yossi and his parents are very attached to each other, but perhaps it would be a good idea for Yossi to make the transition to a new residence while his parents are still well and active in his life. Wouldn't it be much harder for Yossi to cope if he had to adjust to a new home and the loss of his parents at the same time?

Dina was thirty-five years old and had been living in a residence almost all her life. She was profoundly retarded with serious health problems. Her parents were very grateful for the care her residence provided over the years. They assumed that this arrangement would continue even after their deaths, and didn't think it was necessary to make any plans for her future.

Dina's parents were in their eighties. Her mother suffered a fatal heart attack; her father's health deteriorated rapidly and he died within a year. The residence staff had always relied on her father to sign off on medical consent forms, but when her parents passed away, the court had to assign a guardian. The residence staff could only hope that the guardian would be someone caring, understanding and responsive to Dina's needs.

Michael was his mother's darling, her only son. Widowed when Michael was only seven years old, mother and son were practically inseparable. Even after Michael began to show sign of mental illness and had his first breakdown, his mother remained close and supportive.

Michael never attended any formal day program or rehab. As the years passed, a stable pattern formed with Michael spending his days watching TV in their apartment and going for a daily walk with his mother.

They lived simply, but actually Michael's mother had squirreled away almost $500,000 from her husband's life insurance policy. She told herself that she was saving the money for Michael to "go to college when he gets better."

Michael never did get better, but thanks to his mother's care, his living situation was adequate. When Michael was forty-one, his mother died in her sleep. He had not ventured out of the apartment by himself in years and had no idea what to do or how to reach out for help.

Eventually, neighbors found him and Adult Protective Services was called. The court appointed a guardian to manage Michael's money. Without the familiar companionship of his mother, Michael became so agitated that he was placed in a state mental institution. Since he had significant cash assets, Michael was not eligible for SSI or Medicaid benefits.

Within five years, due to the extensive financial demands that his deteriorating mental condition required, Michael's assets were completely depleted. With no one to advocate for his needs and carry on the wishes of his mother, all the money that Michael's mother had saved for his future was unable to help him. The loss of his mother, his community, and a consistent caregiver, were powerful factors precipitating Michael's deep isolation and tragic decline.

Despite her cerebral palsy, Shira was an extremely bright and af-
fectionate child who gave her parents much nachas. She
accomplished a great deal to overcome her severe disability. By the
time she was in her teens, it was clear her medical needs and re-
sultant disability would limit her ability to compete in the
workforce. Her parents were very grateful for the Medicaid and SSI
income she received that allowed them to provide for Shira without
draining the family's resources.

One family member who was particularly proud of her was her
great uncle. Quietly, without anyone's knowledge, he bequeathed
Shira twenty five percent of his estate, stating in his will, "I
want Shira to be taken care of so she shouldn't have to worry
about anything."

Several months after receiving her inheritance, no insignificant
sum, Shira was notified by the Social Security Administration that
her benefits were being discontinued. Not only that, Shira owed
Social Security all the payments they had sent for the last nine
months, since she had acquired her great-uncle's money. Shira and
her parents had to spend her own money for her medical care and
personal needs, significantly reducing the generous sum her uncle
had left her.

ADVOCACY/CASE MANAGEMENT

There are professionals available to oversee the services a disabled child receives throughout his lifetime. An agency hired for
this purpose can have a social worker attend case conferences,
monitor changes in treatment and ensure that the child receives
the highest quality of care.

Beyond the basics of food and shelter, family members may also
want to ensure that their loved one receives that extra special attention that will make his life more meaningful and enjoyable. The
care agreement might stipulate special visits, outings, gifts,
Shabbatonim and other ongoing services the agency would provide that personalize the care of the disabled individual and add
to his quality of life.

TRUST FUNDS

Many parents don't know that if they leave assets directly to
their disabled child, he or she may lose government benefits. A

special law allows for the creation of a supplemental needs trust, which protects the disabled person's benefits while providing funds that will pay for the special services, goods and care he may need.

There is also a special type of trust that allows a disabled person who has large financial assets of his own to become immediately eligible for Social Security and Medicaid without any penalty or waiting period.

Parents of children in residences are often under the misconception that SSI, SSD and Medicaid will cover all of their child's needs and therefore there is no reason to set aside extra money in a trust. This is not always the case. Medicaid will not cover dental implants and bridges required for tooth loss or severe decay, a problem prevalent in the disabled population. New, non-approved medical procedures or advanced prosthetic/mobility devices may not be covered by Medicaid either.

When planning for the future, parents should keep in mind that their disabled child will one day become a geriatric patient. While nursing homes might provide adequate care, they do not provide as much social stimulation as a group home. Funds put aside for the future needs of this child might make all the difference in allowing him or her to remain in his current residence among peers. Additional aides could be hired for an older resident to supplement the house staff and meet the disabled person's complex medical needs.

A trust fund, set up as part of a will or life insurance bequeathal, can make all the difference in the quality of life for a disabled person. Often people with modest financial means make the mistake of thinking narrowly in this regard. Twenty-five or even a hundred thousand dollars sounds like a lot of money, but it is really a small sum in relation to the lifetime care needs of a disabled child.

The typical middle class family may have assets for a trust they may not even be aware of — such as a home of considerable equity, a life insurance plan or pension benefits. Some pension plans provide lifetime payments to children who are disabled. Parents employed by a government agency should look into this carefully. Yet, hard-earned benefits can be completely neutralized by Social Security income limits if they are not put into a trust.

Even young disabled children can amass assets and income, whether it's an inheritance, a substantial bar mitzvah gift or a lawsuit settlement. Unless these funds are put into a supplemental needs trust, the child is in danger of losing needs-based government benefits. Parents who have received a windfall of cash should consider using the money to set up a supplemental needs trust or life insurance policy with the child as a beneficiary.

A trust that has sufficient funds to sponsor intensive case management and other supports can also assure that a moderately disabled person can continue to live in his parents' home, or perhaps an apartment near other relatives or familiar community people.

Parents might consider bequeathing their own home to a community residence program so it may be used to house their child as well as other disabled people. Not only would this be a great merit and charity, it can also assure that the child will be well provided for in a familiar environment.

GUARDIANSHIP

According to the law, a person over the age of eighteen is assumed competent unless proven otherwise. Therefore, it is important that parents take action to formally become their child's guardian during their lifetime, as well as to appoint a standby guardian to take their place should they become incapacitated or die. If this is not done, any future medical procedure or intervention may have to be approved by the court or a court-designated guardian, who may have little knowledge or sensitivity to the child's needs and personal history.

Many parents plan for siblings to take over the care of a disabled child. Instead of creating a trust, parents can economically write the disabled child out of the will. They can give the money to the designated sibling with the understanding that that money will be used exclusively for the disabled sibling. This allows the disabled child to receive benefits that have an income threshold such as Medicaid or SSI without penalty, since technically the money does not belong to him.

But the money legally belongs to the sibling and is subject to whatever financial issues he has. For example, should the non-disabled sibling get divorced or have creditors, this money is equally subject to legal actions of the contesting party and is in no way sheltered or protected. Any inheritance tax implications will become the full responsibility of the non-disabled sibling.

Parents of a disabled child need to make formal and careful financial plans for their child. With the help of a case manager, a trust fund and a guardian, a disabled child can be well cared for the rest of his life.

SECTION SEVEN
Religion and Psychology Intersect

The ideas and values of religion and psychology conflict, yet there is a deep commonality. Both systems of thought seek to probe the inner mind, to explain why people do what they do, and try to help people succeed in their social and personal goals. Both religion and many psychological theories view human behavior not as an accident, but as a product of experiences and choices. In truth, every facet of life has an aspect of both religion and psychology within it.

63

Religious Conflicts in Psychotherapy

Patients are not always comfortable when they enter our psychotherapy practice. Many patients feel their religious values may be violated by seeking the counsel of a professional. But these patients have not yet grasped the method and goal of the psychotherapy process. There really is no contradiction. Let us examine several questions that have been presented to us.

A Guide for Life

> Why can't the Torah or mussar sefarim (works involving character development) solve my problems? Isn't the Torah supposed to be a guide for life?

True, the Torah is not just a legal and moral code — it is a guide for personal development. Rambam (*Mishneh Torah, Hilchos Deos* 2:1) clearly advocates seeking rabbinic counsel for illnesses of the soul. Why should an observant Jew, who is having family strife or other emotional problems, need to consult a therapist? Why not a *mussar sefer* or a rabbi?

To counter this dilemma, let us ask another question. If the Torah is a source for all wisdom, why go to the latest doctors for medical treatment? Torah scholars should be able to treat patients for the most severe physical illnesses. Why go to a mechanic if your car breaks down? Somewhere in the Torah there must be the wisdom necessary to solve even that!

Psychotherapy, though less concrete than medicine, can be categorized as a form of medical treatment. Observant Jews have been taking advantage of the latest medical interventions for centuries. A visit to a psychotherapist presents the same issues as a visit to the doctor, whose knowledge is also obtained from sources outside the Torah realm.

Yes, psychotherapy deals with intangible areas of thoughts and emotions, but in principle it is no different from seeking medical help. Ramban states, "When G-d is pleased with the actions of a man, he has no need for doctors" (*Ramban, Vayikra* 26:11). In the days of the prophets, an ailing individual needed only to visit the prophet of G-d who would direct him on a path of repentance and prayer. In our generation, medical doctors are widely accepted. The same logic applies to psychotherapists.

Still, how does a person choose the best route to solve his problem? Will the advice of a rabbi or the study of *mussar* suffice, or is psychotherapy necessary? Let us compare and contrast these options.

The rabbi is a representative of the Torah. He provides advice on how to live life successfully in accordance with the Torah, the guidebook for how humans ought to act and behave. Though there are many aspects of the Torah that can be personally beneficial and enjoyable, and it is important to take pleasure in leading a Torah life, the Torah perspective does not consider material pleasure — or happiness based on material pleasure in this world — as an ultimate goal.

If a religious person can use the advice and guidelines of the Torah to overcome personal and emotional difficulties and achieve happiness — wonderful. But many people find that despite their efforts to improve their character and relationships through mussar *and other religious advice, they simply cannot get a handle on depression, for example, or maintain peaceful familial relationships.*

There is a popular misconception that a good therapist gives good advice. Actually, a good therapist should not be giving any advice. People experiencing emotional difficulties already have legions of friends and relatives giving them advice, telling them what to do. Even strangers volunteer unsolicited advice!

The real goal is to teach people *how* to fish, not to give them fish. This may sound simple, but it actually takes years of training, experience, and a good deal of natural talent. The psychotherapist must master two opposite and conflicting skills. He must join the patient emotionally, trying to understand the situation completely from the patient's perspective. Yet he must also stay detached enough to help the patient view his own situation more objectively.

The patient has a goal. The therapist's role is to help the patient remove the obstacles that prevent him from accomplishing that goal. The therapist is less concerned with moral right and wrong. Through effective therapy, a patient can recognize what personal feelings and choices contribute to his current difficulties and what other possible feelings, thoughts, actions, and choices are available that may be more conducive to achieving his goal.

How does psychotherapy help? All it does is help people understand their own situation better! Yet many people who have had a true and professionally executed psychotherapeutic process find it extremely valuable and helpful. Why?

Most people experiencing difficulties get way too much advice, and comparatively little patience, understanding and respect. Not many friends have the patience to sit and listen to someone whine. Not many friends will sit and lend encouragement while their friend works through the possible choices and solutions — without persuading him to follow this or that advice. A really good friend may be able to do this for a short while, but a therapist is trained to do this for an extended period of time. People change slowly, and a skilled therapist works accordingly — slowly and with patience.

Therapists are trained to recognize patterns and behaviors that the patient himself may not be aware of. A person can be driven by unconscious motivations — and the therapist will help him become more conscious of them and act accordingly.

For example, a person may come for treatment because he is unhappy in his career. He is fired from job after job because he gets into fights and power struggles with supervisors. His spouse or parents have already given him plenty of advice, such as, "Why do you have to argue so much? Why are you so proud?" Or, "Get a new job first before your current one!"

Why doesn't this advice work? Presumably, some underlying condition prevents this person from making more practical judgments. That is the work of the therapist to uncover. Perhaps the patient has a career goal that he is afraid to follow, so he is constantly restless in his current positions. Is there a more realistic and constructive way to pursue this goal?

Or, maybe the boss is too central in the patient's mind. He looks for compliments and self-esteem from his boss. When he gets criticism instead of praise, he reacts in a non-constructive manner more befitting of an adolescent bickering with his father. The treatment for this person may involve helping him learn to see his boss as less central in his life, and explore other neglected areas of his personal life that can more appropriately meet his needs for positive feedback.

The Torah is a guide for life, and *mussar* works are comprehensive. In some instances, the study of mussar does effect a change in personality. But psychotherapy uses a different means. While *mussar* dictates morals and advice directly, psychotherapy teaches a person about himself, enabling a patient to make the change — if he so chooses.

THE RELIGIOUS LADDER

> *Can I see a therapist who is not as religious as me, not religious at all, or even not Jewish?*

A true professional would not try to impose his views and values on a patient. In fact, the opposite is true. The therapist's goal is simply to help the patient understand himself better. He will endeavor to develop and strengthen the patient's decision-making and judgment capacities.

But not all therapists are able to resist imposing their values on patients. Even a subtle gesture — a slight frown or a raised eyebrow — is a source of influence that has no place in a therapeutic relationship. Imagine a non-religious marital therapist who frowns when the couple is discussing some issue related to family purity, inadvertently trivializing the importance of a key tenet of faith for the couple. How much worse the situation can become if the couple has disagreements over religious matters!

Equally damaging is the religious therapist whose *halachic* views differ from his patient. A patient comes for help with a mental health condition, not to receive guidance on *halachic* issues. Well-intentioned and sincerely devout people can have drastically different values and practices. Should it really be the place of a therapist to mix in?

Ultimately, whether one should choose an irreligious or non-Jewish therapist depends on the quality of the therapist and the judgment of the patient. In our own experience with *halachic* authorities, the general consensus is that it is preferable to work with a therapist who is observant — but there are always exceptions.

All factors have to be carefully considered, on a case by case basis — the reputation of the therapist, the age, character and impressionability of the patient, the depth and severity of the problem, the geographic accessibility to *Orthodox* therapists of quality.

Questions and concerns regarding values and religion should be addressed with the potential therapist from the beginning of treatment, to ensure appropriate care and sensitivity in this matter.

Evil Speech

> *If I speak about my relationship problems, and it involves*
> *complaints against other people, will it be loshon hora*
> *(evil speech)?*

Although we advise our readers to confirm this with their personal rabbi, *loshon hora* is not forbidden when spoken for a constructive purpose without intention to harm. (See Chofetz Chaim, *Shmiras HaLoshon*, Hilchos *Loshon Hora* 10; *Hilchos Rechilus* 9) As for rechilus, speech spoken to spread hatred among people, a therapist's obligatory confidentiality may be a mitigating factor.

A good therapist can recognize the subtle difference between expressing feelings, which is constructive in therapy, and attacking others. If patient intends to malign and hurt the person he is speaking about, not only is it *loshon hora*, it is also very unhelpful to the therapy process. In this situation, a therapist can confront the patient on the grounds that his angry venting without any introspection implies resistance to treatment and self-knowledge.

Observing Mitzvos

> *What if I do not want to keep certain mitzvos or am*
> *unsure if I want to — will you try to convince me one*
> *way or the other? What if my spouse or child disagrees*

with me about a religious issue — will you, an Orthodox
therapist, be forced to take sides based on your beliefs?

The short answer is no. As we have explained, most psychotherapy treatments require the therapist to remain neutral and non-judgmental regarding religious and moral beliefs. In order to understand and solve emotional problems, the patient must be assured that he is free to discuss and explore any issue regardless of how the therapist may personally feel about the matter.

The therapist's personal feelings are not part of the patient-therapist contract and must not be allowed to interfere. Parenthetically, there is an exception to this non-interference rule. By law, if the patient is in danger of harming himself or others, or in cases of child abuse or neglect, the authorities must be notified, and the therapist should make every effort to intervene. But the law makes no such allowances for Torah violations.

The discussion of a patient's moral and religious dilemmas poses more of a problem for the practitioner than the patient. A therapist allows a patient to explore choices and discuss all issues freely and without reservation, an absolutely necessary ingredient for a proper therapeutic environment. What about the therapist's religious obligations?

The Torah prohibits aiding or encouraging sin — not to place a stumbling block in front of someone, not to assist a person in sin. Without issuing a definitive *halachic* ruling on the matter, it is our practice to ascertain that both patient and therapist understand clearly that the therapist is an impartial observer. He does not encourage any particular path to take and so avoids these prohibitions.

But the Torah also commands us to rebuke one's fellow Jew. Not only is a person prohibited to encourage another person to sin, he is also commanded to instruct another person not to sin.

This dilemma can arise in any profession. Let us consider the case of an accountant whose non-observant boss mentions that he's going golfing on Saturday. Does he have to risk his job and tell his boss that he really should keep Shabbos?

Perhaps yes. But maybe not.

A lengthy sermon to his boss on the value of keeping Shabbos will likely be ignored. Wouldn't it be more helpful for this employee to continuously model exemplary moral and family behavior? Would this not subtly but convincingly show the value of the Orthodox lifestyle and serve as the ultimate fulfillment of rebuke?

We have been given to understand, to fulfill the Torah commandment, rebuke does not have to be with words. The Torah injunction is a directive to influence a person to change. With supportive yet objective feedback, psychotherapy enables patients to make morally superior decisions. It is far more effective than simple advice. The very neutrality of the therapy process allows a greater fulfillment of the Torah commandment.

64

A Hypothetical Debate

Due to relatively stable and affluent conditions, Orthodox Jewry has become sophisticated not only in their knowledge of Torah, but in scientific and psychological issues as well. Sometimes, this superior knowledge makes it difficult for committed Jews to understand aspects of the tradition within the context of psychology. It's hard to distinguish moral failings from mental illnesses such as depression or addiction.

If a person is "lazy," should he seek counsel from his rabbi, or should he seek psychotherapeutic treatment for depression? A person feels unable to control certain behaviors such as gambling, drinking or promiscuity. Is he a victim of his *yetzer hara*, requiring a good dose of *mussar* to overcome this vice? Or is he perhaps the victim of a compulsive disorder, which needs treatment?

Let us take an example from Rabbi Yehuda HaLevi's *Kuzari*, who applied the style of classic Talmudic give and take, used by diligent Torah students for thousands of years, to matters of faith and reason. Our hypothetical debate will flesh out the opinions of the *baal mussar*, one who is constantly working on character development, and the psychotherapist. Whose services should be sought and when?

> **Baal Mussar**: Jewish people have always utilized available medical technology to cure their illnesses, but I have serious misgivings about turning to psychology to solve mental problems. Medical doctors treat illnesses that have origins in a body malfunction — such as strep throat or a fractured

bone. The cause of these illnesses can be empirically detected and measured via throat culture or x-ray.

But a mental illness is based on internal attitudes and emotions. This is a matter of the soul and should be dealt with by those who understand the soul — those knowledgeable in Torah and *mussar*.

Psychotherapist: You are echoing the words of Thomas Szasz, a psychiatrist who has been one of the twentieth century's most outspoken critics of modern psychology and psychotherapy. He writes in *The Myth of Mental Illness*:

> Mental illness is a metaphor. The word disease denotes a demonstrable biological process that affects the bodies of living organisms (plants, animals, and humans). The term mental illness refers to the undesirable thoughts, feelings, and behaviors of persons. Classifying thoughts, feelings, and behaviors as diseases is a logical and semantic error, like classifying the whale as a fish. As the whale is not a fish, mental illness is not a disease. Individuals with brain diseases (bad brains) or kidney diseases (bad kidneys) are literally sick. Individuals with mental diseases (bad behaviors), like societies with economic diseases (bad fiscal policies), are metaphorically sick.

When an unconventionally gifted child is diagnosed with ADD (attention deficit disorder) because of his unusual behavior in a school setting, Dr. Szasz's arguments have merit. But this is not the whole picture. Mental illness is as difficult to identify as it is to treat, but this does not disqualify it as an illness and psychotherapy as a treatment.

Alzheimer's cannot be confirmed without an autopsy. And there is no treatment that is 100% effective. Does this mean that doctors who try to treat this condition are not performing any medical service?

A person who is suffering is ill. Freud's definition of mental health is when a person is free to work and to love. Anyone who feels in some way held back from having success at work or in his relationships can consider psychotherapy as a way to remedy his problem.

Baal Mussar: You pointed out that Freud's definition of mental health is when a person is free to work and to love. My question remains — why should a psychotherapist treat such a problem? The inability to love or work is rooted in a moral failing.

A person needs to overcome his evil inclination and find room in his heart to love, find the energy to overcome his laziness! The Talmud teaches us the solution, "[G-d says] I have created the evil inclination but I also have created the antidote — Torah" (*Kiddushin* 30b).

I agree that it is helpful to turn to other people for advice on how to overcome moral lapses. But psychology — based on theories of a known *apikores* (heretic) and atheist — that should be the last place to turn!

Psychotherapist: If the theories are sound and helpful, who cares whether or not they were authored by an *apikores*?

Baal Mussar: Okay, I see your point. In fact, Rambam raised no objection to using appropriate secular sources to aid in moral character development — he included such sources in his commentary on *Avos*. The sources are deliberately not cited so the reader would not reject the advice of a non-Jew.

But this still worries me. Only a sage with the stature of Rambam could sort out the character-building advice from the heretical. People like us can unwittingly be swayed by subtle unholy influences.

Psychotherapist: Fine, let's put that aside. You maintain that many of the so-called mental problems such as depression, marital problems and various compulsions and addictions are due to moral failings. According to your opinion, a person should seek rabbinic counsel, study Torah and *mussar* to improve his character and overcome his evil inclination. Tell me, how successful have you been in helping people suffering from these conditions?

Baal Mussar: Well, it's not easy overcoming the *yetzer hara*. We've been trying to win this battle ever since Adam ate from the Tree of Knowledge. But calling it a disease and trying to treat it doesn't make it any easier to solve! Nowadays, people have no sense of individual responsibility. A person can shoot his parents dead and be let off scot-free because he had a traumatic childhood!

Psychotherapist: As a professional, it disturbs me greatly how psychological theories are distorted and misused by people whose true agenda is to free themselves from any sense of personal accountability.

But what if psychotherapy can offer you a new tool in your arsenal for fighting the *yetzer hara*? Surely, in your counseling you've come across cases where a person feels completely helpless against his own impulses. Perhaps you have been frustrated when counseling a husband who just cannot control his anger, no matter how hard he tries. Or perhaps you have come across someone unhappy and depressed, who just can't snap out of it.

Baal Mussar: I admit, sometimes I come across cases I cannot seem to help, particularly those who are depressed or suffering from compulsions they cannot control. But I think I get frustrated because of my own impatience. Just because the person isn't feeling better right away doesn't mean the *mussar* isn't helping. Time is a very important factor.

Indeed, the Steipler Rav *ZT"L* was often consulted regarding individuals' emotional difficulties. Regarding a yeshiva student who complained of not being able to feel any satisfaction or pleasure in any of his activities, he states:

> People come to me with problems similar to this often and I endeavor to convince them this is a passing condition. I inform them that I am aware of people like them, who after a year or two slowly returned to normal (*Eitzos VeHadrachos Meyosad al Michtavei Maran Baal HeKehilas Yaakov*, 58).

Regarding someone who obsessed over certain ritual requirements, and was unable to stop worrying no matter how many times he verified that the *halachic* requirements were met, the Steipler wrote the following:

Such thinking is a tactic of the *yetzer hara* in order to make observance of the commandments so burdensome that he will eventually, G-d forbid, shirk the yoke of the Torah ... He should realize he will not endure this suffering forever, because it will eventually pass over time. The main point is that he should follow the rulings of rabbinic authorities without analyzing their reasons and without second guessing them (*Ibid*, 55).

Psychotherapist: Many psychotherapists would agree, particularly with the Steipler's observation that cases of depression eventually improve over time. There are certain cognitive treatments that are also compatible with the Steipler's approach to the obsessive-compulsive behavior described above.

But even if you believe that certain emotional problems are rooted in the *yetzer hara*, wouldn't it be helpful to understand how the human mind works? Psychology explains what is behind this *yetzer hara*.

Baal Mussar: That would be very interesting. After all, even though we believe that when the rain falls it is G-d's will, this does not preclude us from studying the science of meteorology. So too, though we believe in the Divine soul, it should not preclude us from studying the mechanisms of the mind.

Psychotherapist: According to traditional psychoanalytic or psychodynamic theory, there is something akin to what you would call the *yetzer hara* within man. In brief, the human personality is divided into three conceptual categories: the Id, the Ego, and the Superego.

The Id is the instinctive part of the mind we are all born with and it seeks immediate gratification, no matter the consequences. The Ego is the agent of the mind that mediates between the inner reality — the Id's demands — and the outer reality, practical considerations such as personal safety. The Ego is developed secondarily as the child learns the dangers of immediately acting on his impulses.

The Superego is the policing agent of the mind, and corresponds with what is commonly known as the conscience.

The Superego is developed last by the child, as he begins to internalize his parents' expectations and standards. (*Collected Writings of Sigmund Freud, The Ego and the Id*, 19:33-39)

To illustrate: A person sees a nice piece of chocolate cake behind the window of a bakery. The Id screams, "I want it now!" If it were up to his Id, the person would jump over the countertop and stuff the entire cake into his mouth.

But at this point the Ego takes over, holding back the impulse. The Ego plans how to get the cake on practical terms, "Hmmm, let me see. Do I have enough money to buy this cake? Where does the line start? Okay, let me wait and politely try to get the saleslady's attention …"

The internal drama may stop there, or depending on a person's internalized values from his parents, the Superego might chime in, "Should I really be eating cake? Is it good for my health? Perhaps it is too gluttonous? Is the cake dairy — am I *fleishig*?"

This oversimplifies it a bit, but that's the basic idea. A mentally healthy person will have all three personality components working together in balance. The Ego should be the strongest and mediating between the two extremes. A person should not be too greedy or impulsive, but neither should he be paralyzed by guilt and indecision.

Baal Mussar: Rambam offers similar advice in the first chapter of *Hilchos Deos*. And Ibn Ezra makes similar observations in his commentary on *Koheles* (7:2). Ibn Ezra notes that character traits such as anger and mirth are alternately encouraged and then discouraged. He concludes that these seeming contradictions imply a need for balance among the different aspects of the personality, which do seem to correspond with what you have described:

> There are within a person three souls. One is the *nefesh*, the living force … that desires to eat. The second soul is the animal soul, which experiences the five senses and allows a person to ambulate from place to place …[The] third soul is called the *neshama*, which discerns between truth and falsehood. The second soul is in the middle between the other two souls and the Almighty planted man's intellect … to help fulfill each desire at

its appropriate time, to assist a person in fulfilling the commandments, to establish everything according to its proper proportion.

Psychotherapist: Our sages were certainly astute observers of human nature. But I have not yet explained how a therapist uses these basic features of human personality in order to help people. When a person tries and tries to change a particular behavior, there may be subconscious reasons preventing him from succeeding. While on the surface he insists he does not want to behave this way, on a subconscious level the behavior may be serving an important need. Unless the subconscious need is understood and satisfied in another way or otherwise taken into account, the person will not be able to change.

Baal Mussar: Are you saying a person has no free choice? That he is under control of his subconscious mind? This completely contradicts the fundamental Torah rule of free will! (See *Avos* 3:15; *Berachos* 33b.)

Psychotherapist: Not necessarily. Let me first explain how the unconscious mind works. A person is aware of only a fraction of the thoughts and feelings that are going on in his mind — the tip of the iceberg. Some thoughts have to be unconscious to protect the general integrity of the personality from feelings and thoughts that may be perceived as too harmful or painful.

For example, imagine a child who is abused by his parents. In this child's mind there must be a multitude of conflicting feelings such as love, fear and rage. But in order to survive, the child must repress his rage — possibly to the point where he is not even aware of it. If he impulsively lets his anger out while he is being abused, he will only suffer more.

As a result of this tumultuous emotional and psychological process, this child will have difficulty acknowledging or responding to his own feelings even as he matures into an adult. Although this repression of rage into the subconscious was a healthy adaptation during his abusive childhood, it could become problematic. He might feel depressed and not know why, or be emotionally unresponsive toward his own wife and children.

Baal Mussar: There is something similar to the concepts of repression and the subconscious in regard to the biblical account of the chief wine steward who "forgot" about Yosef.

The verse states, "And the chief wine steward did not remember Yosef, and he forgot him" (*Bereishis* 40:23). The Ohr HaChaim observes that the wine steward did not want to remember him, therefore he forgot him. Rashi also elaborates on the wine steward's uncharitable attitude toward Yosef. (See *Bereishis* 41:12) Though the wine steward forgot Yosef accidentally, he actually had a wish to forget him and removed him from his mind.

Another proof for the subconscious mind is in the daily service. Many prayer books include a supplication to be recited before prayer attributed to R' Elimelech of Lezhinsk, author of *Noam Elimelech*, who lived in the 1700's. The prayer beseeches G-d to protect us from disruptive thoughts and feelings which "are known to us, and unknown to us." This seems to indicate that one can indeed have unconscious thoughts and feelings.

And how about *hatavas chalom*? Someone who has a troubling dream that may be warning him of impending tragedy will accept a fast upon himself. The fast serves as a penance to help annul the evil decree.

The *halacha* also states that a person should fast even if he dreamed about a tragedy occurring to someone else. Why? Because though it was another person in the dream, the premonition is really about the dreamer himself. (*Mishna Berurah* 220:4)

Psychotherapist: I believe this is what is called an ego defense, when an intolerable feeling is displaced onto someone else. The dreamer was given a premonition about himself, but it was too frightening, so his unconscious mind changed the victim into someone else.

All of these proofs are great! I'm glad you found these examples in the Torah, because actually, the unconscious is an unproven theory with scant empirical evidence affirming its existence.

There is a fascinating study where people were flashed messages without being consciously aware of it. A tachiscope was used to display an image — for example, the word "walk" — for a fraction of a second. Some participants actually responded by getting up to walk, apparently unaware of seeing the command. When they were questioned as to why they arose, they gave some excuse like, "I needed to get a soda."

The subconscious part of the mind saw the original request to walk, but on another level the person was not cognizant of it. To protect against the anxiety of not knowing why he got up to go somewhere, yet another unconscious part of his mind fabricated a reason that the conscious mind fully believed! The experiment is more complex than this and takes on many forms. (Wright, *The Moral Animal*, 275)

Even without the Torah and scientific proofs, just the theory of unconscious mind and its associated mechanisms has proven to be a useful tool in understanding mental processes and dynamics. With this understanding, psychotherapists have found effective treatments of various problems. Of course, this experiment also clearly shows how the mind can rationalize any behavior, even if there is a deeper reason beyond the person's conscious awareness.

Baal Mussar: I understand the concept of the unconscious mind better now. But can you explain how a person still has free will if he is constantly in the grips of subconscious thoughts and motivations?

Psychotherapist: I think we would all agree that every person is a product of his experiences and the decisions made in response to them, both conscious and unconscious. Right?

Let us imagine a person who has a terrible habit of biting his nails. No matter how hard he tries to stop, he cannot do so.

Our nail biter seeks the help of a psychodynamic therapist. The therapist will try to determine what purpose this nail biting habit serves, which may be subconscious at this point. Is the nail biting some form of repressed anger or hostility? Is it representative of a need to inflict pain and/or punish himself?

If this nail biter cannot successfully understand the role his habit serves in his subconscious life, all efforts to change may not be effective if the unconscious need is stronger than the conscious need to bite his nails. Psychodynamic-oriented therapy can conceivably help in this process by making the subconscious motives conscious and providing the person with an opportunity to make a new decision.

So before he seeks treatment, our nail biter is helpless to his unconsciously repressed anger or self-hate. Is this person *halachically* liable if he bites his nails on Shabbos?

Consider that his current situation is a culmination of previous choices, judgments and behaviors that were once conscious. No one made him choose to become who he became, and he could have chosen different ways of handling his anger.

The "self," equally difficult to define spiritually and psychologically, can encompass both the conscious and the subconscious. A person cannot escape the ultimate responsibility of who he is and what he does, no matter what level of awareness he is exercising at that moment.

Baal Mussar: Our sages say, "One sin begets another" (*Avos* 4:2) and, "When a person commits the same sin twice, it will be rendered as if it is permissible in his eyes" (*Yoma* 86b). It's similar to what you are saying. A person made the initial choice to sin and now his compulsion to sin is even more powerful. His free will has been affected by his own previous choice.

Psychotherapist: So, it would seem there are many areas where psychology and the Torah are in agreement.

Baal Mussar: This really should not be so surprising. Our sages knew the workings of man intimately. It helped them understand G-d's handiwork and guide people in the ways of the Torah. To whatever extent modern psychology has uncovered truths about the personality, there no doubt will be reflections of this in our tradition.

65

Controlling
Thoughts and Feelings

Many people feel pathologically guilty about inner thoughts, to the extent that they require psychotherapeutic intervention. But according to the Torah, in many circumstances, we are not required to control our feelings — just our actions.

Ramban supports this notion in his commentary on the verse, "Love your neighbor" (*Vayikra* 19:17), or more correctly translated as, "Be loving toward your neighbor." Ramban asserts that though it is impossible to be forced to *feel* love toward a fellow person, the Torah can command us to *act* in a loving manner.

But there are other instances when the Torah does require us to control our feelings. For example, the Torah prohibits being jealous of a neighbor's possessions (*Shemos* 20:14); immoral thoughts are prohibited (*Shulchan Aruch, Even Haezer* 23:3). Here the Torah does indeed dictate feeling. How can these commandments be explained according to Ramban's principle?

THOU SHALL NOT COVET?

Ibn Ezra (*Shemos* 20:14) poses a similar question to the Ramban's. A person sees something beautiful — he desires it. How can the Torah reasonably command us *not* to want it? How can the Torah command a *feeling*?

Ibn Ezra's position is as follows: A person does not usually covet something totally outside the realm of possibility. It would be ludicrous to be jealous of a bird because it can fly. Everything we have, including wealth and material success, is a gift from G-d that is tailor-made specifically for us. If a person would just take that to heart, he would have no cause to covet another's possessions.

It is not the feeling or desire we are expected to control. The Torah expects us to control the thoughts that set us up for jealousy. If we recognize that everything comes from G-d — that G-d has given each of us that which will enable us to attain our purpose in life — then we have no reason to be jealous. Our obligation is to train our thoughts so certain feelings are less likely to arise.

Cognitive behavior therapy is similar to Ibn Ezra's approach. Feelings can be changed through the conscious change of cognition and behavior.

FORBIDDEN THOUGHTS

The Ezer MeKodesh (*Shulchan Aruch, Even Haezer* 23:3) raises an interesting question: If the Torah forbids certain thoughts, how can a person study the portions of the Talmud and the related laws that describe — in painstaking detail — various forbidden and immoral acts? Would this not also constitute a violation? His response is as follows:

> No young unmarried student should hold himself back from studying from the holy books topics that can possibly cause forbidden thoughts, as found in the many laws that relate to marriage and women ... As long as it is in the manner and form that it is written in the holy books, there is no grounds for concern of even a remote violation ... The prohibition against thinking forbidden thoughts ... is not defined to include a transient thought that occurs in passing ... anyone who [subsequently] changes his train of thought to the best of his ability has no violation whatsoever, for the holy Torah was not given to angels. [But when] a person dwells on forbidden thoughts and awakens a desire in his soul with images in his imagination ... this behavior makes an impression on the person's character to awaken in him, G-d forbid, a chance to be drawn to commit immorality ... and only this kind of thought is forbidden, not anything else.

So there is room within the Torah to allow a person natural feelings and thoughts. But what about actions? Is it possible that a person could be psychologically compelled to commit a sin, and therefore not be held responsible?

From a Jewish philosophical perspective, there are certain categories where a person is acquitted of responsibility for his actions, such as insanity (*Chaggigah* 3a) or an extremely high level of intoxication known as "the drunkenness of Lot" (*Eruvin* 65a). But what about the sane, able-bodied person, who is overcome by temptation for a particular sin to the extent that he cannot control himself?

The Torah stresses and treasures the concept of free will. "All is in the hands of Heaven except for fear of Heaven" (*Niddah* 16b). G-d grants each person different qualities — strength, intelligence and wealth; but the moral decisions each person makes are his own choice and his own responsibility. Each person has the power to choose to do good or evil.

In seeming contradiction to this, there is a fascinating teaching found in the Talmud which appears to speak directly to this issue:

> Rabbi Elai the elder said, "If a man sees that he is succumbing to temptation, he should go to a place where he is not recognized, don black clothing and headdress, and do as his heart pleases so that he shall not come to desecrate G-d's name in public." But this is not so! For we learned in a *braisa* that ..."It is fitting for him to have not been born ... he who commits a sin in secret!" This is not a question. The latter is referring to when he can squelch his desire and the former is referring to when he cannot. (*Kiddushin* 40a)

At first glance, the Talmud seems to be making two revolutionary statements. One, a person may indeed be in a state where he cannot control his temptation. And two, in such a case, there is an accepted and permitted course of action to follow.

But upon closer scrutiny, neither of these two points is proven. The Talmud indicates that it is indeed possible that a person can *feel* as if he cannot control his temptation, but it may very well be within his ability to do so. And the Talmud does not absolve or permit the sin — it advises the best mode of conduct, should a person feel the sin is simply inevitable.

The commentary of Tosafos limits this even further. The Talmud never really expects the person to actually follow through with the sinful act! The process described was merely a way of stalling and making the sinful act potentially uncomfortable and humiliating, so the person will ultimately win over his temptation.

So we see that while temptation can be great, and a person may genuinely feel he cannot overcome it, it is possible for him to withstand.

Let us examine the biblical case of the gentile captive woman who is permitted to be taken as a wife during the course of a war (*Devarim* 21:10-14). Regarding this, the Talmud states, "The Torah is only speaking to assuage the evil inclination" (*Kiddushin* 21b).

War is a bloodthirsty business. A soldier has to throw his inhibition to the wind and become ruthless. In such a free state, a soldier could be overcome with temptation and act immorally. To counteract this, the Torah put in place a process by which he may lawfully take this woman as his wife.

So the Torah does accede that a person can be completely overcome with temptation to sin! But this is the exception to the rule. Marrying the gentile captive is the exception; the general rule is that people can indeed overcome temptation.

There is another case where the Talmud does seem to acknowledge that certain temptations cannot be overcome — but only when the sinful process has already begun. (See the concept of *yetzer albesha*, *Kesubos* 51b) A person who was forced to act sinfully might not be held culpable if the act is continued due to an inability to suppress desire.

The sages did acknowledge that in some situations, sin would be almost inevitable for the average population, and they therefore made appropriate allowances.

For example, the Talmud (*Shabbos* 153a) proactively permits a stranded wayfarer to ask a gentile to carry his wallet on Shabbos, even though this is normally forbidden by rabbinic injunction. The average person would not be able to withstand the sudden loss of a sum of money. If he would not be allowed to ask the gentile to carry the wallet for him — a rabbinic injunction — he would carry the wallet himself in a public domain and violate a Torah prohibition.

Here the sages allowed a legal safety valve, so the common folk would not be forced to withstand such a difficult crisis. But suppose this loophole had not been in place. The rabbis did not discuss the repercussions of one who violated the Torah commandment of carrying in this case. Would he have been exempt from this sin?

THE PSYCHOLOGICAL PERSPECTIVE

To refrain from psychological compulsions is not simply a matter of willpower. Certain conditions, such as obsessive-compulsive disorder, are actual psychiatric illnesses and cannot be corrected by applying willpower or administering additional — and often severe — *mussar*. Such erroneous beliefs only add to the shame and guilt that these people already suffer, and may even serve to increase the unwanted behavior.

Mental illness is an unwanted, unbidden affliction that can ruin a life if left untreated. In some cases, it can even lead to suicide. Proper treatment is a must and sometimes includes powerful medications.

Let us draw a distinction between moral responsibility and free choice. A person suffering from obsessive-compulsive disorder has a limited ability to overcome certain compulsions. Surely the person's moral liability or culpability must be equally limited as well. Blaming such a person or criticizing him harshly is harmful and unjust. A person whose mental condition causes him to lose touch with reality can't be held responsible for his actions.

But there are many gray areas. Not every compulsion is utterly overwhelming. While some forms of depression paralyze a person, others, though debilitating, do not rob the person of free will. A component of treatment for obsessive-compulsive disorder may involve learning how to withstand the anxiety generated by resisting the compulsion. Likewise with depression, a therapist may counsel the patient to choose to become more active, even if he does not feel like it.

A person suffering from mental illness is lost in a maze. It is theoretically possible to find a way out, but it is a difficult task without the help of a guide who is holding the map. Technically speaking, a person can choose to exit the maze of mental illness, but practically speaking, it is all but impossible.

Under expert therapeutic guidance, a person can begin to manage the thoughts and feelings that induce the behavior. Psychotherapy is not a passive experience, and the patient must work at least as hard as the therapist. Obviously, if change can be effected by collaborating with the patient, there must be a degree of free choice.

66

The Humility
of Moshe Rabbeinu

Dear Feuermans,

I have never been able to understand how the Torah could describe Moshe as "exceedingly humble, more than any other man" (Bamidbar 12:3). It seems impossible that Moshe could act as a leader and exercise his authority while still remaining humble.

In the very same portion that discusses Moshe's humility, we also find Moshe getting angry with G-d for burdening him with the Jewish people. Moshe complains, "Why have You done evil to Your servant ...by placing the burden of this nation upon me ... that You should request of me, 'Carry them in your bosom as a nursing mother carries her child'" (ibid. 11:11). And a few chapters later, when confronted with Korach's rebellion, the Torah explicitly states, "And Moshe was very angry" (ibid. 16:15).

How can one maintain two opposite character traits — firm and authoritarian, yet humble? I was hoping your dual perspective of Torah and psychology could help me unravel this mystery.

OUR RESPONSE

We think your difficulties can be resolved by redefining "humility." None of the commentaries explain Moshe's humility in terms of how he thought about himself. His extreme humility is defined in terms of his behavior and emotional responses.

Rashi uses the word "*savlan*," patient. Ramban states, "He does not retort in a quarrel." Targum Yonasan uses the phrase, "*anvesan bedaate*," humble in his opinions. These commentaries seem to be bothered by your same question.

Ibn Ezra concludes that Moshe was humble because he did not actively seek a position of leadership. Moshe wished, "If only G-d would make all of His nation into prophets ..." (*ibid*. 11:29).

The Torah's statement of Moshe's humility immediately follows Miriam and Aharon's criticism of Moshe. Aharon and Miriam complained that Moshe had no right to separate from his wife. They were also prophets, yet G-d did not instruct them to leave their spouses.

Moshe did not react to their accusations. Moshe could have easily retorted and revealed the elevated spiritual attainment he had achieved — his prophecy was qualitatively different from all other prophets, and justified separation from his wife. But Moshe remained humbly silent.

Moshe's humble behavior had nothing to do with his awareness of his abilities and his qualifications to lead the Jewish people. Moshe loathed the thought of his beloved Jewish nation being led by the insincere Korach, whose motive was self-aggrandizement and not the best interests of the people. He faced down his challengers with appropriate wrath.

Rashi seems to be troubled by his anger in this situation as well. Normally translated as "angry," Rashi interprets the verse "*vayichar liMoshe*" (ibid. 16:15) as "Moshe was saddened" about Korach's actions. Note that the verse differs from the standard form, "*vayichar Moshe*," leaving room for alternate interpretation.

Of practical psychological interest, these commentaries suggest that humility is based more on a person's actions than his thoughts. It is less important to think humbly; we must focus our efforts on acting humbly. Not false humility or acting insincerely, but behaving and thinking in the manner of one who is humble — listening to other people's opinions, judging others favorably. This goal is within the grasp of mere mortals to attain.

67

Helping Others, Protecting Ourselves

It is a well-known principle in the addiction treatment community: friends and relatives must not "enable" an addict, by providing any support that helps him maintain his current condition. A person who is abusing substances, or a mentally ill person who refuses to enter treatment or take his medication, must first "hit bottom" so he will stop denying his problem and realize the seriousness of his situation.

Some may feel this to be in conflict with our requirements to perform *chessed*, being kind to a fellow Jew. Is the principle of refusing to enable an addict or a mentally ill person contrary to Torah philosophy?

HELPING OTHERS

Kli Yakkar makes a novel and surprisingly contemporary derivation from the verse, "Do not witness your friend's donkey or ox fallen on the path and hide from them, [rather] you shall surely help raise them up with him" (*Shemos* 23:5). The end of the verse states "with him," excluding you from the obligation to assist an owner who stands idly by and refuses to help out. The Kli Yakkar extends this idea even further:

> From here we have a retort for many of our poor people who refuse to work or in some way take measures to support themselves. You are only obligated to help them if they put in their own efforts. (Kli Yakkar, *Shemos* 23:5)

Though it may be painful to watch, an addict or mentally ill person needs to show the first signs of commitment to treatment. He must commit to help himself if we are to step in to help him up, as proven by the Torah commandment to help "with him."

PROTECTING OURSELVES

An addict or mentally ill individual will often use and abuse his friends, manipulating, stealing or betraying. He may subsequently make a tremendous effort to repent and reform, but alas — his friend can be a friend no longer. Because even if the addict is sincere at the moment, he can easily backslide and hurt his friends again. We would like to avoid hurting his feelings — he suffered so much already. But can we protect ourselves?

Now that he has repented and changed his ways, to criticize him in any way for his past actions is a textbook violation of *ona'as devarim* (hurtful speech). The Talmud (*Bava Metzia* 58b) uses this very case as one of the examples of this prohibition. But the fear that a friend will regress and abuse once more remains.

While we are entitled to tread cautiously, the former addict is also entitled to basic human respect. He cannot be ignored. If he is still doing things that are offensive, he must be informed — if he'll be receptive. After all, the Torah says, "Do not hate your friend in your heart, rebuke him. And do not bear a sin on his behalf" (*Vayikra* 19:17).

If there is hatred bottled up in our hearts, we will hate him. But if we confront the friend directly and respectfully about his wrongdoings as the Torah commands, the hatred will evaporate. (See Rambam, *Mishneh Torah, Hilchos Deos* 6:6 and Ramban, *Vayikra* 19:17)

"Just forget about it, I forgive you" is not reconciliation. This is a superficial forgiveness and it does not take away the pain etched on the heart. The real message given here is, "You are not worthy enough to understand how much you hurt me. I won't give you a chance, or don't trust you, to make full amends by telling you what you did wrong."

But this is a misdeed. This newly reformed friend is denied the opportunity to learn about his failures; denied the chance to make true restitution.

We can never hate him. Does this mean we have to love him? We can fulfill the Torah requirement of "Love thy neighbor" by *acting* lovingly toward him, with the respect and kindness every human being deserves.

68

Excessive Guilt

Guilt is a subjective feeling — for any given offense, there is a significant variance among people as to how guilty they feel. If a loved one is constantly beating himself up over his imagined or real offenses, it will be difficult indeed to convince him that his guilt is unwarranted. After all, who can say what is really a grave offense and what is a minor offense? To a righteous person, even the most minor lapse is a spiritual cataclysm.

MINOR OR MAJOR?

The Mishna states, "Be careful with the minor commandments as with the severe ones, because one cannot know the true reward for each commandment" (*Avos* 2:1). So we cannot compare the relative value of one commandment to another.

Rambam explains that this dictum applies only to positive commandments, as the Torah does not specify the punishment for neglecting them. But the Torah almost always describes the punishment for violating a prohibition — the death penalty for one prohibition, a monetary fine for another. By examining the severity of the punishment, it is quite obvious which commandment carries more weight.

DISPLACING GUILT

According to some psychological theories, a person may feel irrationally guilty due to an unconscious guilt about a serious matter, a matter that the person cannot consciously accept. The person unconsciously displaces this guilty feeling onto more mundane or trivial issues.

An example of this is survivor's guilt, the guilt experienced after safely emerging from a catastrophe that killed or harmed others. In a life-or-death emergency, a person must make split-second, painful moral decisions in order to survive. As he flees, terrified, from a burning building, he hears a sharp, high-pitched noise. Was that a cry for help? he wonders. Then he dismisses it as the sound of twisting metal.

He might repress the memory of this conflict from his conscious awareness to avoid this painful guilt. But the emotion still leaks out and is expressed by feeling unrealistically guilty over other matters.

This unconscious defense may be helpful on a short-term basis. It allows one to cope in the face of overwhelming trauma. But in the long run, the repressed guilt must be confronted in order eradicate the irrational guilt.

THE EVIL EYE

Survivor's guilt is a simple, straightforward example. But guilt can be about highly subjective matters as well. Many young children have the irrational belief that their thoughts can cause people harm. As with other vestiges of childhood, we do not completely grow out of this. Deep down, many adults continue to believe that their thoughts can cause harm.

To complicate matters further, the Jewish tradition of *ayin hara*, evil eye, supports this belief. A great Torah authority explained that the evil eye is the result of another person's jealousy. His unspoken envy is a silent prayer that the beauty or wealth or children should be taken away and granted to him instead. Though such jealousy is forbidden, each Jewish person has power in his prayers, and his evil eye can inflict damage.

Your relationship with your friend or relative is vicarious; there's some hidden anger or hostility. Suddenly, your friend or relative dies or suffers a tragedy. Unconsciously, you may feel you are to blame. Similarly, children of divorce may feel guilty that their parents' marriage ended because of them.

If you suffer from excessive guilt, how can you change your thinking? Aside from psychotherapy — which is helpful if there is a deep and unconscious reason for this guilt — is there anything you can do to remedy the problem yourself, or with the aid of a caring family member?

A USEFUL EXERCISE

If you suffer from guilt, keep a journal for a week. The journal should contain three columns. The first column should describe a particular sin. The second column is for your own subjective rating on the severity of the offense — 1, very mild; 5, moderately sinful; and 10, going straight to *gehennom*.

The third column should be reserved for an objective rating from a trusted *rav* or halachic authority. This might seem too simple to be helpful, but over time, it can be quite effective in subtly changing your faulty and distorted views.

SECTION EIGHT
Social, Religious, and Personal Growth

I t is a challenge to learn how to balance personal needs and emotional health with Torah directives to do mitzvos, perform chessed, and be altruistic. Is it possible to be righteous, zealous in concern and care for others, but still be just as good to yourself? Is it possible to be a devoted servant of G-d and still allow yourself emotional freedom? Torah ideas and lifestyles can be used to promote psychological growth. Let us explore.

69

Pathological Debt

Late one night after the kids went to bed, Mr. and Mrs. Goldberg stared at the pile of bills on their dining room table. They had made purchases on their store-brand credit card — zero down, no interest for six months. But the purchases had added up. "How did we allow ourselves to get into this mess?" they wondered.

First it was just one credit card with low finance rates the Goldbergs used to pay for a summer vacation. Then there were some much-needed renovations and repairs they put on a second card — with frequent flyer miles, of course. Before the Goldbergs knew it, they had accumulated $30,000 in debt. The interest alone was costing them hundreds of dollars a month and the debts were only growing larger.

UNCONSCIOUS ANGER

Unconscious anger is the root of most self-destructive behavior — even running into enormous debt. An angry person plots and plans against the object of his anger. So if his actions are self-destructive, he is plotting and planning against himself — he must be angry with himself.

Someone who is self-destructive is not necessarily actively seeking to be hurt. A reckless driver, or a high-risk investor, behaves the way he does for the pleasure and satisfaction of the experience. A person engages in risky behavior with the awareness that he may suffer, or at least be placed at risk.

You paid top dollar for a hotel room on a vacation and it turns out to be much below your expectations. You complain to the manager, but he is arrogant and unsympathetic. Later that night, you try to turn the air conditioner setting to "high", but the knob is jammed. Now you are really annoyed. You then use all your strength to force it to turn and the knob accidentally breaks.

Was it really an accident? Would you treat your home air conditioner like that? Of course not! But you weren't actually trying to break the air conditioner — otherwise you could have just taken your suitcase and smashed it against the control panel. In this scenario, you were angry enough with the hotel management that you treated the air conditioner recklessly. Reckless behavior is fueled by anger.

And not necessarily just self-anger. When a person cannot bear his anger with another, he may direct the anger inward, especially when it's a loved one. There can be a great deal of guilt and fear associated with the thought of being angry at a spouse, parent or even a child.

How does this play itself out with a person who drives himself into debt? Perhaps the breadwinner resents the financial pressures and care burdens, so he becomes careless with the money. Or sometimes it is the homemaker who resents being stuck at home, burdened with unglamorous domestic tasks, taken completely for granted. Huge bills are racked up as an expression of these emotional needs and resentment.

These are only examples. There may be many reasons for unconscious anger. But as a rule, a family that has pathological debt problems also has communication problems. If the family members learn how to express their feelings constructively and improve communication, some of the unconscious anger and resentment may dissipate.

MANAGING MONEY

Psychology aside, sometimes people also need good advice on how to handle money. Budgeting is a learned skill. Some chronic debtors should destroy their credit cards, just as an alcoholic must swear off drinking. But there are ways for healthy, responsible people to use credit cards safely.

If you are one of these people, here is one easy money management tool. Enter every single credit card charge into your checkbook as if it were a check. Instead of a check number, use a symbol to indicate which card was used. Balance your checkbook with each entry. When you receive the credit card bill, your checking account should reflect your balance as if the bill was already paid for. Then, simply write a check for the full amount. This way, you will never lose track of your expenses and always have enough money to pay the credit card bill.

70

Plenty of Chessed, Zero Intimacy

Dear Feuermans,

I want to share with you an unfortunate experience I had in the hopes that your readers can become more sensitive to an important issue, as well as hear your insights as to why this problem exists. Several years ago, after my husband was diagnosed with a terminal illness, we made the decision to move from out of town to New York in order to be closer to expert medical care and our married children. I don't want to name any neighborhoods, but suffice it to say that the entire block was frum.

During the difficult months of the illness until he passed away, no one on the entire block ever took the time to introduce themselves, say hello, or inquire about our welfare. This was a big disappointment for me, especially because I was used to out of town life, where everyone is open and friendly — Jew and non-Jew alike.

When I recently complained about this to a friend who does not live on my block, she said, "Do you have any idea how much chessed goes on in the frum community?" I don't doubt it. But we did not need chessed, charity, medical advice or favors. We could have used some good old-fashioned friendship and human contact.

*My husband sat outside on the porch in his wheel-
chair and no one ever greeted him or attempted to engage
in conversation. I had to work for part of the day, and it
would have been so kind if someone reached out just to
say hello.*

OUR RESPONSE

Your words speak for themselves. Hopefully they will help raise
the community's awareness. But acknowledging the problem is
only the first step in solving it. Why would members of a good-
hearted, *chessed*-performing community avoid performing the
simple acts of kindness you describe?

Perhaps the most important factor is fear of intimacy.
Befriending a person is much more emotionally demanding than
merely doing *chessed*. In *chessed*, the kindness-performer is in control, and the person on the receiving end is the one down. There's
no fear of rejection and very little chance that the encounter will
raise deep feelings.

But to become intimate with another person involves a relationship of equals. This raises a fear of rejection — and many other
emotional challenges. A new friend may have new things to teach,
or some enviable trait or possession. Some people have a primitive
fear of becoming intimate with those who have diseases or disabilities because somehow they might catch it.

This resistance to intimacy is also reinforced by the value we place
on *tznius*, modesty. It is difficult for people to balance the requirements of *tznius* with the common sense dictates of *mentchlichkeit*
(proper etiquette).

There are stories of holy, righteous sages who were modest, and
still greeted strangers, women or gentiles in a friendly and understanding manner. Elisha the Prophet allowed a grief-stricken mother
to clutch his feet, despite the overly zealous attempt of his assistant
to have her removed for her impertinence. (*Melachim* II 4:27)

Years ago, there lived a chassidic Rebbe and a *misnaged* Rosh
Yeshiva in the same town. Although they were vehemently opposed to each other on an ideological basis, when the Rebbe
became ill, the Rosh Yeshiva did not hesitate to visit the sick Rebbe.

The Rebbe refused the Rosh Yeshiva's company, insisting, "I
don't want to be your *esrog*." The Rebbe felt that the Rosh Yeshiva

was doing the *chessed* of visiting him for the sake of the *mitzvah*, not because he cared about his welfare. Instead of a person, the Rebbe felt he was being treated like an object of a *mitzvah*, an *esrog*, if you will. In fact, an important dimension of the mitzvah of visiting the sick is codified as praying for the person's welfare. You can't do that unless you really care about the person.

A friendship where both sides appreciate the qualities of the other brings equal benefits to all parties, and is no longer a one-sided *chessed*. While it is true that the initial friendly overtures may be a result of *chessed*, a true friendship cannot emerge until both parties move beyond the *mitzvah* and truly connect — thereby developing a uniform relationship.

Tolerating Street Beggars

71

Dear Feuermans,

I am often confronted by street beggars who ask for charity. I usually give to them, but feel conflicted because I am not sure where the money actually goes. Their standard and style of living appears to be quite impoverished, although many of them seem to have at least one large wad of cash from which they are able to produce change.

Some of them tell stories about large families they have to feed either in this country or elsewhere, or how they cannot get welfare and food stamps because they are "illegal aliens" from Israel. I would like to help them financially, but I have two basic questions:

Their appearance and demeanor can easily match that of a junkie or drug addict. If I give them money, is it just feeding a habit?

Even if they really will use the money for food and shelter, perhaps many of these street people are just lazy, anti-social, or suffering from some psychiatric disorder they refuse to get help for. Must I support someone like that? Why aren't they asking for job training or something?

I thought that since you are both social workers and sensitive to halacha, you might have a perspective that could be helpful.

There is a biblical injunction against "hardening your heart and constricting your hand" (*Devarim* 15:7) to the poor. But your fear about such people being junkies or addicts is justified, especially considering what we know about the homeless population at large. Most are suffering from addictions, psychiatric disorders, or both.

The circumstances must be very extreme if a normal, stable person becomes homeless. What happened to his network of family and friends? His community? He must have significantly distanced and alienated himself beyond anyone's ability to tolerate.

What can you do for them that would be helpful? Cash is probably not a good idea. Food is far more helpful and less likely to cause harm. If a person claims to be starving, you must immediately supply him with food and should not waste time verifying or checking up on him. (*Mishneh Torah, Hilchos Matnas Aniyim* 7:4)

If the person claims to have medical bills or other debts, it is preferable to pay his creditors directly. Contacting the creditors provides verification for the poor man's story. Beware of someone who refuses to supply you with this information.

Perhaps the best way to treat the street beggar should parallel that of the addict — friends, relatives, or even strangers should not "enable" him to continue in his ways. Providing him with money or food and paying off his debts allows the beggar to continually ignore his situation. He must seek help, and if he has to hit rock bottom to realize that, then so be it.

The problem is that this attitude violates the command not to refuse a poor person's request for *tzedaka*. True, you can circumvent the prohibition by giving a small token amount. Even a dime or a nickel could void the violation. But this does not answer the philosophical question inherent in the dilemma. Can we refuse to give a poor person *tzedaka* for his ultimate good?

The Torah philosophy on poverty places high value on the destitute recovering financial autonomy. The highest level of *tzedaka* is lending or gifting a poor person money so he can start a business, or helping him obtain employment. (*Mishneh Torah, Hilchos Matnas Aniyim* 10:10) The poor person himself is expected to take even the most menial and degrading work in order to avoid being dependent on others. (*Ibid.* 10:17) But just because the poor petitioner was negligent in obeying these details, we are not permitted to refuse him *tzedaka*.

The lesson of the Kli Yakkar on the verse, "Do not witness your friend's donkey or ox fallen on the path and hide from them, [rather] you shall surely help raise them up with him" (*Shemos* 23:5) can be applied here. (See Section Seven, Helping Others, Protecting Ourselves.) We are not obligated to help a poor person unless he puts in his own effort as well.

A scholar once pointed out a key etymological difference between the English word "charity" and the Hebrew word "*tzedaka*." Charity is derived from care, to love. Indeed, the Christian notion is that charity is done out of love. The Hebrew root for the word *tzedaka* comes from *tzedek*, justice. *Tzedaka* is based on more than love; it is based on justice. A Jewish person is obligated to give *tzedaka* because the money he has does not belong to him. G-d gave it to each one of us to do His will. This is justice, not charity.

Though we should never refuse to give *tzedaka*, a person has the right — no, a moral obligation — to ascertain that this is truly the kind of help the petitioner needs. In our opinion, if, after a careful investigation, it is discovered that the person is using the money in a self-destructive manner, or not making an effort to improve his situation, to refuse him further assistance can be justified.

The Boundaries of Chessed

72

Dear Feuermans,

I am writing to you about a matter that involves both relationships and Torah values. Recently, a middle-aged lady asked me if I could give her a ride to a certain location that was a few blocks out of my way. Given the neighborhood traffic patterns of erev Shabbos, a few blocks could easily take an extra fifteen minutes to drive through.

I was in a rush to get home to my children and to get the Shabbos cooking started, so I told her that I could not take her. The woman persisted and told me, "Are you sure you can't take me? It's a mitzvah." Although I felt guilty, especially since it was a hot day and I was worried about this woman's health, I still refused because of my own personal concerns about getting home on time for my children and other responsibilities.

As I was turning the corner in my car, I noticed the woman entering a car service storefront, I suppose to hire a taxi. After seeing this, my guilt gave way to annoyance. Why should she put me in this guilty position and whine about it being a mitzvah? Why couldn't she spend a few dollars — which she ended up doing anyway! She did not appear to be poor in any way.

What do you think? Was I being selfish, or was she being unfair?

Our Response

You feel this woman was being manipulative, since she could have readily obtained a ride at a moderate cost relative to her apparent standard of living.

Let's assume your assessment of her economical situation was correct. Let's say for argument's sake that she was pathologically cheap, or perhaps engaging in attention seeking behavior. Her request may still be within the boundaries of *chessed*.

Tzedaka, charity, extends to supplying a formerly wealthy person with the accouterments of his previous standard of living. The Talmud instructs that if he is used to riding a horse, "he should be supplied with a horse" (*Kesubos* 67b). The modern day application would presumably include a limousine for one who is genuinely used to a limousine.

In a similar fashion, perhaps the *mitzvah* of *chessed* does not necessarily allow us to make value judgments about the necessity of the request. The woman's request might have to be taken at face value, leaving psychological analyses aside.

There is another point you touch upon in your letter — what degree of personal loss and inconvenience must you absorb at the cost of performing a kindness? Consider the benefit of the other person, compared to your inconvenience.

If those few blocks take you only five minutes to traverse by car, and it would take the woman ten minutes to walk them, and you still will have time to prepare for Shabbos, then there is a net gain in terms of human suffering. If driving her the few blocks costs you an equal amount of time lost sitting in traffic as you navigate back, then the total amount of human suffering versus kindness received remains equal, if not possibly in deficit.

Among the laws pertaining to the return of a lost object (*Shulchan Aruch, Choshen Mishpat* 264:1), there is one particular law that is pertinent here. A person finds himself in a situation — he can save his own object from destruction, or he can save his neighbor's. He is exempt from the obligation to save his neighbor's. Perhaps we can deduce that there is no obligation to grant a favor when it incurs a loss to ourselves of equal or greater amount. However, ultimately chessed is an act of giving, and though there may not be an obligation to give to that extent, you may still choose to do so as an act of piety.

73

If Haman Went for Help

Dear Feuermans,

I, Haman, should feel like the luckiest man alive. You see, I have a supportive wife, ten sons, and I am in the height of my career. King Achashveirosh has chosen to appoint me above all the other ministers in the land. Yet all this feels worthless to me when I see Mordechai the Jew, who refuses to bow before me. (Esther 5:13)

Though I hold a high government position, I am technically indebted to Mordechai because of a rather unusual and embarrassing incident. I was once traveling in the wilderness and ran out of food and water. Mordechai came along and offered to share his food, but only if I agreed to sell myself to him as a slave. I was starving. I had no choice about the matter — I signed a slavery contract. To this day, whenever I try to assert my authority, Mordechai smugly flashes the contract in front of me. (Targum Esther 3:1-4)

This really burns me up. All this success and I still feel like a failure. Do you have any advice for me?

OUR RESPONSE

Although understandably the situation with Mordechai is causing you great distress, the root of your problem lies elsewhere. We would rather address some of the personality issues that seem to have gotten you into trouble in the first place. You crave honor and recognition, yet when you do receive some, it does not seem to satisfy you.

This raises two questions.

‣ Why is the recognition you receive not satisfying you? In your words, "All this success and I still feel like a failure." What is preventing you from feeling good about whatever degree of success you achieve, despite having failures in other areas?

‣ Are the failures just a case of bad luck, or are you somehow unconsciously engineering them as part of a self-destructive behavior pattern? Unless running out of food in the wilderness was due to some uncontrollable event, there appears to be a degree of carelessness. If our supposition is correct, we must then try to analyze what unconscious purpose this self-destructive behavior serves.

The answers to these two questions are related to a psychological condition known as repetition compulsion. Paradoxically, often people who have the greatest need for attention and affection unconsciously cause themselves to continue to be deprived.

Consider the child of abusive parents who marries an abusive and controlling spouse, despite a strenuous and conscious effort to avoid this trap. No matter how many times this person said to herself, "I will never marry someone like my father!" she can still end up marrying someone with the exact same personality. All her friends were able to see the warning signs from a mile away, but somehow, she was blind to them.

In your case, Haman, you crave honor and recognition, yet you deprive yourself of it constantly through poor judgment and petty thinking. You wish to occupy the highest positions in government, but instead of spending your time and energy on your job, you distract yourself with your rivalry with Mordechai.

What is the root cause of the repetition compulsion? When a person is deprived in his development, there is a constant unconscious quest for resolution of the problem.

For example, a young girl abused in childhood never wants to be in such a situation again, but her unconscious mind has a more complicated response. Aside from being angry with her father for being abusive, she longs for a rectification of the problem — that her father be loving, kind, and respectful. So even if it has been years since her father was involved in her life, she unconsciously seeks a marriage partner who has similar traits to her father, a partner from whom she can seek the parental love and recognition she was always missing.

Haman, if early in your development you were deprived of a certain level of care and attention, you may be unconsciously seeking this care and attention. But since you were not allowed to feel satisfaction and security as a child, you may be drawn to recreating similar situations such as this throughout your life. Even when you do receive praise, you are compelled to mock and minimize it in your eyes: "It all feels worthless when I see Mordechai."

How does a person stuck in this unconscious pattern of self-destructive behaviors free himself? Becoming aware of the pattern is a good first step. But it is also necessary to work through past pains and disappointments so they are no longer a burning and unmet need. Therapy is usually a helpful venue, but it may be possible to do it on your own, if you can see yourself honestly.

Note to the Reader

Although this is just a spoof, it may still raise a deep philosophical question. If a cruel or wicked person behaves this way because of how he was treated as a child, does this excuse his evil behavior or absolve him of responsibility?

Even a person who has had an abusive or deprived childhood still chooses how to react to it. Whether the choice is conscious or unconscious, or a mixture of both, it still is a choice and is still a question of good or evil.

We are not making excuses for Haman's behavior. Many individuals from the previous generation witnessed first hand, as children, the horrors and atrocities of the Nazis, and nevertheless went on to become compassionate human beings and productive members of society. They had courage and character; they chose not to pass on the evil they had received to others.

74

Achieving Success in the Workplace

Our parents and role models have transmitted to us a strong ethical foundation. How do you achieve success? With good, honest work, right?

Well, not always. Bosses and supervisors like the good, honest work outlook. Employees do their jobs, they're productive in their positions. But look around. Are the good, honest workers the one who are rewarded and promoted — or are there other factors to success in your company?

Good, reliable, and honest work is ethical and moral, valuable to your employer, and a necessary requirement for personal and career success. But good work habits alone aren't enough. They're like going on an interview without wearing a suit. You must wear a suit to get in the door, even if that is not the basis for obtaining a job. So too, to advance in your career, you may need to learn how to psychologically "dress for success".

If you deliver good work, the boss will keep you on the job, and maybe even promote you. But this is to serve his own interests. What about your interests? You'd like to serve your career needs, without neglecting ethical responsibilities.

There are hidden dynamics that contribute significantly to success in the workplace. You have to understand how others perceive you. You can control your own fate by asserting control over how you define yourself in the workplace environment.

PROMOTING YOURSELF

Employing the philosophy of "Conscious Use of Self" can help increase your awareness of yourself in the workplace. Instead of just going through the daily motions, using the exemplary work habits you have been trained to follow in professional and social interactions, expand your awareness. If you are a worker who wants to take advantage of opportunities, you must become conscious and cognizant of the subtle but major influences that you can have on your supervisors, coworkers and subordinates.

This is not manipulation. We do not advocate immoral or dishonest behavior. The techniques we describe are not intended to be used to gain illicit and unfair advantages at the expense of others, but to project skills and talents in a manner that allows them to be effectively utilized and recognized by yourself and your company. Your conscious actions to foster personal success can be a source of benefit to your company, without requiring self-sacrificing behavior.

Some offices consider themselves to be one big family. In fact, some employees act like squabbling siblings. Psychological theories that are traditionally applied to dysfunctional individuals and families could also be applied to the work environment. Let us examine some personality and character disorders in the workplace and how they may contribute to professional success or failure.

THE CODEPENDENT WORKER

Psychotherapists note common characteristics and dynamics in families of recovering addicts. There are subtle ways in which family helps the addict retain his addiction. The recovery community calls this phenomenon codependency. A codependent is a person or persons within the family who share dependency for the alcoholic or substance abuser's symptoms.

If a man has a drinking problem for an extended period of time, he cannot continue without help from his family. Someone has to cover for him. When he is hung over on Monday, someone has to try to roust him from bed or call his boss to say he is sick. If no one in the family does this, he will not be able to get away with this behavior for long. He will lose his job, run out of money, and go broke.

Eventually he will end up begging on the street. People may feel sorry for him and give him cash. And he won't use the cash to buy a new tie for an interview — he'll hit the bottle again. Even an entire society can be codependent.

Why do family members and friends help this addict remain addicted? They go out of their way to bail out, lend money to, and cover for an addict because they cannot bear to watch him suffer, lose his job, and embarrass the family. Isn't a firm hand kinder than allowing the addict to self-destruct?

The codependent spouse is also known as an enabler because he enables the dysfunctional behavior. In the above example, the wife enables her husband's addiction. Maybe the family needs the addiction in place so there is less fighting, or at least, no divorce. This process is known as homeostasis — the family system unconsciously preserves dysfunction in order to maintain relative stability.

There may be the same type of dysfunctional behavior in your workplace. You, in your position, may be helping to maintain this homeostasis. Sometimes people are treated unfairly at work. Some companies have financial and structural limitations. But many times you, the individual worker, can be as much of a contributor to maintaining the status quo as your supervisors are. Using this approach, dubbed as "Systems Theory" by family therapists, you can look at yourself and your coworkers in a new light, and remedy some destructive patterns.

The codependent worker is similar to the codependent spouse — both are part of a dysfunctional system, and even engage in behaviors that help maintain the dysfunction due to their own unconscious psychological needs.

Sally considers herself to be an exceptionally dedicated worker. Often, Sally works through lunch and stays late, in order to help her boss complete assignments inside the deadline. Mr. Boss constantly tells Sally how much he appreciates her help. When he can, he buys her dinner, and even arranges for a taxi to take her home if they work particularly late. On numerous occasions, Mr. Boss expressed his desire to give her a raise, but he cannot increase her salary significantly due to budget cutbacks. He has also been trying to hire an assistant for Sally, but again, because of budgetary reasons, he can't.

Sally is a happy and cheerful worker. But on occasion, under intense pressure, Sally blows up at her coworkers. It only happens once in while and she is always extremely apologetic. But her coworkers revile Sally because of her temper. One time it happened within earshot of Mr. Boss's supervisor! Sally almost got fired, but Mr. Boss intervened on her behalf.

THE ANALYSIS

On the surface, Sally is a competent worker. She is valued by her company and has reasonable satisfaction in her job. Unfortunately, she has a bad temper that is tolerated because of her otherwise excellent performance.

But if we dig a little deeper, we find that her situation is actually quite tragic. Here we have a bright and talented woman who has remained in the same position for years. True, her boss appreciates her, but how has she progressed in her personal development? She is disliked by her coworkers. The challenges and accomplishments of her work life revolve around making deadlines and controlling her temper.

Of course, it's possible to find fulfillment while holding the same position for your entire life. Great respect is due if you faithfully and happily choose to serve your company. But Sally gives the impression of someone who is bitter and frustrated. She feels she can do more, but something is holding her back.

If her company had a chance to promote her, would they? The way she acts makes it clear that she is definitely not management material. Sally has the ability to accomplish much more and is selling herself short!

Taking a deeper analytic look at Sally's situation raises the following questions:

- Why does Sally blow up from time to time?
- Even if her company truly does not have the money, why does Sally put up with this? Why doesn't she look for a job elsewhere?

Psychologically speaking, we can theorize a possible cause for Sally's behavior at work. She is the type of person who buries her feelings until she reaches a point where she blows up at people.

Sometimes this pattern of behavior is learned early on in life. Perhaps one or both of her parents had a short temper, so Sally learned to push her feelings out of the way to avoid trouble. Sally was probably never taught that her feelings were worthwhile to have and express. And so, over time, Sally began to have a poor self-image. In her adult life, perhaps her job became her sole image.

Sally's anger grew over the years, especially when she felt mistreated or abused. It reminded her of the humiliation she had experienced when her mother would snap into a rage at her.

She's learned to function normally in the adult world, but deep down, Sally feels worthless. Whenever the pressure builds up and Sally feels taken advantage of, she flies into a rage. And she is not only angry with her boss or coworkers; she is angry with her parents, albeit unconsciously. And then she feels guilty, and then even more feelings of worthlessness evolve.

The thought of leaving her company brings up all her old fears of abandonment. Can you imagine five-year-old Sally saying to her mother, "Sorry, but I cannot tolerate this abuse. I am going to live somewhere else"? Sally feels as powerless to change her current work situation as she did when she was five years old, on the receiving end of an abusive parental tirade.

So Sally tolerates working conditions that are unreasonable, partly out of fear of change, partly out of guilt, and partly out of the few crumbs of desperately needed self-esteem her boss throws her. But what can Sally do to change her situation?

Separation and Individuation

Sally needs to become conscious of her own lack of self-esteem and confidence, and not let it interfere with her ability to make an objective, rational assessment of her situation. She must assess her skills and qualifications, her personal needs and priorities, as well as the realistic limits that her company has.

Sally must be able to simultaneously perform well at her current job, discuss her grievances, and look into other opportunities. This requires a degree of personal development and maturity that she has not yet mastered. In psychological and relationship terms, Sally needs separation and individuation.

An infant sees himself and his mother as one object. When mommy is happy, he is happy. If mommy is sad, he is sad. Over time, the child develops the capacity to accept that his feelings and others' feelings are not the same. He can feel one way, and still tolerate others feeling differently.

Sounds simple, right? Actually, it is not, even for adults.

Most difficulties in interpersonal relations stem from poor self-other differentiation. Stop for a moment and think how many times others' feelings and opinions made you irrationally upset. Think of how many nasty fights you could have avoided if you were able to accept and understand the separateness of others' feelings and your own. Sally will need to tolerate separating emotionally from her boss and her company, and not let guilt or misplaced loyalty interfere with her plans for success.

Sally must firm up the boundaries between her personal life and her work life. She works late without pay out of guilt or loyalty to her boss. Psychologically speaking, that is a boundary incursion. Nobody works consistently as a favor — they work for appropriate compensation.

If Sally's company was going bankrupt, would she be able to retain her job based on their feelings of gratitude toward her? A company retains employees who serve the company's needs best, especially in difficult financial times. Loyalty is not a big factor.

It is only fair that a worker be paid and treated in accordance with the objective quality of the work, not more and not less. Of course, some individuals take this to an extreme and refuse to do any additional work that is "outside their job description." Such a tactic is rigid and unrealistic. Every good worker should sometimes do some extra work.

THE SELF-DESTRUCTIVE WORKER

Self-destructiveness is a very human trait. People drive recklessly, endanger their health and take risks on a regular basis. Some people tend to engage in this type of behavior to the point where others wonder why they beg for disaster.

At work, too, there are those who go beyond the normal limits, just asking to be fired. They are subtly or not so subtly insubordinate. They dress poorly, especially when important people are around. They miss deadlines.

Often, the self-destructive person will offer rationales such as, "I don't kowtow to anyone." Or, "I won't fake it." But this is just a defense against dealing with the underlying emotional issues.

What value is there in being perceived as a non-productive, non-conforming, and sloppy individualist? Non-conformity and individualism certainly have their place, but in a manner that is productive to your career and your company. Conform in appearance; leave the freethinking to your own mind.

A person who is fully developed emotionally can have his own opinions and values, work to achieve them, and still conform to the expectations and rules of the corporate culture at large. Adolescents, in their process of separating and individuating, don't want to be phony. Yet to achieve a fulfilling and lucrative career, you sometimes have to be "phony," to become part of the establishment.

Whether you are a subordinate, supervisor, or executive, all of us at times are self-destructive both in our personal and our work lives. The key is to recognize when you are engaging in this behavior, and to stop it.

THE CONSCIOUS WORKER

The conscious worker represents the ideal mental and emotional state people must strive to achieve. The conscious worker has learned to become aware of all his pathological and unconsciously destructive personality traits; he has learned to channel the underlying feelings in a constructive fashion.

The conscious worker will use understanding of the work environment, coupled with emotional realities, to be as objective as possible. He or she is valued as fresh and creative, but steady, ethical, and reliable at the same time. The conscious worker asks and answers the following questions on a daily basis.

- Am I caught in any repetitive patterns?
- What are the current work issues that anger me?
- In what way do I act out my anger?
- How am I perceived?
- What are my short-term plans and goals?
- What are my long-term plans and goals?
- What have I done today to further these goals?

Fortunately, this is not an all or nothing proposition. You can work on this and achieve various levels over time. The more you master these skills, the more you are a master of your own fate. There are many forces in the work environment that are not under your control, but there is so much that is. Most people only recognize a fraction! These opportunities are just waiting for the conscious worker to take hold of them and succeed.

75

A Case of Hidden Hostility

Dear Feuermans,
Recently, I was at an aufruf (party celebrated in the
groom's synagogue the Shabbos before his wedding)
and noticed someone who was preparing to hurl a bag
of candy at the groom with unusual force and gusto.
I attempted to stop the person out of concern for the
groom's welfare. The thrower was indignant, claiming
I was obstructing him from following the minhag
(ritual custom). I have seen on occasion how some
people seem to gleefully enjoy when the groom gets
bonked on the head by a candy bag. Is this really a
mitzvah or just an excuse for people to act out their
jealousy?

OUR RESPONSE

From a religious perspective, Jewish custom is very important and often has the status of a *halachic* requirement. But common sense tells us that the custom here is to shower the groom with sweets — not to assault him. The Talmud (*Berachos* 50b) cites certain foods to be showered on the bride and groom as a sign of blessing and material success, reminiscent of the apple dipped in honey for a sweet new year.

From a psychological perspective, that groom is enjoying a moment in the limelight. You observed a degree of gleeful hostility and enjoyment in someone actually hitting the groom with a well-aimed candy bag. This type of reaction is not surprising.

Freud explores the psychological basis behind customs and observances in primitive societies as well as their modern day equivalents. Rituals and customs, posits Freud, represent an expression of contradictory or ambivalent feelings that people are in conflict about.

Many primitive tribes treated their kings with great veneration on the one hand, while at the same time almost torture them with highly restrictive rules. The Mikaddo of Japan in early centuries would not allow their king's feet to touch the ground or sunlight to directly touch his head, presumably out of respect. But the king was practically deprived of any freedom of movement. If he wanted to travel, he had to be carried by slaves in coaches.

Freud cites many similar examples, most strikingly the Timmes of Sierra Leone. On the eve of the coronation, all the people were allowed to beat the new king. Some kings never survived their coronation. (*Totem and Taboo*, 40-50)

What emotions are at the root of such customs? According to Freud, people want to honor and revere a leader, but they also have hostile feelings of jealousy, fear and hatred. These customs unconsciously arose to express these contradictory and ambivalent feelings.

Savage little school-age boys administer "birthday punches" to the birthday boy. The children are jealous, but at the same time, they admire the one who holds the center of attention.

Let's return to our groom, whom we know is compared to a king. Apparently this is true in more ways than one. His momentary success and high rank attracts feelings of admiration tainted with hostility and jealousy. So instead of being showered with sweet candies, the unenviable groom is pelted with an occasional ballistic bomb.

76

Hating One's Fellow Jew

From a psychological perspective, there are many reasons why we might hate a person — some rational, some irrational. The emotion of hatred may be useful sometimes, but generally it is destructive both for the object of your hatred and for yourself. Hate alone without any constructive action causes stress and bitterness, ultimately breeding more hate.

THE TORAH PROHIBITION

According to the Torah, it is forbidden to hate a fellow Jew. So what do we do if we feel hatred toward another person? Is hate ever justified, or at least permitted?

Our tradition is far from naive about the subtleties of human emotion, and when our sages focused their Talmudic-analytical skills on this topic they yielded important insights about hatred. Their wise discussions relate to our daily lives.

The verse states, "Do not hate your friend in your heart. You must surely rebuke him, and do not bear a sin on his behalf" (*Vayikra* 19:17). The verse can be conceptually divided into three parts. First, the negative commandment prohibiting hate. Second, the positive commandment to rebuke. Third, a rationale for this process — so that you do not bear a sin on his behalf.

Targum and Ramban explain that the latter segments of the verse refer to a fellow Jew who is sinning. If you witness someone committing a sin, you are commanded to rebuke the sinner, to convince him to return to the correct path. You must not remain silent because otherwise you will "bear his sin." Your silence would signify tacit agreement, causing you to share moral liability with the sinner.

Rashi offers a similar interpretation, but the third part is cautioning you, the rebuker, to speak in a manner that will limit the embarrassment of the sinner. "Do not bear a sin" is an instruction not to compound the sin by embarrassing him during rebuke.

But several other commentators give a different twist to the word "sin" — a personal offense. According to this interpretation, all three components of the verse are part of the message. It is prohibited to hate a fellow Jew. Instead of holding on to the resentment caused by a personal offense, rebuke him! You have to tell him about it, give him a chance to apologize and set the record straight. (Ramban; *Rambam Mishneh Torah*, *Hilchos Deos* 6:5)

Speaking openly reduces hatred and anger in all relationships. How many times do people resent us and we don't even know what we did wrong? How many times do people jump to conclusions, misinterpret our remarks or actions, and assume we did something to hurt them when that was the farthest thing from our minds?

The Torah is saying to us that if we want to have healthy relationships, do not keep resentment buried inside. Speak it out. Do it kindly and without hostility to avoid further sin. But only if we speak our feelings can the anger possibly be resolved.

OPEN HATRED

There is still one outstanding question. What if we follow the advice of the Torah, and still there is no change in the person's behavior? Or even worse — sometimes the appeal for change is rudely rebuffed. Now is it permitted to hate this person?

The verse plainly states, "Do not hate your friend — in your heart." In your heart you may not hate him, but openly expressed hatred is not included in the prohibition.

Some may argue that the intention is not to hate, *even* in your heart. Of course open hatred should also be forbidden!

The Steipler Rav (*Kehilas Yaakov* 10:54) suggests this is the opinion of Rashi in *Erchin* (16b). But not everyone agrees with Rashi. The Steipler notes a subtle variation between Rambam and Ramban. Rambam clearly states, "The Torah only forbids hatred in the heart" (*Mishneh Torah*, *Hilchos Deos* 6:5). Ramban emphasizes the command to tell our friends what they have done wrong. And the result is — we will not harbor secret resentments.

According to Ramban, if you tell your friend that you hate him without giving a proper explanation, you will still be in violation of hating a fellow Jew. Anger is only productive when expressed along with an appeal for correction and resolution.

According to Rambam, once you express your hatred, it is no longer "hatred in the heart." Rambam rules that it is an extra *mitzvah* to inform the person exactly what is bothering you (*Mishneh Torah, Hilchos Deos* 6). But once you've shared your feelings, you can leave it up to the other person to figure out why you are upset. You have accomplished something and are no longer liable for the sin of hating your fellow Jew.

The Steipler Rav points out that if you tell the other person what you are upset about and he does not respond or rectify the matter, although you may not be liable for the prohibition of hating your friend in your heart, Rambam (*Sefer HaMitzvos* 302) states that one is still in violation of the prohibition against bearing a grudge.

But not everyone is in agreement with Rambam on this point. Rabbeinu Yonah (*Shaare Teshuva* 3:38) opines that bearing grudges only applies to monetary and service matters, not personal issues. The Torah forbids resenting by holding back a good or service, and obligates repaying selfishness with generosity instead of revenge. (Rabbeinu Yonah's ruling is based on *Yoma* 23a.)

There may be some opinions that permit you to hate a person who has shown no regard for your feelings, even after you try to explain how you were hurt. Nonetheless, to forgive the person is considered an act of piety. (*Mishneh Torah, Hilchos Deos* 6:13)

The Torah commands and the sages' interpretations show understanding of the complex emotion of hatred. We are not expected to shove our feelings aside or swallow them. Instead, the Torah encourages us to discuss our resentments openly with the intention of resolving them.

This is not necessarily our first instinct. It forces us to face unpleasant feelings — and possibly experience even more pain — in order to solve the problem. But worthwhile actions are rarely easily accomplished.

77

Coping with Loss and Grief

Generally, the rituals and close-knit life of the religious community provides generous support for coping with death or other tragic events. But occasionally, even religious people have difficulty grieving and coping with personal loss. Some may be reluctant to express feelings of sadness and anger, in an attempt to avoid their own doubts about Divine providence and retribution. But keeping grief locked inside does not allow the mourner the opportunity to work through emotions and adjust properly.

BLESSING G-D FOR GOOD AND BAD

The *halacha* states, "Just as one must recite a blessing to thank G-d for a fortunate occurrence, one must also thank G-d for an evil occurrence" (*Shulchan Aruch, Orach Chaim* 222:1-3). This statement implies that the Torah does not want a person to be sad, angry or upset about a loss. This can be quite a challenge, especially with the loss of a loved one or an object of great value.

Someone who tries to live up to this expectation and cannot, will feel guilty that he failed to heed this ethical imperative. He will turn angry and resentful, both because of the loss and the religious duty to repress the sadness. And then he'll feel doubly guilty for feeling angry and resentful! This is not healthy mourning. Is this really what the law intended?

The *halacha* is not so straightforward. When we celebrate a good tiding or blessed event, we recite *Shehechyanu*, blessing G-d for sustaining us to reach this day. Or sometimes, when the joyful experience is shared with others, one recites the blessing of *Hatov Vehameitiv*, which affirms that G-d is good and does good.

But the blessing over death and loss is very different indeed — *Dayan Haemes*, blessing the Judge of truth. The blessing over loss implies acceptance of Divine judgment and punishment. Yes, it is painful. Yes, it is worth grieving over. Yes, we can be angry or sad. But at the same time, we must accept the suffering.

THE FIVE STAGES OF GRIEF AND LOSS

Dr. Elizabeth Kubler-Ross, in her famous work *On Death and Dying*, identified five stages people pass through when they suffer a death or other loss:

▸ shock and denial
▸ anger
▸ bargaining, trying to find a way out
▸ depression or a feeling of complete hopelessness
▸ acceptance or adjusting to the new reality.

These stages are important ways in which people adjust to their losses and should be experienced with the full range of emotions that they bring. Let us explain the implications of these stages with a religious perspective.

Shock and denial. A person's first reaction often is, "This cannot be true. There must be some mistake." Of course, there always is a chance that it is a mistake, but people will have this reaction no matter how convincing the evidence.

Anger. A person may feel or say, "Why me? It's unfair!" A religious person may feel guilty about this type of reaction. The occurrence is a result of Divine providence and Heavenly justice, and if he is angry, he is not accepting the sovereignty of G-d.

It is true that in the long term, this attitude is not in consonance with the religious perspective. But initially, under the great shock of tragic news, he may very well be in the *halachic* category of *oness*, one who experiences an irresistible compulsion, and is not culpable for his thoughts.

Bargaining. A person who suffers a loss or hears terrible news will search for a way out. This reaction is healthy and adaptive. After all, there may in fact be a way out. Take the diagnosis of a terminal illness, for example. Aside from physical means, a religious person may understandably take steps to change his fate through prayer and penitence. But all is in the hands of G-d, and even the most righteous and sincere people do not necessarily merit a miraculous cure.

Depression. At this stage, a person will feel a sense of complete hopelessness. A healthy person will eventually move on to the final stage —

Acceptance. A person adjusts to the new reality. He is neither overly optimistic nor excessively pessimistic about his newfound tragic situation. He will feel and respond appropriately and take whatever steps necessary to continue under the new circumstances.

Unresolved Grief

These stages are not necessarily experienced in chronological order, nor are they experienced only once. Some people cycle through these stages several times, perhaps feeling them more deeply each time. But no one should feel rushed to "get it over with."

Sometimes a person can be stuck in this process and suffer from what is known as complex unresolved grief, unusually sad and depressed for several years. This can result from certain unconscious feelings, such as guilt over unacknowledged anger toward a deceased person. In such cases, a person should consider psychotherapy as a way to understand what is preventing him from moving on with life.

78

Resiliency and Trauma

Two people experience a similar trauma. One is damaged for life, and the other emerges emotionally unscathed. How can we account for this difference between people? What allows some people the resiliency to bounce back from tragedy, while others are slow to recover, if they ever do?

BOUNCING BACK

There is a popular notion to defend and rationalize those who perform cruel acts with the excuse that they were abused as children. While this may be a consideration, how can we explain the numerous Holocaust survivors who spent their formative years exposed to sadistic horrors, and still turned out to be productive and normal citizens? Many such individuals have heroically built or rebuilt lifestyles filled with *chessed* and human dignity benefiting all of mankind. How did they do it?

And trauma doesn't have to be as dramatic as a terrorist act to be emotionally damaging. Trauma can be losing a job or the untimely death of a friend. The victim of a crime, the child of a divorce, deal with trauma.

IDENTIFYING THE TRAITS

This is not just a philosophical or theoretical discussion. If we can identify the personality traits, coping mechanisms and behaviors of those who are resilient, then perhaps we can teach people to utilize these skills when faced with traumatic circumstances.

To the criticism of many, psychological theory and interventions are mostly based on studying ill people. Therapists have learned how to help people largely by working with troubled and distressed individuals who sought their care.

Freud, considered by many to be the father of modern psychology, was originally a neurologist. Patients came to him with somatic illnesses such as paralysis, which had no known physical cause. In struggling to uncover the origins of these symptoms, he formulated his ideas about unconscious defenses, physical symptoms as an expression of repressed feelings.

As clever and insightful Freud's observations were about human nature, they should not be the sole basis in forming theories about human behavior and motivation. Some object that psychoanalytic theory sees people in an essentially pessimistic light, driven by primitive drives instead of higher needs — like competence, mastery, and even spiritual attainment.

Although we believe psychoanalytic theory has a prominent place in the treatment of mental illness, we also recognize there may be other factors at work in allowing a person to handle problems and overcome emotional stresses. Researchers in this area are beginning to identify some qualities of psychologically resilient people:

> ▸ A connection to a religion, value system or higher power;
> ▸ A strong network of family and friends;
> ▸ An ability to be flexible and adapt to changing circumstances.

Such qualities seem to allow these individuals to overcome the shock of whatever trauma they suffer. They put their experience in perspective, talk it over, receive support from loved ones, and if necessary, change themselves to adapt to the new realities.

A Torah lifestyle is conducive to sustaining trauma. Belief in G-d as a Higher Power is understood. Family and community are central. And although some may feel religion promotes rigidity, the Torah also emphasizes the value of flexibility. Our sages taught, "One should always make himself soft like a reed, and not strong like a cedar" (*Taanis* 20a). A reed bends in a strong wind, but a cedar tree, strong as it may be, can snap.

Inner Conflict

The psychological theory of the unconscious has become so widespread that terms like "inner conflict" have become everyday vernacular. But this popularization lends a superficial psychological light to personal failures and inconsistencies.

Regarding a chain smoker or overweight overeater, you might say, "He's conflicted. He wants to quit but he can't." Or there may be someone wants to study for a higher degree or switch jobs, but he procrastinates. He thinks of himself as "being in conflict," because he wishes to expand his horizons but he is afraid.

Truthful analysis? Yes, but incomplete. He acknowledges his emotional conflict, but he must now move beyond this point. He needs to know more about himself if he wants to really effect a change.

Wish, Fear and Defense

From a psychodynamic perspective, every emotional conflict can be conceptually understood to be composed of three components: a wish, a fear and a defense. Using the above example, the wish is to grow by obtaining a higher degree of education; the fear is failure; and the defense is to procrastinate, avoiding failure altogether. In most cases, the fear is the least acknowledged part of the conflict, and often it is completely unconscious.

Even if a person can acknowledge his fear, the true meaning and cause of the fear is never accessed emotionally. He knows he is afraid, but why? The entire endeavor to move forward in his education is a success. That he struggles to receive less than perfect grades is trivial.

When the fear is completely unconscious, it is even more difficult to escape the defense pattern. The overeater — his wish is to
be healthy. What is the fear and what is the defense? Eating can be
self-soothing, a method of warding off depression or loneliness.
His fear is the pain and anxiety of feeling lonely and uncared for.
The defense — he indulges in sweets that substitute for the rewards of genuine human comfort.

This defense is not limited to people who have no friends; it's
also used by those who are dissatisfied with their current relationships. Regarding his tendency to eat away his frustration, one
patient observed, "Faithful married men don't get angry, they just
order another slice of pizza." This can be applied to the opposite
gender as well. No one feels more alone than a person surrounded
by others who don't understand him.

The first step is awareness. A person has to recognize that he is
in emotional conflict or in turmoil over some goal. But fear, often
unconscious, can't always be dealt with alone. Psychotherapy,
based on a psychodynamic theoretical model, can be effective by
helping a person understand, acknowledge and accept the fear,
unleashing a person from his avoidance dance. With proper help,
a person can be free to fulfill his personal goals.

Relapse is Normal

When a person makes a resolution to change, no matter what it is, often there will be times when he relapses to his old habit. It makes no difference what the resolution is. It could be to lose weight, do exercise, not let loose with rage — or even a more serious resolution, such as to quit an addiction. Why do people relapse? How can it be prevented or handled?

PEOPLE OF HABIT

Humans are hard wired to follow their habits. This is a survival and efficiency mechanism that allows a person to manage routine tasks without requiring much attention. A new driver must dedicate most of his conscious attention to the demands of ever-changing road conditions. But a seasoned driver can automatically respond to the demands of the road without conscious thought. After a certain point, driving has been turned over to the more automatic and habitual functions of the mind.

Similarly, adults more or less sight-read. They recognize entire words and even phrases, as opposed to beginning readers who must slowly sound out each letter.

A person can easily fall back into an old habit, particularly if the habit is rewarding and pleasurable. Indeed, our sages observed, "One who transgresses and then repeats the transgression, will feel as if it is permitted" (*Yoma* 86b). Relapsing is not just reverting to an old habit. It's an important part of the process of learning and change.

Studies of child development have observed that children regress as part of the normal developmental and growth process. A toddler striving for independence will scoot away from her mother — only to come running back a few moments later. She needs the physical reassurance of her mother's presence before she can run off again. This may occur repeatedly during a particular play period; each time, the child may venture further and further away.

A child who has come close to mastering toilet training might paradoxically react to his parents' praise by having several accidents. Psychologically speaking, this is no different from the toddler who runs back to her mother, although a bit more frustrating and inconvenient for the parents. The new level of independence that comes along with toilet training may frighten a child — so he goes back to wetting himself.

But this regression may also serve as a function of learning. Much of what we learn is based on distinctions between opposites. It is impossible to know what light is without experiencing darkness. Part of the human learning process is to experiment with opposites; it's a way of reinforcing a newly learned skill.

The child may be intuitively wetting himself as part of re-organizing his personality within the context of the changes he has made. In a certain sense, the child needs to compare who he was with who he is, in order to define his self-image. This is an important point, because if this supposition is true, it mitigates some of the guilt of those who slip-up after making a commitment to change.

THE GUILT CYCLE

Guilt is important. If we never felt guilty, we might never work to improve ourselves. But guilt can also be debilitating. Many habits are self-soothing — overeating, smoking, or even biting nails. Sucking or touching something to our mouths is instinctively gratifying, since our first pleasure as infants was centered on our mouths.

If a person relapses and breaks her resolution, she will feel guilty and sad, driving her even further toward her old habit because it brings emotional comfort. Guilt is an enemy to those who want to overcome a bad habit. Instead of obsessing over past failures, view each future moment as its own accomplishment.

A FINAL WORD

This section is a fitting conclusion to our book, in that it should lend comfort to all who are trying to incorporate new ideas and emotional responses into their life. Change and growth is an uneven process. Do not give up, and do not get discouraged!